T0302316

Commodity Investing

Founded in 1807, John Wiley & Sons is the oldest independent publishing company in the United States. With offices in North America, Europe, Australia and Asia, Wiley is globally committed to developing and marketing print and electronic products and services for our customers' professional and personal knowledge and understanding.

The Wiley Finance series contains books written specifically for finance and investment professionals as well as sophisticated individual investors and their financial advisors. Book topics range from portfolio management to e-commerce, risk management, financial engineering, valuation and financial instrument analysis, as well as much more.

For a list of available titles, visit our Web site at www.WileyFinance.com.

Commodity Investing

Maximizing Returns through Fundamental Analysis

ADAM DUNSBY

JOHN ECKSTEIN

JESS GASPAR

SARAH MULHOLLAND

WILEY

John Wiley & Sons, Inc.

Published by John Wiley & Sons, Inc., Hoboken, New Jersey.

Published simultaneously in Canada.

S&P GSCI™ is a registered service mark and trademark of Standard & Poor's.

Limit of Liability/Disclaimer of Warranty: While the publisher and author have used their best efforts in preparing this book, they make no representations or warranties with respect to the accuracy or completeness of the contents of this book and specifically disclaim any implied warranties of merchantability or fitness for a particular purpose. No warranty may be created or extended by sales representatives or written sales materials. The advice and strategies contained herein may not be suitable for your situation. You should consult with a professional where appropriate. Neither the publisher nor author shall be liable for any loss of profit or any other commercial damages, including but not limited to special, incidental, consequential, or other damages.

For general information on our other products and services or for technical support, please contact our Customer Care Department within the United States at (800) 762-2974, outside the United States at (317) 572-3993 or fax (317) 572-4002.

Wiley also publishes its books in a variety of electronic formats. Some content that appears in print may not be available in electronic formats. For more information about Wiley products, visit our Web site at www.wiley.com.

Library of Congress Cataloging-in-Publication Data:

Commodity investing : maximizing returns through fundamental analysis / Adam Dunsby ... [et al.].
  p. cm. – (Wiley finance series)
  Includes bibliographical references and indexes.
  ISBN 978-0-470-22310-9 (cloth)
  1. Commodity futures.   2. Commodity exchanges.   3. Investment analysis.
I. Dunsby, Adam, 1967–
  HG6046.C636   2008
  332.63'28–dc22

                                                    2007041568

Printed in the United States of America

10 9 8 7 6 5 4 3 2 1

Contents

Acknowledgments   ix

PART ONE

  Basics   1

CHAPTER 1
  Introduction   3

CHAPTER 2
  Commodity Futures as Investments   9

CHAPTER 3
  Commodities for the Long Run   29

PART TWO

  Understanding Energy   37

CHAPTER 4
  Crude Oil   39

CHAPTER 5
  Heating Oil   57

CHAPTER 6
  Gasoline   67

CHAPTER 7
  Natural Gas   79

PART THREE

   Understanding Grains and Oilseeds   **93**

CHAPTER 8
   Corn   **95**

CHAPTER 9
   Wheat   **107**

CHAPTER 10
   Soybeans   **117**

PART FOUR

   Understanding Livestock   **131**

CHAPTER 11
   Hogs   **133**

CHAPTER 12
   Cattle   **141**

PART FIVE

   Understanding Industrial Metals   **151**

CHAPTER 13
   Copper   **153**

CHAPTER 14
   Aluminum   **165**

CHAPTER 15
   Zinc   **177**

PART SIX

   Understanding the Softs   **187**

CHAPTER 16
   Coffee   **189**

CHAPTER 17
Sugar 197

CHAPTER 18
Cocoa 207

CHAPTER 19
Cotton 213

PART SEVEN
How to Invest 221

CHAPTER 20
Some Building Blocks of a Commodity Futures Trading System 223

CHAPTER 21
The Rise of the Indexes 245

CHAPTER 22
Conclusion 265

APPENDIX
The London Metal Exchange 269

Notes 273

References 283

About the Authors 287

Index 289

Acknowledgments

We thank Kumar Dandapani for reading and helping to prepare the manuscript, Henry Luk for helping to procure the Chinese rice data, Judy Ganes-Chase for reading and helping with the softs chapters, and Jeff Smith for reading the grain chapters.

Basics

CHAPTER 1

Introduction

In 1980 Julian Simon and Paul Ehrlich bet $1,000 on the future price of five metals (chromium, copper, nickel, tin, and tungsten). Simon, who believed that human ingenuity would consistently improve the lot of humanity, bet that prices would fall in real terms, while Paul Ehrlich, who believed that a growing human population would increasingly strain the Earth's resources, bet that they would go up. The Simon–Ehrlich basket of metals was not the first commodity index (that title apparently belongs to the Economist Commodity Price Index), but their bet on the future change in price may have been the first derivative on a commodity index. The prices of all five metals declined in real terms, and Simon won the bet.

Today huge numbers of investors are taking similar bets, except they are betting not thousands of dollars but billions. Passive long-only indexing in commodities has grown from very little in 1991 to probably over $100 billion in 2007. Much of the inspiration (or sales pitch) behind the move to commodity investing is the same as Ehrlich's inspiration in taking the bet with Simon: a general belief that the world's growing population is increasingly straining the Earth's ability to supply commodities such as oil, grains, and metals. Inevitably China is mentioned. Demand is going up, supply is going down. What could be simpler? Or is it? After all, the world's population has been increasing for a long time yet, as we will show, when measured over the course of centuries, the price of commodities has gone down in real terms, not up.

When approaching commodities from an investment perspective extra care must be taken. The prima facie case for investing in commodities is weak. Put simply, commodities are produced to be consumed, and they do not naturally produce investment returns. Contrast commodities with the more standard investments of stocks and bonds. Stocks and bonds by design produce cash flows in the form of dividends, interest payments, or capitalized earnings. They are financial instruments, and the sole reason they exist is to provide investment returns. If they did not provide investment returns, no one would own them. However, even if natural gas did not belong in one's 401(k), one would still buy it in order to heat one's home.

The purpose of this book is to provide those who would approach commodities from an investment perspective with information, tools, and modes of thinking that will inform their analyses. We do not take the position that commodities are going *Up! Up! Up!* nor do we take the position that they are going *Down! Down! Down!* Rather, we hope that upon completion readers will have a base of knowledge that will allow them to analyze specific commodity investments and strategies according to their individual characteristics and their own times. Undoubtedly, there will be opportunities to profit in the commodity markets for those who have the requisite skills. That being said, it is fair to say that the authors of this work are skeptical that the current rush to passive, long-only commodity investments will yield the intended results.

The selection of commodities as a major investment theme is relatively new. Of course, commodities have been around for a long time, but the notion that an investor or pension fund would allocate a substantial portion of an investment portfolio to plain old commodities such as coffee is recent. Because of this, the investment industry is still learning. There is a shortage of trained commodity analysts, and there is a shortage of good books on the subject of commodity investing. It is our goal to make this book an addition to the short shelf of good ones.

Many academics have written about commodity investing, and much of it is good and useful; on the whole, however, it is detached from the commodities themselves. Academics generally do two things when researching the commodity markets. The first is to look at the overall historical returns of a commodity portfolio and compare them with the returns of other assets such as equities. The second is to explore the shape of the futures curve with the obligatory discussion of Keynes's theory of normal backwardation. These two approaches are useful, and we will apply them to some extent in what follows, but notice that no mention was made of specific commodities. Whether the portfolio contains egg futures or oil futures is not considered interesting. The *academic approach* generally employs the same modes of analysis without regard to the specific commodities analyzed. There is no notion of how an industry is changing or what the long-term supply–demand dynamic is. One of the premises of this book is that investors should have a basic understanding of the individual commodities. If you are approached by a manager who wants you to invest in a North Pole coffee plantation, you should be able to do more than just recite the mantra that commodities have yielded equity-like returns during the past 30 years.

It is important to emphasize that this is a book on commodity *investing* and, for that reason, we will be constantly trying to bring everything back to the theme of investing. There are many other economically interesting approaches to thinking about commodities. For instance, one might be curious how oil shocks affect the economy. This would fall under the category of the macroeconomics of commodities. One might be interested in the prices of commodities, such as coffee, because these prices affect the terms of trade in developing countries and therefore affect the prosperity of these countries. There are other perspectives, of course, many of which are interesting but none of which will be addressed here.

Another premise of this book is that investors need to understand the source of returns from commodity investments. Can commodities go *Up! Up! Up!* while investment returns go *Down! Down! Down!* Yes; they can and they have. The reason is that investment returns are composed of more than just the change in the price of the commodity. First, it must be pointed out that investors actually do not invest in physical commodities themselves but in commodity futures. Thus *commodity investing* is really short for *commodity futures investing* and *commodity index* is usually short for *commodity futures index* and so on. Since investors own futures, this puts a wedge between the change in price of the spot commodities and the change in price of the futures. This wedge is also a source of returns, and it can be positive or negative. The final source of return is the interest that investors receive for the cash and margin they put up to support their futures investments. Investors in passive, long-only indexes should understand how these different sources have affected returns historically and how they might affect them going forward. For example, commodities have earned positive returns during periods of high inflation, but these are periods when interest rates are also high, increasing the portion of return due to margin interest. Historically the distant oil futures have been priced lower than nearby oil futures, generating positive roll yield and contributing to the positive historical returns from investing in oil futures.

There are various approaches to investing in commodities. The most common, of course, is to invest in an index. But there are others. For example, one could buy commodity-based equities, invest with a trend-following commodity trading advisor (CTA), use judgment to assess the commodity environment and to make the appropriate decision, or construct a quantitative strategy that uses many pieces of information. It is desirable that investment strategies pass two tests: (1) that they make sense and (2) that they have worked historically. For passive indexing there is a debate as to whether condition 1 is satisfied. Certainly many people are convinced that it is. Condition 2 can be addressed more firmly, and we provide that analysis.

The conclusion one draws as to the historical performance of commodity indexing depends on the time period selected. Since 1500, the price of wheat has gone down substantially in real terms and not up all that much in

nominal terms. The commodity price index with the longest history is the
Economist Commodity Price Index which dates to the mid-1800s. Since its
introduction, it has also gone down in real terms and has been completely
inferior to equities as an investment. The Economist Commodity Price Index
also dropped in value when the U.S. stock market crashed in the late 1920s,
something that should be kept in mind by those who consider commodities
a hedge in their equity portfolio.

Most analyses of commodity market returns focus on recent years, say
from the middle of the twentieth century onward. This is simply because
there is more and better data available in recent decades. The New York
Mercantile Exchange (NYMEX) crude oil future was not listed until 1983,
for example. Thus, most of what we know or *know* about commodity
returns is based on analyses from this time period. When looked at in this
way commodity investments have done better. They have provided equity-
like returns with little correlation to equities.

The authors of this book specialize in the construction of quantitative
investment models and have included sections on it. We are quite forward
in saying that we do not give away the shop, but we do not tease either.
We provide some specific variables to consider, ones we use, and offer insight into methodologies that investors may find helpful. For example, when
constructing a model it is always comforting to have an *anchor variable*,
a factor to which the commodity of interest should be attracted. Examples
might be the price of substitutes or the price of inputs.

The remainder of this book is laid out as follows: Chapters 2 and 3 assess
the historical performance of commodities. Chapter 2 presents an analysis
of commodity returns over the recent period of modern financial markets
with its tremendous richness of futures contracts to use. The available data
is more than ample for detailed statistical analysis. We can test how commodities have done compared with equities and bonds. We can explore how
commodities performed during periods of inflation and recession. We can
see how profitable buying commodities was relative to buying commodity-
based equities. For example, would an investor have done better by buying
oil futures or by buying shares in Exxon? Chapter 3 uses long-term histories of wheat and the Economist Commodity Price Index to construct long
histories of commodity returns as measured by these series. This approach
has the advantage of reaching far back into time, but the disadvantage of
having only a small number of series to analyze.

The middle section of the book is devoted to the commodities themselves. It can be read through or referred to for the commodities of interest.
It is here that the reader will come to understand the commodities, the state
of their industries and, where we have something useful to say, the long-term
outlook. For example, how much oil is out there? Are we running out soon?

Are we sliding down Hubbert's peak? Will it last forever? We collect the data from the primary sources and summarize it in a useful way. Along with the big-picture issues we present the nuts-and-bolts information that investors will need to understand, such as why the natural gas futures curve has a bumpy shape? There are chapters on energies, grains and oilseeds, the softs (coffee, sugar, and cocoa), and base metals. One category of commodity we do not cover is the precious metals. Precious metals are fundamentally different from other commodities in that they are not produced primarily to be consumed. They are more like currencies and stores of value. Consequently we have less to say about them. Readers interested in gold, for example, can refer to Peter Bernstein's excellent book *The Power of Gold*.

Chapter 20 is titled "Some Building Blocks of a Commodity Trading System," and in this chapter we begin to pull together and explain various components that may prove useful in either constructing an investment strategy or in evaluating a commodity-based investment strategy. Most of the chapter deals with the shape of the futures curve. Next to the price movement of commodities, the shape of the futures curve is the most important factor in determining the outcome of a buy-and-hold strategy. This chapter introduces the theories that are typically used to understand the shape of the futures curve. They include arbitrage, Keynes's theory of normal backwardation, and Hotelling's theory of the economics of exhaustible resources. None of these can provide the complete answer, but that is because there is no complete answer. Commodity markets differ, and there is no one-size-fits-all explanation. Taking the shape of the curve as a given, it is shown that the shape of the futures curve can substantially affect investment returns. Also presented in this chapter are trend-following strategies, anchor variables, and a simple trading strategy. The chapter concludes with a discussion of risk control. So that focus does not drift too far away from commodities the discussion is kept brief (fortunately, because this is a very tedious subject). We focus on two risk control methodologies that are commonly used: value-at-risk and maximum drawdown.

The final chapter deals with the boom in passive, long-only commodity indexes. The amount of money invested in these indexes has dramatically increased in recent years. The king of these indexes is the S&P GSCI Index (S&P GSCI). Originated in 1991, this index now has investments of around $60 billion linked to it. Many investors might be surprised to learn that there is much more to the return of these indexes than just the change in the price of commodities

To summarize some of the main themes and findings of this book, from the perspective of what makes a good investment, the case for owning commodities is not clear. Therefore investors must be both careful and thoughtful when evaluating commodity investments. Commodities have performed well in recent years, but their long-term performance has not been so good, especially when compared with equities. There is information available to investors that can help them improve returns and avoid investments that are likely to have a poor return profile. Chief among these is the shape of the futures curve. Nobody knows definitively what commodity prices are going to do in the future, but if the futures curves are steeply contangoed (i.e., spot prices below futures prices) it is going to be difficult for passive, long-only indexes to yield attractive returns. In such an environment, an investor who desires exposure to commodities may want to explore other opportunities, such as investments in commodity-based equities.

CHAPTER 2

Commodity Futures as Investments

Are commodities good investments?[1] Investors have poured billions and billions of dollars into commodities believing the answer to this question to be "Yes!" Have commodity investments done well historically? Even when they are not good investments, perhaps commodities can offer insurance; doing well when inflation is high or when there is a stock market crash or some other wealth destroying event. Assuming one decides to invest in commodities, how does one actually do it? Should an investor buy a silo of grain, individual commodity futures, an investable index, or can an investor do better by buying stocks that offer exposure to the commodities of interest? These are the questions of interest in this chapter. We will address these issues primarily from a quantitative and historical perspective, relying heavily on analysis of historical data.

This chapter will consider commodity investments primarily from a passive, long-only standpoint. The interesting questions of whether commodity returns are forecastable and whether dynamic trading strategies can be constructed is left for a later chapter. The specific investment vehicles an investor may wish to consider, such as the S&P GSCI Index or a trend-following CTA, are also presented in a later chapter.

What makes something a good investment? The most basic consideration is whether it earns a positive return. If you put money in, do you expect to end up with more money than when you started? People who invest in stocks or bonds do so expecting to end up with more money than when they started. There are both practical and philosophical aspects to this question with regard to commodities. The first is whether, *a priori,* we should expect commodities to have positive returns. Not everything that exists is necessarily a good investment. Pet rocks, lottery tickets, and old newspapers are examples of things that provide a negative return, at least in expectation. Stocks and bonds are purely *financial* assets. That is, they exist solely to provide a financial return to their owners. They generally produce positive cash flows over their lives. Commodities do not exist to provide investment returns; they are produced to be consumed (precious metals being the exception). Wheat is not grown to be held in perpetuity, but to be turned into bread; oil is not pumped from the ground to be kept as a store of wealth, but to be used to heat homes or to propel cars.

There are two basic arguments generally given as to why commodity prices should go up. The first basically goes: We're making more and more people who demand more and more stuff but we're not making any more planet Earth. Therefore increasing demand and decreasing supply should drive up the price of commodities. The second argument states that commodities are real things and therefore they should go up at least at the rate of inflation. They should not lose value simply because a sovereign currency, such as the U.S. dollar, does. These arguments may or may not be true. In regard to the first argument, supply may be increasing in some cases. Improved technology has increased grain yields immensely during the past 100 years. Oil reserve estimates are often raised, at least slowing the pace at which the world will run out of petroleum.[2]

Famously, in 1980 environmentalist Paul Ehrlich bet economist Julian Simon that the price of five metals (chromium, copper, nickel, tin, and tungsten) would increase in real terms over the coming decade. Ehrlich was a proponent of the first argument: An increasing population would begin to use up the Earth's resources at an increasing rate. What happened? All five metals declined in real terms and three declined in absolute terms (and Simon made $576). This happened even though the world's population increased by 800 million during that time period. Not surprisingly, since then no major investment bank has come forward with an investable index based on the prices of chromium, copper, nickel, tin, and tungsten.

The point is that commodities are not financial assets. They exist to be consumed, not to produce investment returns. They may increase in price, or they may not. The onus is on the commodities and the commodities-are-an-asset-class believers to establish the utility of commodities in an investment portfolio. A good place to start is the historical data.

Before we can turn to the data, however, there are a few issues that need to be addressed. The first is which commodities should be analyzed? We restrict ourselves to commodities for which there are futures contracts. This is quite a big leap, because while many commodities have listed futures, many do not. There are no apple futures, no carrot futures, and no used-car futures. This bifurcation also brings to the foreground the important distinction that investors in commodity markets invest almost always in commodity future contracts and not in the underlying commodity. This has important implications for returns that will be explored in Chapter 20, "Some Building Blocks of a Commodity Trading System."

Commodity futures are listed on exchanges all over the globe. There are tapioca chip futures listed in Thailand, greasy wool futures listed in Australia, West Texas Intermediate (WTI) crude futures listed in the United States, and many, many more. Some of these futures contracts trade very little or not at all. For example, future contracts on urea, a major component of human urine, are listed on the Chicago Mercantile Exchange (CME)— Bloomberg symbol TCA. In December 2006 the open interest was zero. (Urea is used in fertilizer.) Milk futures are also listed on the CME (Bloomberg symbol DAA). In December 2006, the open interest across all of the listed milk contracts was a few thousand, but any given day's volume was only a few hundred. By contrast, at the same time the corn future on the Chicago Board of Trade (CBOT) had an open interest of nearly 600,000 just in the front contract, and this single contract had a volume of about 30,000 a day.

Another issue is redundancy in contracts. For example, the United States and Canada have four wheat contracts between them. The New York Mercantile Exchange (NYMEX) and the Intercontinental Exchange (ICE)—formerly the International Petroleum Exchange (IPE)—both have very successful crude oil contracts. Similar stories can be told for other commodities. A more subtle issue is commodities that are downstream products of other commodities. For example, heating oil and gasoline are made from crude oil, and all three have contracts listed on the NYMEX. Their prices tend to move together. Similarly, soybean oil and soybean meal are made from soybeans. All three have future contracts listed on the CBOT, and their prices also typically move together.

The commodities we chose for analysis include those that (1) are the most liquid, (2) are nonredundant, (3) are primarily traded on U.S. exchanges, and (4) have high investor interest. The list is presented in Table 2.1. Of these, canola is the only one not denominated in U.S. dollars. It is traded on the Winnipeg Commodity Exchange and denominated in Canadian dollars.[a] The industrial metal contracts aluminum, nickel, and zinc are traded outside of the United States on the London Metals Exchange (LME) but are denominated in U.S. dollars. The copper contract chosen is the one that trades in the United States on the COMEX. The COMEX contract is less heavily traded than its London counterpart, but it has the advantage of being a future contract, as opposed to a forward contract and is thus easier to work with analytically. We have chosen to include for individual analysis the downstream products such as heating oil and bean oil with the justification that there is strong interest in these commodities in their own right.

Not on the list are commodities that are no longer traded. There used to be egg futures, potato futures, and chicken futures along with others. These

---

[a] It is converted to U.S. dollars in the following text.

TABLE 2.1   List of Commodities

Commodity	Start Date	Exchange
Crude Oil	5/31/83	NYMEX
Unleaded/RBOB Gasoline	2/28/85	NYMEX
Heating Oil	2/29/80	NYMEX
Natural Gas	5/31/90	NYMEX
Canola	4/30/90	WCE
Wheat	8/31/59	CBOT
Corn	8/31/59	CBOT
Soybeans	8/31/59	CBOT
Soybean Meal	8/31/59	CBOT
Soybean Oil	8/31/59	CBOT
Cotton	8/31/60	CSCE/NYBOT
Cocoa	9/30/59	CSCE
Coffee	5/31/75	CSCE
Sugar	2/28/62	CSCE
Lean Hogs	2/28/70	CME
Live Cattle	4/30/65	CME
Copper	8/31/59	COMEX
Gold	1/31/75	COMEX
Silver	2/28/67	COMEX
Aluminum	2/29/80	LME
Zinc	2/28/77	LME

contracts failed for various reasons. When studying returns, it is potentially a serious mistake to ignore the returns of instruments that used to exist but exist no longer. For example, if in a study of equity returns one ignored all of the companies that had gone bankrupt, the remaining return series would be an upward biased estimate of what investors would have actually earned. This is probably not a concern, or at least less of a concern, in commodities because commodity futures tend to get delisted not because the underlying commodity goes to zero but because there is no demand for a derivative on the underlying commodity. For example, there may be insufficient hedging interest or there may be a problem with the delivery mechanism. An early study by Bodie and Rosansky (1980) studied the returns of 23 commodity futures from 1950 to 1976. Of those 23, 5 are no longer listed (broilers, plywood, potatoes, wool, and eggs). Bodie and Rosansky report that four of those five had positive returns.

The futures data comes primarily from the Commodity Research Bureau (CRB). More recent data has been updated from the data set kept at the Cornerstone Quantitative Investment Group and that has been primarily taken as reported by Bloomberg. In the more recent data we restrict the data to day sessions only. All data has been checked. The spot price data is also taken from the CRB with the exception of RBOB (gasoline) which is taken from the Department of Energy website. Additional information is presented in the data appendix to this chapter.

RETURNS

Computing investment returns from futures contracts is less straightforward than for other instruments. The reason is that futures are free. Unlike a stock or a bond, when a futures contract transaction takes place no money changes hands. The buyer and seller are agreeing to exchange the commodity at a time in the future at a price that is fixed now. (They are also agreeing to pay or receive money as the price changes day to day.) Margin must be posted, but this is generally small relative to the face value. For example, a WTI crude oil contract that trades on the NYMEX is for 1,000 barrels. If a barrel of oil costs $60.00, then the face value of one contract is $60,000. The initial margin that must be posted, however, is only $3,375 dollars, which is 5.6 percent of the contract value. So one could control 1,000 barrels of oil with only $3,375. This would be a highly levered position and a movement in the price of oil of $3.37 would wipe out the entire investment. Another way to approach the investment would be not to lever at all but to actually put up the $60,000. When this is done, the futures investment is said to be fully collateralized. The interest earned on the $60,000 is another source of investment return in addition to the change in price of the future contract. Putting up $60,000 is arbitrary, but people often find it intuitively appealing to have the cash investment equal to the face value of the futures contracts.

As an example, consider a cash investment in the S&P GSCI Index. Assuming XYZ Investment Bank was the manager, an investor would give XYZ, say, $1,000. XYZ would then buy the appropriate basket of futures contracts; they would post margin for the futures contracts, and they would invest the balance of the $1,000 in interest-bearing securities such as T-Bills. Most of the margin could also be posted as interest-bearing securities, so the investor would earn approximately the return on the futures position, plus interest on the $1,000, less any fees the investor might be charged.

In what follows we will compute returns as the percent change in the relevant future contract. We will fully collateralize (i.e., include T-Bill interest) or not, depending on the question at hand.

HAVE COMMODITY FUTURES EARNED
POSITIVE RETURNS?

The answer to this question is "Yes." The results that show this are presented in Table 2.2. The returns in this table are presented with no interest included (i.e., they are not collateralized). This allows us to focus solely on the performance of commodities without mingling it with the performance of T-Bills. At this stage, we are interested in the simple issue of whether commodities by themselves tend to go up or not. Following Erb and Harvey (2006), we take the period since the introduction of the NYMEX crude oil contract as particularly important in the history of commodity

TABLE 2.2   Commodity Future Returns

Panel A: Full Sample: August 1959–March 2007				
	Annualized Geometric Returns	Annualized Arithmetic Returns	Annualized Standard Deviation	Sharpe Ratio	t-Stat
Equal Weight Portfolio	*6.04%*	*7.00%*	*13.67%*	*0.51*	*3.54*
Crude Oil	9.26%	15.10%	32.95%	0.46	2.24
Gasoline	19.62%	28.98%	40.60%	0.71	3.36
Heating Oil	12.40%	19.09%	35.48%	0.54	2.80
Natural Gas	−6.73%	7.06%	53.46%	0.13	0.54
Canola	−2.01%	−0.43%	17.85%	−0.02	−0.10
Wheat	−4.55%	−2.10%	22.77%	−0.09	−0.64
Corn	−4.15%	−1.86%	22.26%	−0.08	−0.58
Soybeans	1.89%	5.12%	25.96%	0.20	1.36
Soybean Meal	5.27%	9.63%	30.15%	0.32	2.20
Soybean Oil	3.15%	7.40%	29.33%	0.25	1.74
Cotton	0.81%	3.18%	21.89%	0.15	0.99
Cocoa	−1.93%	2.70%	30.96%	0.09	0.60
Coffee	1.94%	9.56%	39.44%	0.24	1.37
Sugar	−6.84%	2.43%	45.10%	0.05	0.36
Lean Hogs	2.94%	6.79%	27.26%	0.25	1.52
Live Cattle	5.27%	6.94%	17.77%	0.39	2.53
Copper	9.01%	12.98%	27.17%	0.48	3.30
Gold	−2.18%	−0.41%	19.10%	−0.02	−0.12
Silver	−2.01%	2.86%	31.35%	0.09	0.58
Aluminum	0.16%	2.20%	20.39%	0.11	0.56
Zinc	4.82%	7.61%	23.16%	0.33	1.80
Nickel	10.27%	16.65%	35.90%	0.46	2.45

(Continued)

TABLE 2.2 (*Continued*)

	Panel B: May 1983–March 2007				
	Annualized Geometric Returns	Annualized Arithmetic Returns	Annualized Standard Deviation	Sharpe Ratio	t-Stat
Equal Weight Portfolio	*4.80%*	*5.40%*	*10.64%*	*0.51*	*2.48*
Crude Oil	9.26%	15.10%	32.95%	0.46	2.24
Gasoline	19.62%	28.98%	40.60%	0.71	3.36
Heating Oil	13.62%	21.06%	37.18%	0.57	2.77
Natural Gas	−6.73%	7.06%	53.46%	0.13	0.54
Canola	−2.01%	−0.43%	17.85%	−0.02	−0.10
Wheat	−6.30%	−4.08%	21.70%	−0.19	−0.92
Corn	-6.16%	−3.68%	23.26%	−0.16	−0.77
Soybeans	−1.14%	1.26%	22.05%	0.06	0.28
Soybean Meal	2.57%	5.38%	23.53%	0.23	1.12
Soybean Oil	−1.35%	1.87%	25.79%	0.07	0.35
Cotton	−0.97%	1.63%	23.02%	0.07	0.35
Cocoa	−7.44%	−3.76%	28.38%	−0.13	−0.65
Coffee	−6.35%	0.43%	38.56%	0.01	0.05
Sugar	−5.41%	1.66%	39.42%	0.04	0.21
Lean Hogs	2.33%	5.61%	25.21%	0.22	1.09
Live Cattle	5.30%	6.39%	14.36%	0.44	2.18
Copper	9.08%	12.86%	26.94%	0.48	2.34
Gold	−3.16%	−2.26%	13.73%	−0.16	−0.80
Silver	−5.30%	−2.37%	24.71%	−0.10	−0.47
Aluminum	1.80%	3.87%	20.37%	0.19	0.93
Zinc	5.94%	8.64%	22.82%	0.38	1.85
Nickel	13.54%	20.69%	37.59%	0.55	2.69

Note: Returns are uncollateralized.

investing. The NYMEX WTI crude oil contract is arguably the most important commodity contract listed today, and it makes up a large part of the S&P GSCI Index, the most widely followed commodity index. In our sample, the first oil return is in May of 1983, so we divide the sample here. In addition to the 22 contracts examined individually, we create a simple portfolio in which all contracts that have returns for a given month are included with an equal weight.[b] As shown in Table 2.1, the earliest contracts in the sample are the CBOT grains, and the most recent is NYMEX natural gas.

---

[b] This implies monthly rebalancing.

Both annualized geometric and arithmetic returns are considered. Geometric returns represent compounded investor returns that encapsulate the overall return performance in a single number. Arithmetic returns are just the series of simple returns, but they are easier to analyze statistically given that a series is needed in order to compute something like a standard error. One very useful property of a geometric return is that if it is positive the investor made money.[c] Geometric returns are always less than (or equal to) arithmetic returns.

For the full sample, annualized geometric return is 6.04 percent and the annualized arithmetic return is 7.00 percent (again, no interest has been included). The returns are lower in the more recent subsample. Since May of 1983 the annual compounded return is 4.80 percent. As measured by t-statistics these returns are statistically significant, with a t-statistic of 3.54 on the equally weighted portfolio for the whole period and a t-statistic of 2.48 for the more recent period. The Sharpe ratios over the two periods are both roughly 0.5. The smaller return since May of 1983 was matched by a fall in volatility.

These returns also beat inflation, as measured by the consumer price index (CPI). This is presented in Table 2.3. For the full sample the compounded real return was 1.87 percent. The real return was also positive in each of the subperiods. It was 2.04 percent prior to May 1983 and 1.71 percent since then. Thus returns are also lower in real terms in the more recent period.

TABLE 2.3 Real Commodity Future Returns

Panel A Monthly Real Returns (Arithmetic Returns)			
Date Range	Equal Weight Portfolio	CPI	Real Return
8/31/59–3/31/07	0.57%	0.34%	0.22%
8/31/59–4/30/83	0.69%	0.43%	0.26%
5/31/83–3/31/07	0.44%	0.26%	0.18%
Panel B Annualized Geometric Returns (Geometric Returns)			
8/31/59–3/31/07	6.04%	4.18%	1.87%
8/31/59–4/30/83	7.31%	5.27%	2.04%
5/31/83–3/31/07	4.80%	3.09%	1.71%

---

[c] Unfortunately, this is not necessarily true of arithmetic returns. If an investment goes up 75%, up 75%, and then down 100%, the arithmetic return would be (75% + 75% − 100%)/3 = 17%, but the investor would have lost all of his money.

Turning to the individual compounded commodity returns, over the entire period 14 of the 22 commodities had positive returns. From May 1983 onward, 10 of the 22 had positive returns. Not all contracts existed prior to May 1983 and some that did had short histories, so we do not report separate results for that period. Over the full period, grains (with the exception of the soy complex) and precious metals are negative. The other contracts with negative returns are natural gas, cocoa, and sugar. In the more recent period the same commodities yield negative returns along with soybeans, soymeal, cotton, and coffee. The best performing commodity future was unleaded gasoline, which earned a compounded annual return of 19.62 percent since it entered the sample in February 1985. The other two petroleum commodities, crude oil and heating oil, also produced positive returns.

It is interesting to compare the returns earned from commodity futures to the percent change in price of the spot commodities. This will bring into relief any differences there may be between the change in physical commodity prices and the change in commodity future prices. As a reminder, investors' exposure to the commodity markets is by way of commodity futures, not the physical commodity. This disconnect is potentially important inasmuch as the shape of the futures curve can have significant implications for returns. This effect of the future curve on returns is developed in detail in Chapter 20, "Some Building Blocks of a Commodity Trading System." However, to introduce some of the concepts now: The spot price is the price of a commodity now, the future price is the price at which a commodity will be exchanged at a fixed date in the future. If the spot price is above the future price the market is said to be backwardated. If the spot price is below the future price the market is said to be in a state of contango (or a normal market for grains). In a backwardated market, a long position in the future can earn a positive return even if the spot price does not change, because the future price will creep up the curve as it converges upward to the spot price. The reverse is true in a contangoed market.

The commodity spot price data is taken primarily from the CRB. More information is given in the data appendix to this chapter. Displayed in Table 2.4 are the futures returns, as previously discussed, showing the monthly arithmetic percent change in the spot price and the difference between the two. For each commodity the spot price and the future price are aligned to cover the period over which both exist, so some of the future returns may differ from what was presented previously. As before, an equally weighted portfolio is created consisting of the commodities that had returns for a given month. Results are presented for the entire sample, which begins as early as August 1959 for the CBOT grain contracts.

On average, commodity spot *returns* are higher than commodity future returns. The annual compounded *return* for the physical commodity portfolio is 7.77 percent compared with 5.53 percent for the portfolio of futures, a

TABLE 2.4 Comparison of Spot Change with Future Returns (Annualized Geometric Returns)

Commodity	Future Return [A]	Spot Return [B]	Future − Spot [A] − [B]
WTI Crude	9.26%	3.23%	6.03%
Unleaded Gas/RBOB	19.62%	4.12%	15.50%
Heating Oil	12.40%	3.40%	8.99%
Natural Gas	−0.47%	12.90%	−13.36%
Canola	−2.01%	0.79%	−2.79%
Wheat	−4.55%	1.57%	−6.12%
Corn	−4.15%	2.21%	−6.36%
Soybeans	1.89%	2.50%	−0.61%
Soybean Meal	5.27%	2.66%	2.61%
Soybean Oil	3.15%	2.56%	0.60%
Cotton	−0.21%	1.04%	−1.25%
Cocoa	−1.93%	2.06%	−3.99%
Coffee	1.94%	1.74%	0.21%
Sugar	−6.84%	3.38%	−10.22%
Live Cattle	5.27%	3.05%	2.22%
Lean Hogs	2.94%	2.00%	0.94%
Gold	−2.18%	4.01%	−6.19%
Silver	−2.01%	6.03%	−8.04%
Copper	5.13%	5.21%	−0.08%
Aluminum	1.46%	2.41%	−0.95%
Zinc	6.97%	7.10%	−0.13%
Nickel	18.17%	13.46%	4.71%
Equal Weight Portfolio	5.53%	7.77%	−2.24%

Notes: Futures and spot prices are aligned over same time period for each commodity, so future returns may differ from previous tables if the cash has a shorter time period. The period spans August 1959 through March 2007.

difference of −2.24 percent. This suggests that, overall, the positive returns of commodity futures are not due to curve effects. If anything, the curve effects lowered the return of the commodity future portfolio.

Examining the individual commodities, in 8 cases the future outperformed the spot, and in 14 cases the spot outperformed the future. As a group, petroleum-based futures all outperformed spot prices. This is because these markets have typically been backwardated (the spot price above the future contract price). In the majority of the remaining markets, the spot price outperformed the future. This is consistent with the standard theory that the owner of a future must *pay* the carrying costs. These theories are discussed more fully in Chapter 20, "Some Building Blocks of a Commodity Trading System."

COMMODITY RETURNS COMPARED WITH STOCKS AND BONDS

How have commodities fared relative to stocks and bonds? This is obviously an important question to investors since for most investors equities and fixed-income instruments are their typical investment alternatives. In this section we compare the returns of the equally weighted commodity portfolio to the returns of stocks and bonds. For this we use the returns of the S&P 500, 10-year U.S. Treasury Bonds, and T-Bills. The data for these series are explained in the appendix to this chapter. For commodities we now switch to a fully collateralized measure. This is done by simply adding T-Bill interest to the previously constructed equally weighted commodity index. The reason for now switching to a fully collateralized index is that we are now interested in comparing investment alternatives on a total return basis and, as discussed previously, the total return a commodity future investor receives includes interest. The time period analyzed is the period from February 1962 through March 2007, as this is the period for which 10-year bond returns are available.

Correlations are displayed in Table 2.5. The first panel presents correlations for monthly holding periods, the second for annual holding periods. At

TABLE 2.5   Correlation, February 1962–March 2007

Correlation of Monthly Returns					
	Commodities	S&P 500	Bonds	T-Bills	CPI
Commodities	1.00	0.03	−0.15	−0.05	0.01
S&P 500	0.03	1.00	0.20	−0.03	−0.15
Bonds	−0.15	0.20	1.00	0.03	−0.10
T-Bills	−0.05	−0.03	0.03	1.00	0.54
CPI	0.01	−0.15	−0.10	0.54	1.00

Correlation of Annual Returns					
	Commodities	S&P 500	Bonds	T-Bills	CPI
Commodities	1.00	−0.20	−0.28	−0.03	0.27
S&P 500	−0.20	1.00	0.29	0.00	−0.22
Bonds	−0.28	0.29	1.00	0.10	−0.26
T-Bills	−0.03	0.00	0.10	1.00	0.70
CPI	0.27	−0.22	−0.26	0.70	1.00

Notes: Commodity returns are the equally-weighted portfolio with T-bills included (i.e., they are collateralized). Annual periods are overlapping.

monthly horizons, the correlation of commodities with the other asset classes and inflation is low. The highest is −15 percent with bonds and, interestingly, the correlation with inflation is only 1 percent. At monthly horizons, commodities are basically uncorrelated with stocks. At annual horizons, the results change somewhat. The correlation with inflation is now 27 percent and the correlation with equities is now −20 percent. This suggests that commodities have been a somewhat useful hedge against inflation and have tended to perform somewhat above average when equities have performed below average.

Table 2.6 displays summary statistics of the asset classes, and Figure 2.1 displays the cumulative, compounded portfolio returns. The top panel of Table 2.6 presents annual compounded returns for the entire sample and for the period from May 1983 to March 2007. Over the full period, commodities had an annual return of 12.45 percent compared with 10.46 percent for stocks and 6.98 percent for bonds. After 1983 the situation is reversed: The annual return for commodities is 9.85 percent whereas

TABLE 2.6   Return Comparison

	Annualized Geometric Returns				
	Commodities	S&P 500	Bonds	T-Bills	CPI
Feb 1962–Mar 2007	12.45%	10.46%	6.98%	5.62%	4.35%
May 1983–Mar 2007	9.85%	12.31%	8.65%	4.82%	3.10%
	Monthly Arithmetic Returns				
	Commodities	S&P 500	Bonds	T-Bills	CPI
Feb 1962–Mar 2007					
Average	1.06%	0.92%	0.58%	0.46%	0.36%
Median	0.82%	1.11%	0.46%	0.42%	0.31%
St. Dev.	4.00%	4.24%	2.07%	0.21%	0.31%
Max	25.08%	16.81%	11.36%	1.30%	1.81%
Min	−12.76%	−21.54%	−7.42%	0.07%	−0.65%
May 1983–Mar 2007					
Average	0.83%	1.06%	0.71%	0.39%	0.25%
Median	0.91%	1.29%	0.74%	0.40%	0.25%
St. Dev.	3.08%	4.22%	1.92%	0.17%	0.22%
Max	10.42%	13.47%	7.08%	0.84%	1.22%
Min	−8.31%	−21.54%	−5.72%	0.07%	−0.65%

Note: The commodity portfolio described here is collateralized.

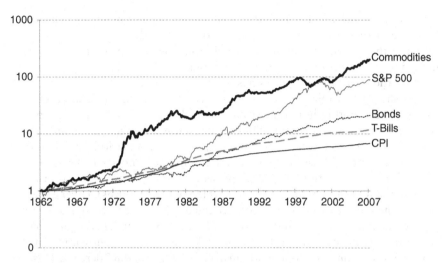

FIGURE 2.1 Cumulative Performance (log scale)

equities returned 12.31 percent. Examining the cumulative return chart it can be seen that the outperformance of commodities over the entire sample is due to their strong returns in the early 1970s, an inflationary period. Over this period there were 13 commodities in the portfolio, mostly agriculturals, and all of them rallied strongly. This was the period before energy futures were introduced. Stocks also did poorly over this period, augmenting the outperformance of commodities.

The lower panel of Table 2.6 presents a more detailed analysis of comparative performance based on monthly arithmetic returns. The results, as expected, mirror the results of the annual returns, with commodities outperforming equities over the entire sample but underperforming since the introduction of the crude oil contract. In addition, it is shown that for the entire sample the commodity portfolio and the S&P 500 had similar volatilities. Over the more recent period the standard deviation is significantly less than that of equities. The standard deviation of the commodity portfolio was 3.08 percent while that of equities was 4.22 percent. In addition, for the entire sample the worst month of the commodity portfolio was much smaller in magnitude than the worst month for the S&P 500—12.76 percent versus −21.54 percent. The worst month for equities was October 1987, reflecting the stock market crash.

The results of Tables 2.5 and 2.6 clearly show that, at least from a backward-looking perspective, commodities would have served a useful role in an investment portfolio. For the entire sample, commodities had higher returns than stocks and bonds; they had a low correlation with stocks and bonds, and their volatility was similar to the volatility of equities. More recently, the return of commodities has been lower than that of equities (and only a bit better than bonds) but their volatility has also dropped whereas the volatility of equities has not changed much.

As shown in Table 2.5, commodities' correlation with inflation is close to zero at a monthly horizon. At an annual horizon it is higher—27 percent. This suggests that commodities are not a useful hedge against inflation over short horizons but may have some modest value over longer horizons. It could also be the case, however, that commodities do well during periods of very high inflation. Table 2.7 presents this return breakdown for the 5 percent of months in which inflation was highest (27 months). During these months the monthly rate of inflation averaged 1.15 percent. Stocks did very poorly earning average monthly returns of −0.46 percent. This is consistent with the negative correlation between stocks and inflation shown in Table 2.5. The commodity portfolio made an average return of 0.87 percent. This is much better than stocks or bonds, but it is below the commodity portfolio's return for the entire period of 1.06 percent. However, it is also the case that when inflation is high the Federal Reserve raises rates, which increases short-term interest rates. When inflation is high, the return on short-term T-Bills will be high. Since the commodity portfolio we are now examining contains returns from T-Bills, it is interesting to look at the commodity portfolio's return without the T-Bill interest. This is shown in the last column of Table 2.7. Without the T-Bill interest, the average monthly return is only 0.08 percent—still positive, but barely. So, in months with very high inflation it is not the commodities as such that do well, but the T-Bills.

Table 2.8 presents the performance of commodities during the worst 5 percent of months for stocks. Over these months the commodity portfolio returns 1.51 percent which is higher than the overall average of 1.06 percent. How this should be interpreted is unclear.

TABLE 2.7 Commodity Returns and Periods of High Inflation: Returns in the Top Fifth Percentile of Inflation

	CPI	S&P 500	Bonds	T-Bills	Collateralized Commodity Portfolio	Uncollateralized Commodity Portfolio
Average	1.15%	−0.46%	0.22%	0.79%	0.87%	0.08%
Std. Dev.	0.18%	5.16%	3.57%	0.22%	5.93%	5.98%

Note: Twenty-seven months over the period February 1962 through March 2007.

TABLE 2.8 Commodity Returns and Periods of Low Stock Returns

	S&P 500	Bonds	T-Bills	CPI	Collateralized Commodity Portfolio	Uncollateralized Commodity Portfolio
Average	−8.94%	0.24%	0.49%	0.52%	1.51%	1.02%
Std. Dev.	3.12%	2.62%	0.26%	0.43%	7.54%	7.56%

Note: Low returns are defined as the bottom fifth percentile of stock returns. Twenty-seven months over the period February 1962 through March 2007.

Investments that do well during recessions are valued by investors. During recessions incomes drop, and an investment that can offset this drop is a good thing. To explore this we look at the recession periods as identified by the National Bureau of Economic Research (NBER). We take the months identified as peaks through the periods identified as troughs. There are 71 recession months over the period February 1962 through March 2007. The results are displayed in Table 2.9. Over recession periods the commodity portfolio earns an average monthly return of 0.62 percent. This is below its full-sample return of 1.06 percent. Without T-Bill interest added in, the average return would have been slightly negative. That commodities would perform below average during recessions is perhaps explained by low economic growth reducing demand for commodities.

In summary, since 1962 a commodity portfolio would have outperformed the S&P 500. However, this outperformance occurs mainly in the 1970s, and since 1983 stocks have outperformed commodities. Commodity investments would have done well during inflationary periods, but much of this was due to elevated T-Bill rates and thus higher interest income.

TABLE 2.9 Commodity Returns During Recessions (Average Arithmetic Returns)

	S&P 500	Bonds	T-Bills	CPI	Collateralized Commodity Portfolio	Uncollateralized Commodity Portfolio
Average	0.26%	0.97%	0.65%	0.56%	0.62%	−0.03%
Std. Dev.	5.97%	3.10%	0.24%	0.41%	5.54%	5.55%

Notes: Recessions as dated by the NBER. Seventy-one months from February 1962 through March 2007.

COMMODITY RETURNS COMPARED WITH COMMODITY-BASED EQUITIES

Investors who wish to have commodity price exposure in their portfolios potentially have opportunities beyond commodity futures. Producing and processing raw materials and foodstuffs is an ancient industry and, consequently, there are many publicly traded firms that engage in these businesses. Given that it is the purpose of publicly traded firms to make profits, investors should expect to earn positive returns from investing in these equities. Since the future price direction of commodities is less certain, investors could reasonably choose to invest in commodity-based equities rather than in the commodities themselves. Such a choice might make sense if the commodity future curves are in a state of contango (i.e., the futures prices are above the spot prices) as has been the case in the mid-2000s. In any case, these issues can be addressed from a backward-looking perspective by exploring how commodity futures performed relative to commodity-based equities.

As a simplification, one can think of the profits of a commodity company as coming in two pieces: the change in price of the commodities they own and the margin they earn from processing the commodities. For example, Conoco–Phillips, one of the oil majors, owns crude oil and also refines it into useable products such as gasoline. If the price of oil goes up, Conoco will be able to sell its products at a higher price, increasing its profit and stock price. However, even if the price of oil does not change Conoco will still earn a refining margin. Thus commodity companies can be profitable and produce positive investment returns, even if commodity prices do not change. However, investors do need to be aware that the profit stream from processing the commodity will make any commodity company an imperfect substitute for the commodity itself.

Companies can use the futures markets just as investors can, and they will often sell futures to lock in the price at which they sell their products. (This practice is a building block of Keynes's theory of normal backwardation.) For example, in its 2006 third quarter earnings announcement Encana announced that it had hedged one-third of its expected 2007 natural gas production. Clearly, the more a company hedges its outputs the less sensitive its profits will be to price movements in the commodity.

In constructing indexes of commodity companies it is helpful to understand the industries. In the energy and metals (both base and precious) industries, companies typically control their inputs—oil companies own their reserves,[d] mining companies typically own the mines or have very long-term

---

[d] This may change over time as nations exert more control over richly priced natural resources.

leases. In the agricultural markets this is less true. The cattle industry is very fragmented, for example. There are thousands of privately held farms producing corn, wheat, and soybeans. This makes it tougher to find companies that are exposed to these markets in ways that are interesting to potential commodity investors. In what follows we divide commodities into three group—energy, metals, and agriculturals—and use equity indexes that are sensible for each commodity group.

The energy category consists of crude oil, heating oil, unleaded gas, and natural gas. As in the previous construction of the commodity index, the return for the energy future portfolio is the equally weighted return of each future contract plus T-Bill interest. For comparison to the energy future portfolio the Dow Jones Oil and Gas Titans index is used. This is an index of the world's largest oil and gas companies. The metal category consists of aluminum, copper, zinc, nickel, gold, and silver. The equity comparison index is the Dow Jones Basic Resources Titans index. The agricultural group consists of canola, corn, wheat, soybeans, soybean oil, soy meal, lean hogs, and live cattle. There does not exist an index that is obviously comparable to this group, so a group of equities was selected and equally weighted.[e]

The results based on monthly arithmetic returns are displayed in Table 2.10. The sample covered begins in February 1992, when return data becomes available for the Dow Jones equity indexes. Starting with energies, the correlation between the futures and the index is .47, so there is a reasonable relation. The energy future portfolio has an average arithmetic monthly return of 1.78 percent with a standard deviation of 9.33 percent. The energy equity index has a monthly return of 0.97 percent and a standard deviation of 4.83 percent. Roughly, the energy futures have twice the return and twice the volatility of the energy equity index. The correlation of metal futures and the basic resources equity index is .56. Again, this shows a reasonably strong relationship. The metal futures portfolio earns 0.91 percent a month with a standard deviation of 4.44 percent and the equity index earns a return of 0.80 percent a month with a standard deviation of 6.00 percent. In this case, the futures have both a higher return and a lower standard deviation. For the agriculturals the correlation is only .01, effectively zero. The equity index constructed is not a good substitute for the agricultural future portfolio. That being said, the average monthly futures return is 0.40 percent with a standard deviation of 3.95 percent. The equity index has an average return of 1.21 percent and a standard deviation of 5.45 percent.

---

[e] Smithfield, Tyson Foods, Hormel, Premium Standard Farms, Archer-Daniels Midland, Bunge.

TABLE 2.10 Commodity Returns versus Commodity-Based Equities (Monthly Arithmetic Returns)

	Energy Futures	Energy Equities
Average	1.78%	0.97%
Std. Dev.	9.33%	3.10%
Correlation	0.47	
	Metal Futures	**Metal Equities**
Average	0.91%	0.80%
Std. Dev.	4.44%	6.00%
Correlation	0.56	
	Agriculture Futures	**Agriculture Equities**
Average	0.40%	1.21%
Std. Dev.	3.95%	5.45%
Correlation	0.01	

Notes: The time period is Feb 1992 through March 2007. Energy futures are Nymex Crude oil, heating oil, unleaded gas, and natural gas. Energy equities are the Dow Jones Oil and Gas Titans. Metal futures are copper, zinc, aluminum, nickel, gold, and silver. Metal equities are the Dow Jones Titans Basic resources index. Agricultural futures are canola, corn, wheat, soybeans, soybean oil, soybean meal, lean hogs, and live cattle. Agricultural equities are Smithfield, Hormel, Premium Standard Farms, Archer Daniels Midland, and Bunge.

Ignoring the agriculturals, where comparison with equities is difficult, the commodity future portfolios in both cases outperformed the comparison equity index. In the case of the energies, normalizing by volatility makes the two portfolios' performances roughly similar. So historically, one could make the argument that commodity futures have been at least as good as commodity-based equities as investments. Whether this will be true in the future depends, of course, on one's view of future movements in commodities. If commodity prices were to remain flat, commodity-based equities would still make money from their processing margin. If commodities go up, ignoring curve effects, then commodity futures investments will likely outperform commodity-based equities since they are a pure play on commodity price movements.

The result that equity indexes with nontrivial correlations to commodity futures exist is interesting in its own right. It suggests that investors have the ability to gain exposure to the commodity markets through equities. In some cases, circumstances may favor equity investments over pure commodity investments. In the case of energies, part of the return of the energy future portfolio is due to T-Bill interest and creep up the curve, because the energy markets have typically been backwardated. (This is dealt with in more detail in Chapter 21, "The Rise of the Indexes.") Oil prices have also gone up over time. Say that one thought that oil prices would continue to go up but T-Bill rates were low and the futures curve was contangoed. In this case, it might make sense, depending on valuations, to implement one's view on oil prices in equities in the oil industry.

CONCLUSION

This chapter has explored the historical return characteristics of commodities during the recent era. This is a good first step in evaluating the potential for commodity investments. Commodity futures investments have earned positive returns historically. They have generated similar returns to equities, with similar volatility but with very little correlation to equities. However, much of this outperformance occurred during the 1970s. Commodities have outperformed equities in periods of high inflation, but whether they are a good hedge against inflation is less clear. They are profitable in the months with the highest inflation, but most of this return is due to T-Bill interest. Commodities have also done well compared with commodity-based equities.

It should be emphasized that what has been accomplished in this chapter is very much a backward-looking exercise. It has been shown that commodities have done well historically, but why this is so—what the economic mechanism is exactly—remains unclear. Unlike stocks and bonds, commodities do not generate earnings or interest payments. Investors who wish to consider commodities from an absolute return standpoint should not do so unless they have reason to believe that commodity futures will generate positive returns in the future. The remainder of this book will provide information and tools to help investors reason through the potential for commodities as investments. First, however, we look further back into history.

DATA ADDENDUM

Futures Data

The gasoline series is actually a combination of the older unleaded contract and the newer RBOB contract. The switch comes in June 2006. The contract change occurred due to the dropping of MTBE as a gas additive in favor of ethanol.

The lean hog contract was the live hog contract up until 1996.

The soymeal contract switches from 44 percent protein to 48 percent protein with the expiration of the September 1992 contract. We used data from the U.S. Department of Agriculture (USDA) in order to compute a continuous percent change in the cash price over this transition period.

The London Metal Exchange (LME) contracts aluminum, nickel, and zinc are forward contracts, not futures.

Aluminum: Until September 1987, the change in the three-month forward price is used as a proxy for the return. From September 1987 enough data is available to interpolate a return using either the cash price or a two-month price.

Zinc: Until January 1988, the change in the three-month forward price is used as a proxy for the return. From January 1988 enough data is available to interpolate a return using either the cash price or a two-month price.

Nickel: Until February 1987, the change in the three-month forward price is used as a proxy for the return. From February 1987 enough data is available to interpolate a return using either the cash price or a two-month price.

Spot Data

All of the spot commodity price data is from CRB with the following exceptions and augmentations.

RBOB: Data from June 2006 onward (when RBOB replaces unleaded in the sample) is from the EIA.

Natural Gas: February 1992 through October 1993 is weekly Henry Hub Prices taken from Bloomberg.

Soymeal: Data is adjusted over the October–November 1992 period to account for the change from 44 percent protein to 48 percent protein.

Cotton: January 1975 through December 1975 uses monthly *average* prices obtained from the National Cotton Council.

Sugar: January 1960 through July 1979 uses monthly *average* prices obtained from the USDA.

Non-Commodity Data

Ten-Year Bond Returns   Through January 1980 these are approximated total returns using 10-year rates from the Federal Reserve. From February 1980 from Citigroup index 7 to 10 year sector U.S. Treasury. Bloomberg symbol SBGT710 Index.

Bills   Through January 1978 these returns are approximated total returns using three-month bill rates from the Federal Reserve. Starting February 1978 they are returns based on the Citigroup one-month Treasury index. Bloomberg symbol SBMMTB1.

Commodities for the Long Run

In the previous chapter we examined the performance of commodity investments during the past several decades. In this chapter we will explore, as best as we can, the long-term performance of commodities. As with most economic studies that seek to reach far back into history the primary difficulty is the availability and quality of data. Though commodity prices and commodity futures are everywhere today, the salience of commodities in financial markets is a relatively recent development in the history of humanity. True, the Chicago Board of Trade was formed in 1848, but crude oil futures were not introduced until 1983. It is arguably with the introduction of crude oil futures that the modern age of commodity investing began. The S&P GSCI Index, today's most important, was not formed until 1991. In this chapter we will look at two series, the price of wheat and the Economist Commodity Price Index,[1] to get a sense of the long-term performance of commodities. Unlike the last chapter, we will be focusing on the price of physical commodities, instead of futures, as that is what data availability allows.

Why wheat? Wheat is one of humanity's most important foodstuffs. It is the prime ingredient in bread, and bread, of course, is the staff of life. Cereal crops such as wheat have been in continuous use since humans first became farmers 10,000 years ago. In contrast, the commodities humans have used for energy have changed over time. Humans first lived in warm climates where fuel was not necessary. As they moved out of Africa into cooler areas, they first burned wood, then coal, and now oil. Other commodities such as gold or coffee have been around for a long time, but each has its flaws. Gold has served primarily as a form of currency, and coffee is a luxury, not essential to life. Wheat also has the advantage that a long history has been assembled. The primary source for wheat data is Clark (2003), which is also available on that author's website. Clark draws on various sources to put together long histories of agricultural prices in England. This data is supplemented with spot data from the Commodity Research Bureau (CRB) beginning in 1900. The data is restated in terms of U.S. dollars. More information is given in the data appendix to this chapter.

The Economist Commodity Price Index is the longest commodity price index publicly available. Though early data is incomplete, it is collected as far back as 1845. The weightings and commodities have changed over time, and it currently contains 25 items based on United Nations import data for 1999, 2000, and 2001. It currently consists of 56.4 percent food items, 28.2 percent metals, and 15.4 percent non-food agricultural items. It contains no energy and no precious metals. Aluminum has the highest weighting, 14.0 percent, followed by wheat, 8.2 percent. It is U.S. dollar based and the prices are averages over the year, though some of the earlier years are point samplings. The real series is deflated using a GDP deflator and the CPI in earlier periods.

Figure 3.1 displays the nominal price history of wheat since 1500. The price of wheat does appear to have an upward trend, but it is very volatile. Wheat could have been had for less than one hundred cents a bushel in both the 1930s and in the 1530s. From 1501 to 2006 wheat appreciated by 0.54 percent a year. This has been good for consumers; less so for those who might have wished to invest in physical wheat.

Though volatile in general, the price of wheat is punctuated by some significant spikes. Until recently, these tended to be associated with wars. Before the 1970s, the highest price for wheat occurred (in England) during

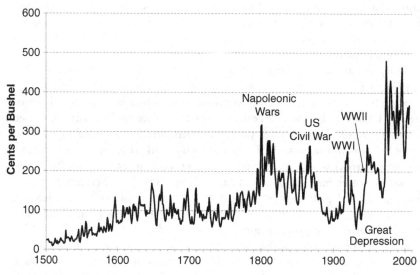

FIGURE 3.1 Nominal Cash Price of Wheat

the Napoleonic wars. There were also significant spikes associated with the Crimean War, the U.S. Civil War, and both world wars of the twentieth century. The spike to new highs in the 1970s was due to the generally inflationary environment and the after-effects of the *Great Grain Robbery*, in which the Soviet Union bought large amounts of U.S. grain to alleviate domestic food shortages. See Ulrich (1996) for a good account of this episode and a good narrative of grain prices in general over the past 200 years. It is also interesting to note that wheat prices declined with the stock market in the late 1920s and the early 1930s. This is important because one of the main factors determining whether commodities fit into an investment portfolio is how they do during times of bad equity market performance. Over the period for which there exists a lot of data on commodities, and hence the periods that are typically analyzed (including those in this book), there are few stock market crashes.

Figure 3.2 presents the real price history of wheat. In real terms, the price of wheat has gone down. It has lost −0.39 percent a year in real terms. Even though the real price of wheat spiked in the 1970s, it did not keep pace with inflation and in 2006 was near its low in real terms.

Approaching wheat from the perspective of investing in physical wheat, Figures 3.1 and 3.2 substantially overstate performance. The reason is that actually holding physical wheat would entail costs. To store and maintain

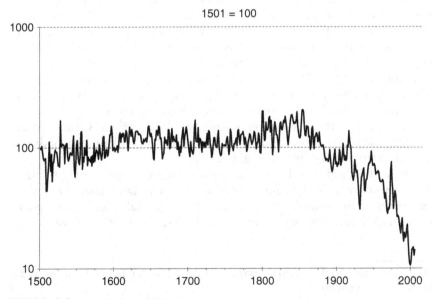

FIGURE 3.2   Real Price of Wheat

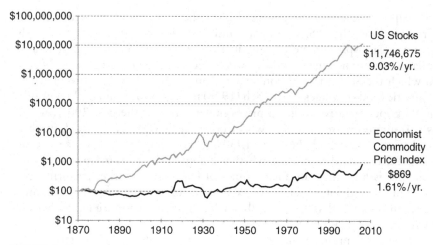

FIGURE 3.3   Commodities versus Stocks (log scale)

a wheat inventory costs money. Assuming a wheat price of 400 cents per bushel and a daily storage of .15 cents (1.5 tenths of a cent a bushel a day), it would take somewhat over seven years for storage costs to eat the entire value of the wheat investment. And there are financing costs as well.

The Economist Commodity Price Index (ECPI) has the advantage over wheat in that it is more broadly based, but the disadvantage that it is available for a shorter history. Figure 3.3 shows the ECPI since 1871, which is when equity returns become available.[a] Normalizing the ECPI to be $100 in 1871, it would have increased in value to $868.87 by 2006. Over the 135 years this would have been an annual (geometric) appreciation of 1.61 percent. As mentioned previously, this 1.61 percent is not what investors would have actually earned, because of storage and financing costs. Over this same time period the annual return on equities was 9.03 percent. Clearly, from a return standpoint, over the most recent century and a half, commodities were an inferior investment to equities.

As with wheat, the ECPI does poorly over the period of the 1929 stock market crash and the initial years of the Great Depression. Over this time period commodities would not have been a useful hedge against poor stock market performance. Later, in the 1970s, when inflation was high,

---

[a] Equity returns are taken from the website of Robert Shiller and updated by hand. See the data appendix.

commodities did do well when equities did poorly. It is interesting to contrast these two periods. The Great Depression was characterized by a drop in overall demand whereas the inflationary period of the 1970s was effectively a debasing of the currency. Equities did poorly in both periods whereas commodities did poorly only when demand shrunk. For commodities, this makes sense: a drop in demand typically does lead to a drop in price and high inflation is nothing more than increasing the amount of currency needed to purchase goods. Overall, the correlation of these two series over this time period is about –9 percent.[b]

Figure 3.4 displays the real returns of the ECPI from 1857 (the beginning of annual reporting for the index) through 2006. Since 1857, commodity prices have declined in real terms. They have lost 0.66 percent annually. Real commodity prices surged during the World War I period, and they were firm during the World War II period, but aside from that they have moved steadily downward. Even the inflationary period of the 1970s provided only temporary support.

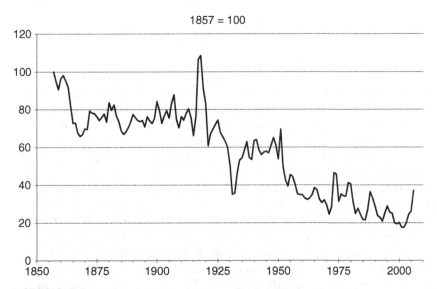

FIGURE 3.4   *The Economist* Real Commodity Price Index, $ Terms

---

[b] This is imperfect since both the equity and commodity series are averaged. The ECPI is generally an average of the prices that occurred in that year, whereas the equity prices are the averages for December.

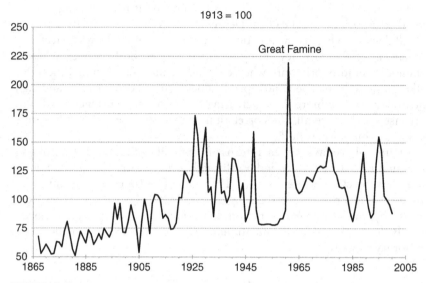

FIGURE 3.5   Chinese Real Rice Price Index

The exploration so far deals with commodity prices in the West. Looking to the East, there has been work to construct long histories of rice prices in China (Feng and Kaixiang 2006). It is again worth emphasizing that it is difficult to construct price series that stretch back into the haziness of distant history, both because good data is hard to get and because currencies are not always stable. That being said, Feng and Kaixiang show that from 1644 until the beginning of the twentieth century, the nominal price of rice was approximately unchanged. The twentieth century contained a significant period of hyperinflation and change in monetary regimes, making nominal prices less informative over this time period. Therefore switching to real terms, the price series of Feng and Kaixiang imply that the real price of rice rose at an annual rate of about .20 percent over the period from 1867 to 2000. Figure 15 from their paper is reconstructed using data provided by the authors and reproduced as Figure 3.5 here. This is positive real appreciation, but obviously very small and, again, it is unlikely to have been sufficient to cover the cost of storage and financing.

In summary, over the broad sweep of history commodity prices have gone up, but not rapidly. Comparing stock returns to commodity appreciation shows that stocks have gone up much more, not even taking account of the storage and financing costs that would have been necessary to maintain physical commodity inventories. Commodities have gone up during periods of war, but during the 1929 stock market crash and the ensuing economic weakness, they went down just as did stocks.

DATA ADDENDUM

Equity Returns

Equity prices and dividends are taken from the website of Robert Shiller. The year-end prices used are averages for the month of December. From 2004 the data is updated with S&P 500 data.

Wheat

Wheat prices from 1501 through 1900 are taken from the website of Gregory Clark (see Clark 2003). Wheat data since 1900 is taken from the CRB and is annual averages. To provide continuity all wheat prices are converted to US dollars, see officer (2006). Prior to 1791 the first entry in the Officer series is used ($4.55/pound). To adjust to real prices the inflation indexes from Officer and Williamson (2007) are used.

Understanding Energy

Crude Oil

Crude oil, also known as petroleum, was formed millions of years ago by the remains of plants and animals that inhabited the seas. It is thought that the majority of these organisms were single-celled and as they died their remains fell to the sea bed and were covered with sand and mud creating a rich organic layer. This process repeated itself over and over and the layers eventually developed into sedimentary rock. Over time increased pressure and heat from the weight of the layers caused the organic remains to slowly transform themselves into crude oil and natural gas, among other things.

Crude oil is made up of hydrocarbons, which are molecules made from both hydrogen and carbon atoms. These hydrocarbons are the basis of all petroleum, but they differ in their configurations of both hydrogen and carbon atoms. The carbon atoms may be linked in a chain formation with either a full or partial balance of hydrogen atoms. An important characteristic of hydrocarbons is that each chemical compound has its own boiling point. If you took a pot of water and boiled it to 212°F, all the water would boil off because this is the temperature at which the chemical compound of water, H_2O, boils. If you took a pot of crude oil and heated it to a 150°F boil you would notice that after some time the crude stops boiling. Raise the temperature to 200°F and the crude will boil again but eventually it would stop. You could repeat this process over and over by raising the temperature. Each time more and more crude would boil off. This creates the distillation curve, the plot of temperature versus evaporation. Each type of crude oil has a unique distillation curve dependent on the kinds of hydrocarbons that make up that crude.[1] The amount of carbon atoms in the crude oil determines its density or weight. Gases typically have between one and four carbons, whereas heavier grades of crude oil can have 50 carbons. Both the weight and the distillation curve of a specific crude oil are important to refiners who need to separate the different components of the crude oil to make various products such as gasoline, heating oil, diesel, and jet fuel.

OIL PRODUCTION

Conventional Oil

The most common way to produce crude oil is to use drilling rigs to create an oil well that will extract oil from a crude oil field. Oil wells can be located onshore, as in West Texas, or offshore, as in the Gulf of Mexico. The type of production process used is dependent on how much pressure is within the oil reservoir and whether additional pressure is needed to pump the oil towards the surface. Most oil is first produced using the natural pressure within the oil reservoir that forces the oil to the surface. Eventually this natural pressure dissipates, and a pump is needed to extract the remaining oil. At some point during the life of an oil well it is no longer economically viable to continue to operate the well because it no longer produces or production is very poor. At that point the well is abandoned, and the flow to the surface is plugged.

Technology has played a critical part in the advancement of energy production. The change in seismic testing from two dimensional to three dimensional, advanced imaging systems, and stronger material used for both pipes and drill bits are a few of the common advances. Another major technological advance is horizontal drilling. The drill path formed by horizontal drilling begins vertically into the oil field and continues in an arc shape into the reservoir where it proceeds horizontally. The objective in horizontal drilling is to allow the well to be exposed to more reservoir rock than under the vertical drilling method. The horizontal drilling method is applied to fractured conventional reserves, fractured source rocks, and also to older wells in order to increase production.

Unconventional Oil

Both the oil sands and shale oil are sources of oil where extraction is more costly than conventional drilling methods. Since the extraction of oil does not use conventional drilling methods, these oil sources are called unconventional oil. The United States has the largest oil shale deposits in the world in two main deposits. The Eastern U.S. deposits are in the Devonian-Mississippian shale located in the central Appalachian basin. The Western U.S. deposits are in the Green River formation within Colorado, Wyoming, and Utah. Shale oil is a rock-like substance that is rich in the organic matter kerogen, which is the primitive precursor to crude oil. The oil can be extracted in two ways. In the first process, oil shale is mined from the ground and then processed at a facility where it is heated and enriched with hydrogen in order to extract hydrogen vapors. The second method is called in-situ processing and involves heating the shale underground until it fractures. When the shale fractures it releases gases and liquids, which are then captured.

Oil sand deposits are found in many countries across the globe, but the majority of oil sands are located in Venezuela and Canada. The oil is trapped in a complex mixture of sand, water, and clay, which is why crude oil extraction from the oil sands is costlier than current conventional drilling methods. The crude oil within the oil sands is called bitumen and is separated from the waste in the oil sands using one of two methods. The first method applies to approximately 20 percent of the oil sand reserves; the sands are mined in an open pit, and the bitumen is extracted using a hot water technique. The other 80 percent of the oil sands are buried deep below the surface and cannot be extracted using open pit mining.[2] In this case, drilling occurs and steam is injected into the deposit to lower the viscosity of the bitumen. The hot bitumen is then brought to the surface using producing wells, and the sand is left beneath the surface. This process is sure to become a large future method of oil production, because most of the oil within the sands must be extracted in this way.

PRODUCERS—OPEC AND NON-OPEC

Oil producers are classified according to two groupings. The first and most famous of these is the Organization of Petroleum Exporting Countries (OPEC). OPEC was created on September 14, 1960 in response to pressure from major oil companies to lower payments and prices to oil producers. The 12 member states are Algeria, Angola, Indonesia, Iran, Iraq, Kuwait, Libya, Nigeria, Qatar, Saudi Arabia, the United Arab Emirates, and Venezuela. Indonesia's membership is currently under review as it is no longer classified as a petroleum exporting country. In addition, Iraq has had no quota since March of 1998 because it is still trying to restore its oil production lost during the Gulf Wars. OPEC members hold the majority of the spare oil production capacity in the world and use it to change their production levels dependent on both prices and demand for crude oil. OPEC is often thought of as a cartel, yet it lists one of its primary missions as trying to achieve stable oil prices which are fair and reasonable to both the consumer and producer.[3] OPEC's actions on the oil market have not always had stabilizing affects however. It shocked the world and heightened inflation by using oil as a weapon in the 1973 oil crisis.

The other producer group is non-OPEC, which consists of all oil producers that are not members of OPEC. Within non-OPEC, the Former Soviet Union (FSU) is often cited as a group because it is the largest single producer

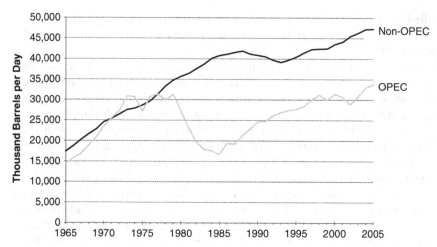

FIGURE 4.1 OPEC versus Non-OPEC Crude Oil Production
Source: BP Annual Statistical Review of Energy 2006

outside of OPEC. In 2005 OPEC's share of world oil production was 42 percent with non-OPEC production being 58 percent. The FSU accounts for 25 percent of non-OPEC production.[4] As shown in Figure 4.1, the oil crisis of 1973 really marked the end of OPEC as the dominant oil producer. By 1980 the rest of the world had surpassed OPEC in oil production. Internal conflicts ensued as Saudi Arabia, eager to gain market share, increased production in the mid-1980s, which further decreased prices. The major characteristic of non-OPEC producers is that the large majority of them are net oil importers. Most of the non-OPEC oil production is run by private oil companies, with the notable exception of Mexico. In addition, production costs tend to be higher for non-OPEC countries than for OPEC countries, making them more vulnerable to price collapses.

OPEC is important to the world because as a whole those countries have the most spare production capacity available. Since OPEC institutes production quotas for its members, production tends to run below total capacity. This enables OPEC to react to changes in the global oil market quickly. Unexpected increases in demand that raise the price of oil can be met by increases in the OPEC production quota. If there is a long-term supply loss from a non-OPEC country, OPEC is able to use spare capacity to make up this shortfall if necessary. This ability makes OPEC the swing producer in the global oil market, and at times the market is at the whim of OPEC's decisions.

HUBBERT'S PEAK

During the past few years numerous alarms have been raised about the peak of global oil production. The concept of peak oil has been talked about almost since the first barrel of oil was produced, given that oil is not a renewable resource. At some point in the future we will run out, but the question of when has been hotly debated. M. King Hubbert was an American geologist who worked within research at Shell in Houston, TX. Hubbert was the first geologist to treat the issue of oil field depletion using quantitative methods. Because an oil field's production is finite, its production both starts and ends at zero. Working with this concept in mind, Hubbert observed that cumulative oil production, as a function of time, followed a logistic growth curve. Taking this concept he was able to quantitatively model production of any given oil field based on discovery rates, production rates, and cumulative production. Hubbert assumed that after discovery of oil, production increases almost exponentially as new wells are put into place. At some point peak output is reached, and the production goes into exponential decline as the resource is depleted. This creates a bell-shaped curve that traces the production of oil. This econometric model became widely known as Hubbert's Peak. It is displayed in Figure 4.2, which shows the bell-shaped curve structure that applies to U.S. oil field production. Based on this chart it is evident that U.S. oil production peaked sometime between 1970 and 1971. In a 1956 speech to the American Petroleum Institute (API) Hubbert

FIGURE 4.2   U.S. Crude Oil Field Production
Source: Energy Information Administration

had predicted that continental U.S oil production would peak somewhere during the early 1970s.[5]

Since Hubbert's speech to the API there have been numerous estimates and date claims for world peak oil production. Although Hubbert was able to use his model to successfully estimate the peak in U.S. oil production, it is not as easy to do so for world oil production. It is imperative to remember that no physical or chemical law compels production to follow a logistical growth curve. Oil production is determined by a number of factors, including political and economic. These factors can keep the production of oil below the maximum possible flow rate for a long time. Hubbert's mathematical model also relied heavily on credible world oil proven resource estimates. These proven oil reserve estimates, published by each producing country and private companies, have not always been freely accessible. According to the *BP Statistical Review of World Energy* in 2006, OPEC's proven reserves have more than doubled from 1980 to 2005, even though we have been consuming OPEC oil during that entire time.[6] This shows that proven reserve estimates are almost useless for predicting future trends. This is just one example of the many limitations of Hubbert's econometric model as a way to predict global peak oil production.

RESERVES

An oil reserve is a known supply of oil held underground that is economically recoverable. Proven reserves are oil reserves that are reasonably certain to be able to be extracted using current technologies at current prices. Outside of proven reserves there are other classifications for oil reserves that do not have the same reasonable certainty of being produced. Probable reserves are defined as oil reserves that have a reasonably probable chance of being produced using current or similar technology at current prices. Possible reserves have a chance of being produced under favorable circumstances. These reserves may need a higher price to be profitable for extraction or may require technology yet to be tested. Unconventional oil sources such as shale oil, oil sands, biofuels, and the conversion of natural gas or coal to liquid hydrocarbons may be classified as possible reserves.

Sixty-eight percent of proven reserves are held by OPEC; and out of the remaining 32 percent of reserves held by non-OPEC countries, 7.5 percent is held by the Former Soviet Union (FSU), as shown in Table 4.1. According to the *Oil and Gas Journal*, the world has approximately 1.31 trillion barrels of proven oil reserves as of January 1, 2007.[7] At the current rate of global consumption, 82.5 million barrels a day, there is enough oil in proven reserves to last for approximately 44 years.[8] Furthermore the *Oil and Gas Journal* estimates world oil proven reserve growth at

TABLE 4.1   Oil Production and Proven Reserves

Country	Proven Reserves	Daily Production (Thousands of Barrels)	% World Reserves
Saudi Arabia	259,800,000	8,990	19.72%
Iran	136,270,000	3,850	10.34%
Former Soviet Union	98,886,000	11,569	7.51%
Iraq	115,000,000	1,915	8.73%
Kuwait	99,000,000	2,200	7.51%
United Arab Emirates	93,800,000	2,501	7.12%
Venezuela	80,012,000	2,563	6.07%
United States	21,757,000	5,135	1.65%
OPEC	902,343,000	33,836	68.49%
Non-OPEC[1]	415,104,415	47,251	31.51%
Total Proven Reserves	**1,317,447,415**		

Source: Oil and Gas Journal, December 18, 2006
[1]Data includes former Soviet Union.

730 billion barrels and undiscovered proven reserves at 938 billion barrels.[9] Reserve growth consists of increases in reserves from technological contributions that increase an oil field's recovery rate. Including reserve growth and undiscovered reserves, there are approximately 2.98 trillion barrels of proven oil reserves.[10] This supply could last for approximately 99 years given current consumption levels. Table 4.2 shows the breakdown of proven, probable, and possible reserves globally. It does not include unknowns such as biofuels or the conversion of natural gas or coal to liquid hydrocarbons.

Heavy hydrocarbons, also known as the oil sands and extra heavy oil, are an unconventional oil resource in which the majority of reserves are not listed in the proven reserves category. This oil resource will become essential for meeting future global oil demand. For 2005, the Canadian Association of Petroleum Producers reported Canadian oil sands production at 992,000 barrels a day.[11] The International Energy Agency reports that at the end of 2000, global oil sands and extra heavy oil accounted for 4.29 trillion barrels of oil resources, of which 580 billion barrels were recoverable.[12] This leaves approximately 3.7 trillion barrels of heavy hydrocarbon resources that would be classified under probable or possible reserves. Given current oil consumption, the oil sands and extra heavy oil could possibly give the world an additional 123 years of supply.

The other major unconventional oil resource is oil shale. In the United States, where the majority of oil shale resources are located, there is not yet sustained production from this resource. In fact Estonia is the world's

TABLE 4.2 Total Oil Reserves: Proven, Probable, and Possible

	Amount (1,000 bbls)	Global Consumption[i,a] (1,000/bbls per day)	Years Supply[b]
Potential Proven Reserves	2,986,547,415	82,500	99
Total Proven Reserves[ii]	1,317,447,415		
Proven Reserve Growth[iii]	730,200,000		
Undiscovered Proven Reserves[iii]	938,900,000		
Oil Sands/Heavy Oil Probable and Possible Reserves[iv]	3,710,000,000	82,500	123
Oil Shale Possible Reserves[iv]	3,500,000,000	82,500	116

[i]*BP Statistical Review*, 2006. (No growth rate applied.)
[ii]*Oil and Gas Journal*, December 18, 2006.
[iii]*Oil and Gas Journal*, November 27, 2006.
[iv]International Energy Agency.
[a]Using consumption as of 2005.
[b]Years supply assuming given global consumption levels and size of reserves.

leading producer of shale oil at 3,000 barrels a day.[13] The International Energy Agency reports that worldwide oil shale resources exceed 3.5 trillion barrels. These oil shale resources would be listed under probable or possible reserves. Given current oil consumption levels, shale oil could provide the world with 116 years of supply.

So how much oil supply is presently on hand, and how long will it last? The figures given previously provide a general idea of how much oil may be left globally. They are by no means final, as each year new estimates of reserves are announced. The true answer is dependent on technological advances along with the price of oil in the future, given that the unconventional oil resources discussed are much more expensive to develop than conventional oil resources. In its Annual Energy Outlook 2006, The Energy Information Administration (EIA) states that oil sands are economically viable to produce when crude oil is above $30.[14] The EIA also cites a study prepared for the National Energy Technology Laboratory that determines the first shale oil production operation would be profitable with WTI oil prices in the range of $70 to $95 per barrel.[15] Keeping these figures in mind it is reasonable to suggest that the world has approximately 222 years of oil supply if proven reserves and the oil sands reserve estimates are included. One issue with this estimate is the energy content of these unconventional oil sources. At this point additional supplies of oil are not of the light, sweet, high-energy type. They are heavy crudes with less energy content per barrel. This results in using more barrels of heavy crude to maintain current consumption levels, cutting into the long-term estimate regarding years of supply. In addition, heavy crudes are more energy intensive to extract and to process. It is obvious that the true problem with unconventional oil sources is the issue of recoverability. It will take higher oil prices, technological advances, research, and time to determine whether these reserves will be worth extracting. Overall, global oil supply could last for more than 300 years if shale oil became a feasible source of oil production, but the issues cited previously would still remain.

CONSUMPTION

Oil is used in a variety of applications. It can be burned to power a car, generate electricity, or heat a home. It also can be used as a raw material to create plastics, petrochemicals, and many other products. The United States and Canada use oil more for transportation than for heat or electricity, but in the rest of the world oil is used more for heat and power than for transportation. Globally the largest consumers of oil have traditionally been industrialized countries such as the United States, England, Germany, and Japan. Figure 4.3, which shows consumption by region, documents that the Asia Pacific region has had a large expansion in demand during the past 20 years. A large portion of this demand increase in Asia has come from China, which in 2003 surpassed Japan as the second largest consumer of

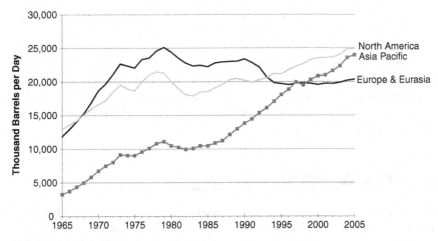

FIGURE 4.3   Oil Consumption by Region
Source: BP Annual Statistical Review of Energy 2006

TABLE 4.3   Yearly Oil Consumption (1,000 bbls)

Country	1980	2005	Avg. Yearly % Increase
United States	17,062	20,655	0.84%
Japan	4,936	5,360	0.34%
China	1,694	6,988	12.50%
Germany	3,056	2,586	−0.62%
France	2,262	1,961	−0.53%
India	643	2,485	11.46%
South Korea	475	2,308	15.44%
Canada	1,915	2,241	0.68%
United Kingdom	1,672	1,790	0.28%
World Total	61,678	82,459	1.35%

Source: BP Statistical Energy Review, 2006

crude oil after the United States.[16] Table 4.3 shows oil consumption growth in various countries from 1980 to 2005. China, South Korea, and India have shown huge increases in demand for oil whereas industrialized countries such as Germany and France have actually exhibited a decline in oil demand. This is partly because the industrialized countries are using energy more efficiently than the emerging economies. In addition, manufacturing has been moving out of countries such as the United States and Germany and into China and South Korea.

As these emerging economies such as China, India, and Brazil continue their growth, their consumption of oil will continue to increase. It is not unreasonable to suppose that these countries may have a growth pattern similar to that of the United States after the Great Depression. Although China and India are the most populous countries in the world, their global share of oil consumption is extremely small. As their economies grow and consumption increases, demand for energy is sure to grow as well. This will create competition for oil imports between the industrialized countries and these emerging economies.

PHYSICAL CRUDE AND REFINING

Physical crude oil comes from a wide variety of locations and in a wide variety of packages. The Energy Intelligence Group reports that there are about 161 different internationally traded physical crude oils.[17] The oil industry first classifies crude based on its production location. The important physical characteristics of crude oil are whether it is light or heavy and whether it is sweet or sour. Light crude oil has low wax content whereas heavier crude has higher wax content and thus higher viscosity. This higher viscosity makes it harder to both pump and transport through pipelines. Sweet crude oil refers to the amount of sulfur in the crude oil, and sweet crude usually contains less than .5 percent sulfur. Lower sulfur content in a crude oil allows it to be more cheaply processed into lighter products than sour crude. With sour crude (more than 1 percent sulfur) the impurities need to be removed before it can be processed into light products. Sweet crude oil is generally the ideal crude for refining into gasoline and other light end products.

Refining is the act of taking crude oil and processing it to make finished petroleum products that we use on a daily basis such as gasoline, heating oil, diesel, and jet fuel. Refining begins with simple distillation, which separates the hydrocarbons in the crude into its fractions, or categories of its hydrocarbon components. This is done by heating the crude oil in a simple distillation chamber. Different products boil off at different temperatures and are then captured. The lighter products such as liquid petroleum gases, naphtha, and straight-run gasoline boil off first. The middle distillate family, which consists of jet fuel, kerosene, heating oil, and diesel boil off next. The heaviest product, residual fuel oil, is the last product to boil off.

Refineries in the United States use much more complex processes than the simple distillation because end-user demand is focused on light products. These light products create high value for the refinery; so after simple distillation, refineries reprocess the heavier products and change them into higher-value light products. A process called cracking uses the heavy distillate captured in the simple distillation and puts it into a catalytic cracker in order to produce lighter distillates and gasoline. Hydrotreaters are used to remove sulfur in petroleum products so that when burned for fuel or energy they emit lower levels of sulfur dioxide. The heaviest output of simple distillation, residual fuel oil, is put through a coker in order to process it into lighter products and petroleum coke. Reforming units create high-octane components used in making gasoline from lower-octane byproducts captured in the simple distillation process.

The quality of the crude oil used in the refining process is important in determining how much processing is needed to achieve an optimal mix of products. Light sweet crude oil like WTI has a high yield of premium light products such as naphtha and straight-run gasoline using just simple distillation. On the opposite end of the spectrum, heavy crude like Iran Heavy yields a high level of residual fuel oil in simple distillation that must be reprocessed to create lighter products. Refineries are aiming to process crude that yields an optimal mix of products, taking into account the cost of the available crude. However, not all refineries have the ability to process heavy crude and heavy products, so the type of crude a refiner can use depends on the refinery's equipment.

Most of the U.S. refining capacity is located on the Gulf Coast. Products are then shipped to the East Coast and the Midwest through pipeline and on tanker ships. According to the *BP Statistical Energy Review*, U.S. refinery utilization from 1996 to 2005 averaged 90.5 percent.[18] In the United States refinery runs have seasonal patterns. Peak utilization occurs in the summer along with the demand for gasoline. Refineries also have two maintenance periods, in the fall and in late winter/early spring. The depth and duration of these maintenance periods depends on the current profit margin. If margins are high due to demand for refined products, refiners will put off routine maintenance or go offline for a shorter time than initially anticipated. If refineries put off necessary and scheduled maintenance too long, accidents at the plant are more likely to occur. An unplanned outage results in the refinery being down for a longer time in the future. Thus, refineries need to balance the need for maintenance with their profit margins and the probability of an unexpected outage. Refineries will also produce products depending on consumers' needs. For example, if the profit margin for gasoline is higher than for heating oil due to market demand for gasoline, refiners will switch to make as much gasoline as possible in lieu of heating oil. Refineries will also make adjustments to output levels dependent on their profit margin.

FUTURES

Both of the two most liquid futures contracts on crude oil are those of the light sweet variety. The first one is West Texas Intermediate (WTI), traded on the New York Mercantile Exchange (NYMEX). WTI crude oil is produced in the United States and is of very high quality, making it ideal for refining into gasoline. The second contract is Brent crude oil, which is traded on the Intercontinental Exchange (ICE). Brent crude oil consists of a variety of crudes produced from the North Sea and includes Brent Crude, Oseberg, and Forties. It is not as light or sweet as WTI but it is ideal for the production of gasoline and distillates. The name *Brent* is taken from the Brent goose, but it is also an acronym for the formation layers (Broom, Rannoch, Frieve, Ness, and Tarbat) of the Brent oil field. The Brent crude oil trades on an electronic trading platform, whereas the WTI crude oil trades side-by-side on both an electronic trading platform and in the exchange pit. These two future contracts are highly correlated, and because of its physical characteristics, WTI usually trades at a premium to Brent.

WTI crude oil futures, traded on the NYMEX, were launched in March, 1983. The WTI future is deliverable to Cushing, Oklahoma which is accessible to the spot market via pipeline. The NYMEX lists the specific sulfur and API gravity for both domestic and foreign crude allowed to be delivered to the WTI futures contract. WTI futures are the most liquid market for crude oil hedging and trading. In comparison the Brent crude oil contract was launched in July, 1989 by the International Petroleum Exchange (IPE). The IPE was acquired by the Intercontinental Exchange (ICE) in July, 2001. For the purposes of the speculative investor the Brent futures contract is cash settled, although it can be a deliverable contract if two parties agree to enter into an exchange for physical and register to do so with their brokers and the exchange. Volume and open interest information for the most liquid oil futures are displayed in Table 4.4.

In March 2006 the trading of oil futures changed when the ICE launched an electronically traded WTI futures contract. This new contract drew many participants who were eager to trade on a transparent screen at their own discretion instead of calling the exchange floor pits to find a market. In June 2006 the NYMEX moved their futures contracts to side-by-side trading, which allows a trader to execute electronically or on the exchange floor. By that time the ICE had picked up some market share in the WTI futures trading, and it is uncertain whether the marketplace will continue to trade both contracts or one will win out.

There are other oil futures contracts listed globally, but the WTI oil future listed on the NYMEX and the Brent oil future listed on the ICE are the two most liquid in the world. Other futures contracts include the Urals oil future listed on the Russian Trading System and the Dubai/Oman crude oil future listed on the Tokyo Commodities Exchange.

There is also an E-mini NYMEX WTI crude oil futures contract that is available for smaller investors. This contract trades electronically and is half of the size of the IPE crude oil future. It is financially settled to the NYMEX standard-sized WTI crude oil future.

PRICE HISTORY AND MARKET REPORTS

Crude oil prices have an extremely volatile past. Much of it started in 1973 with the Arab oil embargo that halted shipments of crude oil to the United States and its allies in retaliation for supporting Israel during the Yom Kippur War. As imports dropped the price of oil in the United States soared, creating demand rationing and gasoline lines. The second oil crisis of the 1970s occurred in 1979 during the Iranian Revolution when changes in the governing regime caused a decline in oil production and in exports from Iran. OPEC increased production as a result, but consumers panicked as the previous

TABLE 4.4   Crude Oil Futures

Name	Electronic or Pit	2006 Avg. Volume	2006 Avg. Open Interest	Units	Tick Size	Tick Value
NYMEX WTI Futures	Both	227,917	1,061,799	1,000 barrels	$0.01	$10.00
ICE Brent Futures	Electronic	174,177	464,631	1,000 barrels	$0.01	$10.00
ICE WTI Futures	Electronic	122,301	251,223	1,000 barrels	$0.01	$10.00

Source: NYMEX Exchange and Intercontinental Exchange

oil crisis was fresh in their minds. This panic increased prices even further, and lines appeared at gas stations yet again.

Since the 1970s the United States has not had a supply cut severe enough to require demand rationing. A short-lived price increase occurred during 1990–1991 with Iraq's invasion of Kuwait and the uncertainty surrounding oil production and exports from both countries. The longest price increase began in 2003 and has been attributed to an increase in global oil demand, especially from Asian and emerging economies such as China, South Korea, India, and Brazil. This price increase occurred gradually over a few years, unlike the sudden price increases of the 1970s. This has allowed consumers to steadily grow accustomed to higher prices. Large price declines occurred when Saudi Arabia increased production substantially in 1986, during the Asian economic crisis of 1997–1999, and again for a short time after September 11, 2001 reflecting uncertainty surrounding the U.S. economy. Figure 4.4 shows these events and their effect on price in the NYMEX WTI prompt month futures contract.

Outside of these major political and economic events, the market receives other fundamental information that can affect the future price of oil. One of the most important fundamental reports for the market is the *Weekly Petroleum Status Report (WPSR)* issued by the Energy Information Administration. The *WPSR* is a snapshot of the U.S. petroleum balance sheet and is issued on Wednesday mornings at 10:30 AM EST. The *WPSR* numbers for crude oil and products are analyzed by market participants as they look for

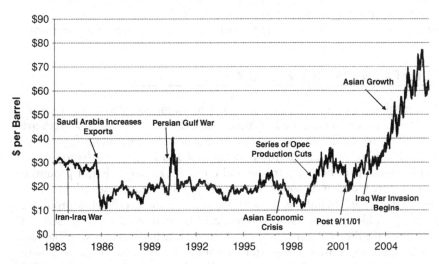

FIGURE 4.4 WTI Crude Oil Futures Price

trends in supply and demand that could affect the future price of oil. The most important data within the WSPR consists of the weekly stock change for crude oil, gasoline, and distillates. Trends such as a draw or build of stocks within the petroleum complex are extremely important when trying to establish the future price of oil. The EIA also publishes a Short-term Energy Outlook on a monthly basis along with an Annual Energy Outlook. Both of these reports paint a more in-depth picture of the fundamentals in petroleum by looking at the global markets in addition to the domestic market.

Another important fundamental report is the Oil Market Report published by the International Energy Agency (IEA). The IEA publishes this report monthly and it encompasses the global petroleum balance sheet. The Oil Market Report is closely watched for changes that the IEA makes to global oil demand. Both the IEA and the EIA are good public sources of fundamental information in the petroleum markets.

The outlook for crude oil prices hinges on the availability of oil production at a specific price. Ultimately it is profit that will drive companies to search for new methods and forms of oil production. If the cost to produce shale oil is $90 a barrel, production will occur when the oil can be sold above the cost of production plus margin. Of course the production of oil cannot be turned on and off like a water faucet. Current prices and expectation of future prices would have to remain above the production price for a period of time to entice a company to start a new production source. Increasing demand brought on by global growth has moved the world away from an era of cheap oil. The most populous countries on the planet are just starting their expansion and their demand for oil, and other forms of energy will rise and fall with their changing economic growth. This growth, along with the search for new supplies, is likely to create a rise in the price of oil over time.

ALTERNATIVE ENERGY SOURCES

It is hard to discuss crude oil without mentioning the development of alternative energy sources, or bio-fuels. These alternative energy sources are substitutes for crude oil or petroleum products and are not made from fossil fuels. The most popular bio-fuels are ethanol and biodiesel. Ethanol is currently made from both sugarcane and corn. Brazil uses ethanol produced from sugarcane as automotive fuel, and the United States uses ethanol produced from corn mainly as an additive to gasoline. Biodiesel is produced from vegetable oils such as soybean oil, canola oil, or palm oil. It is used as a substitute for diesel in automotive fuel or as a heating fuel in residential and commercial applications. Research continues in the area of biofuels with focus on cellulosic ethanol from agricultural sources such as corn stalks, hay, and switchgrass, to name a few. Other alternative sources such as wind power, solar energy, wave power, nuclear energy, and methane hydrates can also be considered partial substitutes for crude oil products. While some of these alternative sources of energy have been around for some time and others are still being tested for real world application, the global marketplace continues to search for energy sources to compete and possibly take the place of nonrenewable crude oil. Additional discussion of ethanol is located in Chapter 6, "Gasoline," while discussion on bio-diesel is in Chapter 5, "Heating Oil."

ADDITIONAL SOURCES OF INFORMATION

The fundamental drivers of crude oil can be explored in depth from many sources. Within the United States the Energy Information Administration (EIA) is the source for official energy statistics from the U.S. government. The EIA also puts out monthly and annual reports on crude oil and various other energy sources. The *BP Statistical Review of World Energy* is published every June by British Petroleum. It contains global numerical data for production, reserves, and refining within the petroleum complex. Another good source for global energy information is the International Energy Agency (IEA). The IEA publishes a monthly oil market report, an annual world energy outlook, and a variety of global petroleum statistics. All of these additional sources are available on the Internet.

CHAPTER 5

Heating Oil

Heating oil is one of the many products produced from refining crude oil. It is classified as a distillate along with diesel, jet fuel, and kerosene. All of the distillates have a similar chemical make-up, and in some areas heating oil is the same product as diesel fuel with the exception of a few additives. Heating oil goes by many names in the United States, including No. 2 fuel oil, distillate fuel, and home heating oil. Outside of the United States it is called gas oil.

Heating oil is used primarily in the northeastern United States to heat both residential homes and commercial buildings. The Energy Information Administration (EIA) reports that in 2001, approximately 7.5 percent of residential houses in the United States used heating oil as their main heating fuel. Approximately 78 percent of these houses are located in the northeastern United States.[1] It is transported by tank trucks to homes and buildings and held in storage tanks that are usually located above ground in basements but can also be below ground. The oil is burned in a boiler or furnace to generate heat for the building. Other regions of the United States typically use natural gas as a heating source, because it has historically been cheaper and the infrastructure is in place in those areas to take the natural gas directly to the homes and commercial buildings. Older homes in the Northeast generally do not have this natural gas infrastructure in place.

Heating oil is very safe to use for heating. It has no self-ignition issues, and it also has a high flash point. The flash point is the lowest temperature at which something can form an ignitable liquid with oxygen. Heating oil's flash point is 52°C or approximately 125°F. This means it cannot ignite under a temperature of 125°F, which makes it pretty safe for the typical household and commercial building.

PRODUCTION AND STORAGE

When refined, one barrel (42 gallons) of crude oil produces approximately 10 gallons of diesel and heating oil along with 4 gallons of jet fuel.[2] Slightly higher yields of these distillates may be possible through further refining or use of different crude oil grades. Also, since these products are from the light gas oil streams, refiners have some ability to change the final product mix. U.S. refiners typically ramp up production of heating oil just prior to winter, when demand for the fuel is at its peak. But because they are limited in the amount of heating oil they can produce to meet demand, both storage and imports must cover the shortfall. Heating oil production increases are often limited by refiners' need to have an optimal mix of products to sell in the winter months. In the United States during 2005, total distillate production averaged 4 million barrels a day. During the same time period, gasoline production averaged 8.3 million barrels a day.[3] This shows that gasoline production and demand still is the number-one concern of U.S. refiners.

Because gasoline production has priority over production of distillate fuels in the United States, there is a focus on both storage and imports during peak demand times. The majority of U.S. distillate imports come from Europe, where the focus is more on distillate production. Diesel is a popular fuel option for cars in Europe, and, along with a much more extensive public transportation system of trains and buses, this encourages fuel demand to be more focused on distillates than in the United States.

Heating oil storage in the United States plays an important role in balancing supply and demand during the winter months. Most heating oil storage in the United States is located on the East Coast with easy access to waterways for transportation. As shown in Figure 5.1, the peak storage level occurs just before the start of winter at the end of September, while the trough in heating oil storage occurs at the end of winter around the middle of April. Storage drawdowns are expected to occur within this time frame, as winter demand exceeds the refineries' production of heating oil. Storage is rebuilt throughout the summer months when overall distillate demand is lower.

CONSUMPTION

According to the EIA, during 2005, 84 percent of residential heating oil use was concentrated in the Northeast.[4] Since heating oil is used as a heating fuel, it is highly dependent on the winter weather. A warm or above-average winter in the Northeast would result in lower than normal seasonal demand

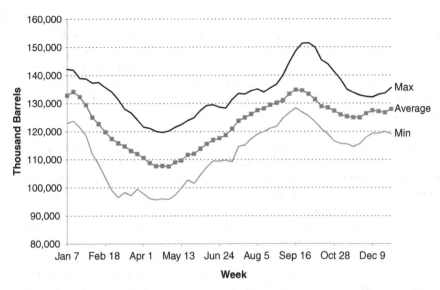

FIGURE 5.1 U.S. Distillate Fuel Stocks: 2002–2006
Source: Energy Information Administration

for heating oil. In the other case, an extremely cold winter can cause a spike in both the demand and the price of heating oil. Traders in the heating oil market are very focused on both short-term and long-term forecasts for winter weather. Meteorologists often study longer-term weather patterns such as La Niña and El Niño when trying to determine the winter weather pattern for the northeastern United States. Both the La Niña and El Niño weather patterns refer to sustained sea surface temperature anomalies greater than .5°C across the central tropical Pacific Ocean, with La Niña being a negative anomaly and El Niño being positive. With regard to the northeastern United States, an El Niño pattern is expected to bring a warmer than normal winter whereas a La Niña pattern could bring a colder than normal winter.

Because heating oil is considered a middle distillate along with diesel, jet fuel, and kerosene, the demand factors for these other products are also important. For example, strong demand for diesel may pull supply away from the heating oil market as refiners focus on yielding more diesel fuel from their distillates pool. Diesel fuel is used in the United States in diesel engines for cars, trucks, trains, buses, boats, farm equipment, and military vehicles. In 2005 diesel fuel consumption by on-highway vehicles accounted for 80 percent of diesel use, and the remainder was consumed by off-highway vehicles, farm and construction equipment, and diesel–electric generators.[5] Diesel fuel accounted for 75 percent of total distillate consumed in the United States in 2005.[6] Diesel is thought of as a very dirty fuel, but in the fall of 2006 the ultra low sulfur diesel (ULSD) program was initiated. This program requires 80 percent of on-highway diesel fuel to have only a 15 parts per million (ppm) sulfur content. This low sulfur level results in a cleaner burning diesel that releases fewer emissions than before.

Both jet fuel and kerosene are the lesser known distillates, but each can have an impact on the supply and price of heating oil. After September 11, 2001 airports around the United States were closed for days. In the months following, demand for air travel fell sharply. This had a significant impact on jet fuel demand because planes were flying less often, which in turn resulted in distillate fuel oil stocks building over 11 percent from mid-September 2001 through the end of the year. This compares to a 10-year average distillate stock build of 1 percent over the same time period.[7] As a result of the sudden drop in demand for jet fuel, refiners changed their mix of products. Jet fuel and its components are similar to heating oil and diesel, so refiners naturally made more of these two products instead of jet fuel. The switch to a production mix of more heating oil and diesel resulted in the rapid increase in distillate fuel stocks in the United States during the fourth quarter of 2001.

FUTURES

Heating oil futures trade on the New York Mercantile Exchange (NYMEX) and heating oil was the first successful energy contract on the exchange. It was launched on November 14, 1978, trading only 22 contracts on the first day.[8] This was five years before the launch of the WTI crude futures contract. Heating oil futures are deliverable in New York harbor. This is the main trading location for the cash or physical heating oil market. Consumers of both jet fuel and diesel fuel often use the heating oil future for hedging purposes, because both jet fuel and diesel cash markets are often traded using a differential to the heating oil price.

The futures contract trades in cents per gallon, and one future is equal to 42,000 gallons of heating oil. One barrel of oil is equivalent to 42 gallons, so the heating oil future is also equal to 1,000 barrels of oil. This is identical to the crude oil futures contract; this is important because a common trade for speculators and a hedge for refiners is the heating oil crack spread. The crack spread is the difference in price between the crude oil futures and the heating oil futures with the same delivery month. A crack spread containing only heating oil and crude oil would be computed as follows:

WTI crude oil January 2007 future = $61.00 per barrel

NYH heating oil January 2007 future = $1.58 per gal

$$\text{Crack Spread} = \text{Heating Oil} - \text{Crude Oil}$$
$$= (1.58 \times 42) - 61.00$$
$$= \$5.36 \text{ per barrel}$$

The crack spread is crucial for refiners because their profit is directly linked to the price of their input—crude oil—and their output—refined products such as heating oil. By trading the crack spread refiners are able to lock in a price to buy their crude oil and sell their refined products simultaneously. The crack spread previously mentioned implies that one barrel of crude oil would produce one barrel of heating oil, which in reality would not occur. The 3:2:1 crack spread better approximates the results of a real-world refinery. The 3:2:1 crack spread comprises 3 barrels of crude oil, 2 barrels of gasoline, and 1 barrel of heating oil. Still the 3:2:1 crack spread is not a true real-world refinery result, but it is the best approximation using futures contracts. It does not take into account additional by-products from the refining process or pricing differentials between heating oil and other distillates.

Supply and demand changes in the crude oil market will filter down to the heating oil market. This is why heating oil futures are highly correlated with the other futures contracts within the oil complex. If you expect crude oil to go down in price, it is highly likely that heating oil will move down in price also, although the magnitude of the price movement may not be the same. This is shown in Figure 5.2, which displays the price of the prompt month crude oil and heating oil contracts in dollars per barrel. From this chart you can also see that the price of heating oil does not trade below the price of crude oil. This is because refiners need to have an incentive to refine crude oil into heating oil. If the refining company is not going to make a profit from doing so, it would just sell the crude oil on the physical market.

PRICE HISTORY AND MARKET REPORTS

Like prices of crude oil, heating oil prices have a history of volatility. Events that have had a major impact on the price of crude oil, such as OPEC production changes, the Gulf Wars, and the Asian economic crisis

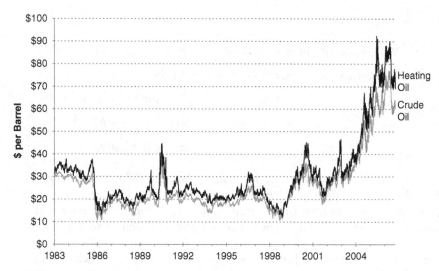

FIGURE 5.2 NYMEX WTI Crude Oil and NYH Heating Oil Futures

from 1997 to 1999 have all had a similar effect on the price of heating oil. As mentioned previously, prices for the entire oil complex are correlated. Heating oil price volatility does increase during the winter months. Figure 5.3 shows some significant price spikes that look unusual compared to the majority of the price action. These price spikes all occur during the winter months in conjunction with extreme cold weather in the northeastern United States that pushed up demand for heating oil. With this in mind, market participants keep a keen eye on the medium-term weather forecasts published by the National Weather Service (NWS). The NWS daily forecasts give an outlook for above- or below-normal temperatures for one week to two weeks forward.

The *Weekly Petroleum Status Report* (*WPSR*) issued by the Energy Information Administration is the most frequently issued report that contains important fundamental information regarding the U.S. heating oil and distillate markets. The *WPSR* is a snapshot of the U.S. petroleum balance sheet and is usually issued on Wednesday mornings at 10:30 AM EST. The *WPSR* heating oil stocks are grouped with diesel in the total distillate stock data. This stock data is also broken down by regions or Petroleum Administration for Defense Districts (PADDS). The PADDS were created during World War II to facilitate oil allocation. There are 5 PADDS in the United States: PADD 1 (East Coast), PADD 2 (Midwest), PADD 3 (Gulf Coast), PADD 4 (Rockies), and PADD 5 (West Coast). It is valuable to focus on the amount

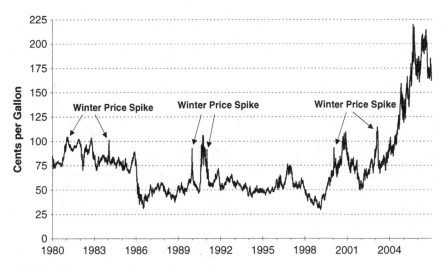

FIGURE 5.3 NYMEX Heating Oil Futures Price

of distillate stock within each PADD, and to look at the ratio of heating oil stocks compared to other distillate stocks. Given that the demand for heating oil is focused within PADD 1 in the Northeast, if a majority of the stocks in the United States are located within another PADD, it will take time to get supply to the major demand area. This could result in price increases if demand suddenly shifts higher as a result of cold weather or lack of supply within PADD 1. The *WPSR* also reports weekly statistics such as distillate production, imports, and implied demand. Trends within all of these statistics are important for determining the fundamental picture that will influence the future price of heating oil.

HEATING OIL VERSUS NATURAL GAS

Heating oil can also be used as a substitute for natural gas in power generation. Some power plants have the ability to burn either natural gas or heating oil to generate power. Plant managers will make this decision based on which fuel is cheaper for them to burn and still generate the same amount of electricity. Natural gas is almost always the cheaper fuel, but in the past heating oil has been cheaper for short periods of time when natural gas prices spike due to short supply or high demand. Figure 5.4 shows a graph of the spread between heating oil futures and natural gas futures in terms of $ per MMBTU. A BTU, or British thermal unit, is the unit of energy in

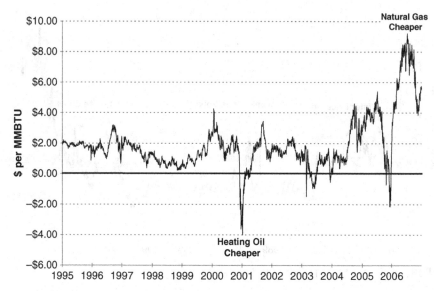

FIGURE 5.4 Heating Oil–Natural Gas Price Spread

which natural gas futures prices are quoted. The EIA shows that 2001 was the year with the largest deliveries of distillate to electric generators over the past decade.[9] What made this extra demand for heating oil occur? From December 2000 through February 2001 heating oil was cheaper than natural gas, as shown in Figure 5.4. During this time, electric generators that could burn heating oil instead of natural gas would have switched to heating oil as their fuel of choice. This created an upward shift in heating oil demand on the part of electric generators.

ALTERNATIVE ENERGY SOURCES

Another possible substitute for heating oil and diesel is biodiesel or bioheat. Biodiesel is fuel created using biological sources; in this case vegetable oils such as palm oil, canola oil, and soybean oil are used. The biodiesel can be used in pure form or blended with regular diesel to achieve a fuel mix. The concept of biodiesel originated in 1895, when Dr. Rudolf Diesel developed the first diesel engine to run on peanut oil. In the United States, singer Willie Nelson created his own brand of biodiesel called BioWillie, which is sold in outlets in eight states.

In the future heating oil prices will have a closer relationship with its substitutes, such as natural gas, as price will continue to create competition between the fuels in some sectors. Heating oil prices will continue to be volatile in the winter months and dependent on the realized weather in the northeastern United States. Demand for both diesel and jet fuel will grow globally with the need to transport both goods and people. Supply issues such as refining capacity must be addressed in order to produce enough distillate to meet demand over the long term. Overall, prices will continue to be correlated with both crude oil and gasoline. In the longer-term, higher prices should prevail to attract companies to invest in future refinery and pipeline infrastructure to increase supply of refined products.

ADDITIONAL SOURCES OF INFORMATION

Additional information about heating oil, diesel, and other distillates can be found at the U.S. Energy Information Administration (EIA) website (www.eia.gov), which is the place for official energy statistics from the U.S. government. The EIA also puts out monthly and annual reports on distillates, along with a special heating oil and propane update that focuses on these fuels during the winter. Additional resources for information on heating oil, distillates, and other petroleum products can be found at the end of Chapter 4, "Crude Oil."

CHAPTER 6

Gasoline

Gasoline is one commodity that most people know something about. You are bound to pass a gas station while driving to work, running errands, or dropping the kids off at school. Most people know that there are different octane levels available and that higher octane levels are better because they are at a premium price. Most people will tell you that they drive more during the summer when the weather is better and they are taking vacations. Drivers usually know how many miles per gallon they get from their vehicles. Gasoline has become a topic of conversation and is a commodity that many people are constantly aware of. Yet, it is also the most complicated of all the energy commodities. Gasoline has evolved throughout history as society has become more aware of the damage it has inflicted on our environment. It is a fine line between maximizing the energy value of the fuel while minimizing its impact on the environment. This has resulted in many changes in how gasoline is made in the United States.

When you pull into a gasoline station you usually are given three choices. There is regular unleaded gasoline, mid-grade gasoline, and premium gasoline. Each of these fuels is differentiated by its octane rating, with regular usually having an 87-octane rating, mid-grade an 89-octane rating, and premium a 93-octane rating. What does the octane rating represent? It is the amount of fuel that can be compressed before it spontaneously ignites. Compression occurs in gasoline engines as a cylinder of air and gas is compressed and ignited with a spark plug. When gasoline ignites from compression rather than the spark of a spark plug, it causes knocking on the engine. Knocking usually occurs just prior to the spark plug flashing and is aptly named because it sounds like a thud or knock. Knocking can cause mechanical damage to the engine and it is not something that you want to occur.

So which grade do you choose to fuel up with? Your car maintenance manual's fuel recommendation will suggest a minimum octane level. There is no benefit in using a fuel with an octane level higher than what your engine needs. This is because octane and energy content are not related. Contrary to popular belief, all gasoline contains approximately the same energy content and detergents to clean the engine.[1] If you drive a Ford car for which regular gasoline with an 87-octane rating is recommended and you are purchasing premium gasoline then you are throwing money out the window. Experts say you will not receive any extra performance by using gasoline with a higher octane level than the one recommended for your vehicle. Most car manufacturers recommend regular gasoline, although some sport and luxury brands with higher compression engines require premium gasoline. The higher compression results in more power for these cars.

Today's cars come equipped with knock sensors that detect detonation and will change timing of the spark accordingly. This means the guy down the street who spent $50,000 on his BMW but is saving $3 each tank by purchasing regular fuel may not hear the engine knock. His car's knock sensors have already compensated for the lower octane level, but the result is reduced performance and lower mileage.

THE RECENT CHANGES—RFG TO RBOB

Gasoline in the United States has gone through many changes as the government has become aware of health issues related to its components. Since the 1980s there have been many changes to gasoline specifications to make it safer for people and the environment. During World War II it was discovered that adding lead, in the form of tetraethyl lead (TEL), was the easiest and most economical way to increase the gasoline's octane rating. Leaded gasoline was phased out beginning in July of 1975, because TEL was found to be extremely toxic even in low concentrations. A full ban of leaded gasoline in the United States was made on January 1, 1996.[2] The new Environmental Protection Agency (EPA) restrictions created conventional unleaded gasoline, which was more expensive for refiners to produce because there was no easy way to increase the octane rating.

Refiners experimented with many blending components to come up with the most economical way to increase the octane rating of conventional unleaded gasoline. Methanol was one of the first additives used. Methanol is the simplest alcohol compound, also called methyl alcohol. Over time interest in methanol as an additive died down for two main reasons. Methanol has an affinity for water and would separate from the gasoline mixture if it came into contact with water during transit. In addition, when burned in an internal combustible engine, it emitted formaldehyde into the air through the exhaust.

The Clean Air Act initiated in 1990 resulted in the requirement of reformulated unleaded gasoline (RFG) in cities with the worst smog.[3] RFG is oxygenated gasoline, with minimum 2 percent oxygen by weight, which is blended to have fewer pollutants than conventional gasoline. The addition of oxygen to the fuel reduces the amount of carbon monoxide and unburned fuel in the exhaust, reducing smog. Methyl tertiary-butyl ether (MTBE) was chosen by refiners as oxygenate of choice in RFG, and its use in the gasoline pool increased even more. It is a chemical compound manufactured from the chemical reaction of methanol and isobutylene. At room temperature it is volatile and flammable and dissolves easily into water. Prior to the Clean Air Act of 1990, MTBE had been used at lower levels in the gasoline pool as an octane enhancer. It helped refiners meet two separate needs—the 2 percent oxygen requirement and the octane requirement. Yet, like methanol before it, MTBE was discovered to have potential health risks associated with it. MTBE has been known to contaminate drinking water through leaks in storage tanks and pipelines, fuel tank damage during accidents, and poor disposal of old gasoline. The first major incident of this occurred in Santa Monica, California in 1996. The EPA concluded that MTBE could be a potential carcinogen at high levels of exposure, although research was not conclusive.[4] States reacted anyway, enacting bans on MTBE with the largest consumer, California, banning MTBE use in gasoline effective January 1, 2004. Finally, the EPA announced that as of May 5, 2006 it would drop the 2 percent oxygen requirement for reformulated gasoline.[5] The dropping of this requirement, the ban on MTBE by various states, and the lack of liability protection in connection with lawsuits arising from MTBE water contamination resulted in a switch away from gasoline with MTBE to gasoline using another oxygenate—ethanol.

ETHANOL

Ethanol, also known as grain alcohol or ethyl alcohol, is an alcohol-based fuel made from the simple sugars of various crops. Globally, ethanol is primarily made from sugarcane or corn, although it can be made from wheat, sorghum, and other starch crops. Fuel ethanol has been around for a long time. Henry Ford's Model-T ran on a version of ethanol. Today the largest use of ethanol is as a fuel and fuel additive.

There are many reasons why ethanol is attractive to refiners even though the oxygenate requirement is no longer valid. Adding oxygen to fuel results in complete combustion of the fuel and lowers carbon monoxide emissions, helping refiners to meet the EPA emission control requirements. Ethanol is the highest octane fuel on the market and it has the advantages of MTBE without being harmful. Ethanol is economically attractive because ethanol blending is subsidized by a federal tax credit of 51 cents per gallon. Finally, ethanol allows refiners to meet the Renewable Fuel Standard Program. This program increases the volume of renewable fuel required to be blended in gasoline. It started in 2006 with a mandate of 4.0 billion gallons and is expected to reach 7.5 billion gallons by 2012.[6]

Still, ethanol does have its weaknesses. Ethanol added to the gasoline pool comes at a higher cost than MTBE. In addition, ethanol tends to separate from gasoline if stored for a long time, and it has an affinity for water that could contaminate the gasoline if the two came into contact. This affinity for water results in ethanol being shipped separately from gasoline, usually by rail car or truck, and blended along with reformulated gasoline blendstock for oxygen blending (RBOB) at the distribution center. This adds an additional transportation layer to what is already a complex process.

Ethanol production in the United States is centered in the Midwest because that is where most of its feedstock, corn, is grown. As shown in Figure 6.1, fuel ethanol production didn't surpass production of MTBE until the MTBE ban by California, which resulted in refiners switching to ethanol oxygenate in 2003. Since then production has increased sharply as refiners have opted away from MTBE and towards ethanol. The common ethanol-gasoline mixture consists of 10 percent ethanol and 90 percent gasoline, called E10. This is the current fuel available in major metropolitan areas of the United States. Flexible fuel vehicles can run on either straight gasoline or any blend of ethanol up to 85 percent. This fuel, called E85, is 85 percent ethanol and 15 percent gasoline. There were approximately 6 million flexible fuel vehicles on the road in the United States as of 2006.[7] This compares with

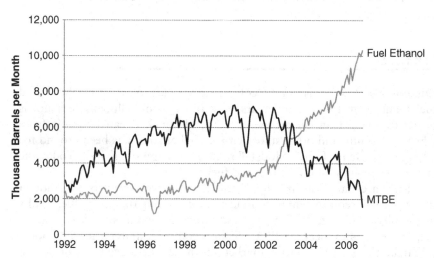

FIGURE 6.1 MTBE and Fuel Ethanol Production in the United States
Source: Energy Information Administration

a total of 230 million trucks and passenger vehicles on the road as of 2004.[8] E85 fuel is available at several hundred gas stations throughout the United States, with most states having at least one pump. Since the percentage of flexible fuel vehicles on the road is quite small, gasoline stations have not been quick to add E85 pumps.

Fuel ethanol contains more than a third less energy content per gallon than conventional gasoline, resulting in fewer miles per gallon for fuel ethanol.[9] The U.S. Department of Energy (DOE) reports that it would take 1.41 gallons of E85 fuel to equal one gallon of conventional gasoline. In 2005, the United States consumed 9.16 million barrels of finished gasoline a day.[10] This is equivalent to consuming over 12.9 million barrels of fuel ethanol on an energy content basis. Since one bushel of corn makes approximately 2.8 gallons of ethanol, it would take 193.7 million bushels of corn a day or approximately 70.7 billion bushels of corn a year to feed the American appetite for fuel ethanol.[11] Given that United States farmers produced only 11.8 billion bushels for the 2004–2005 corn year and that the United States is the largest worldwide producer of corn, a switch to E85 fuel for the entire United States seems an unlikely prospect.[12] Fuel ethanol's use as an oxygenate additive may be helpful for the time being, but a change to higher usage of E85 fuel could harm the current corn supply for food in the United States.

In the end what do all these changes in specification mean for the price of gasoline? Each change to gasoline is costly for both refiners and consumers. The push for cleaner fuels requires upgrades to refining units and lighter and more expensive inputs. Upgrades to refineries will take refining capacity away for a while, and the market may have to rely on current product stocks or imports during that time. With the new gasoline grade of RBOB the market is dependent on both refineries and farms. If the corn harvest is poor one year, the cost of ethanol will rise, resulting in price increases in gasoline as well. Furthermore, as previously discussed, the energy content of ethanol is less than the energy content of both gasoline and MTBE. So blending approximately 10 percent ethanol with gasoline will result in higher overall demand, because a full tank of gasoline will now contain less energy than it did before ethanol was added to the gasoline pool.

PRODUCTION AND STORAGE

Gasoline is the main product produced from refining crude oil. When a barrel of crude oil is refined, it produces about 20 gallons of gasoline, a yield of 47 percent.[13] In 2005, U.S. refineries and blenders produced 3.05 billion barrels of finished motor gasoline.[14] U.S. refiners typically increase production of gasoline during the spring, right after the winter maintenance season. The increased production is to build stocks to meet the peak demand that occurs in the summer. The peak driving season in the United States occurs between Memorial Day and Labor Day when school is out and weather is good for traveling or vacationing.

No new refinery has been built in the United States since 1976. All additional refinery capacity has been the result of expanding current facilities or technological efficiencies in refining. During the summer, refineries are often close to maxing out their capacity due to the strong demand for gasoline. This results in little open refining capacity in the summer; therefore, unplanned refinery outages due to fire or other mechanical issues can create quite a stir in the gasoline markets. Refinery outages in the summer cut into gasoline production expectations, so price rises in order to entice other refineries to increase gasoline production. This rise in price also acts to attract additional imports and to curb gasoline demand.

Since refining capacity growth has not increased as fast as gasoline demand, both imports and storage help meet the production shortfall that occurs during the summer months. Gasoline imports can come in the form of finished gasoline or blending components which are then combined in the United States to make finished gasoline. The majority of gasoline imports come from Caribbean, Canadian, and European refineries. These refineries make gasoline based on specifications and standards solely for export to the United States. Currently, the United States faces little competition from

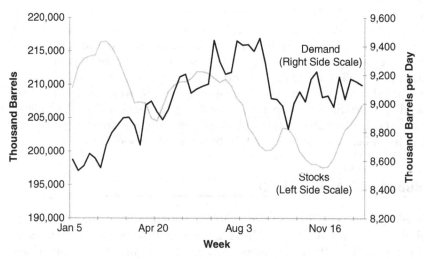

FIGURE 6.2 Gasoline Stocks versus Demand: 2002–2006 Averages
Source: Energy Information Administration

other nations for these gasoline imports, but continued global economic growth will result in additional demand from India and China for gasoline.

Gasoline storage in the United States follows a pattern opposite to that of the distillate market. During the winter when it is cold and snow is building up, gasoline demand decreases. This allows refiners to build up storage. Once the winter maintenance season ends, usually in February or March, gasoline production is increased to build supplies up in anticipation of the summer demand period. Throughout the summer, storage decreases as gasoline demand exceeds production and imports. Figure 6.2 shows that the gasoline storage usually peaks sometime in February when demand is near its lowest point. Gasoline storage typically hits its lows for the year coming out of the summer demand season and from the refinery maintenance that occurs in October and November.

CONSUMPTION

In 2005 finished gasoline accounted for 49 percent of demand for all finished products.[15] Gasoline is far and away the most utilized refined product in the United States, but demand is seasonal. Gasoline demand rises over the summer vacation period, with peak demand occurring in the months of July and August. The lowest demand for gasoline occurs in the winter, usually during the month of February. Weather affects demand in the gasoline market to some extent, but not to the degree that it does so for heating oil. A lot of snow or other precipitation can lower demand for gasoline as people stay indoors whereas sunny, warm weather can entice people to go outdoors.

Gasoline demand in the United States has grown each year for the past 14 years (1992–2005) with an average yearly growth of 1.75 percent.[16] Over this 14-year time frame the average annual spot price of gasoline has increased more than 9 percent a year.[17] The two slowest periods of demand growth occurred in 2000 with growth of .76 percent and in 2005 with growth of .32 percent.[18] These two periods of slow demand growth happen to coincide with the largest year-on-year increases in the average annual spot price for gasoline during the same period. From 1999 to 2000 the average annual price of gasoline increased over 60 percent, and from 2004 to 2005 the same price increased 35 percent.[19]

Is gasoline demand elastic or inelastic? If gasoline demand is elastic, changes in price will have an effect on its demand. If gasoline demand is inelastic, changes in price will have no effect on demand. The elasticity of demand can be different in the short and the long run. In the short run, if gasoline prices doubled overnight and you had a long commute to work with no alternative transportation options, you would be forced to pay the high price for gasoline. In the short run your demand for gasoline is inelastic. Yet, in the long run you may make changes such as buying a more fuel-efficient car or looking for a job closer to home. These changes make your long-run demand for gasoline more elastic. With regard to gasoline, the ability people have to substitute other means of transportation is important in determining the short-run elasticity of demand. In the long run, there are options open to many people who want to lower their demand for gasoline.

As shown in the preceding data, gasoline's demand and price have seen strong growth since 1992. This would suggest that price increases have not harmed growth in demand and that the long-run demand for gasoline is fairly inelastic. However, the pace of demand increases has slowed considerably through 2005 as prices have increased at an above average pace. In fact, the average yearly growth from 2002 to 2005 of gasoline demand is only slightly over 1 percent and under the longer term average. Prices have increased almost 30 percent a year during the same time frame.[20] This shows that periods of sharp price increases may slow down the pace of demand growth as people do change some of their gasoline consuming habits. Yet demand was still increasing during this period, implying that the inelastic nature of gasoline demand may be tied to how quickly the price appreciates.

FUTURES

Gasoline futures trade on the New York Mercantile Exchange (NYMEX) and have gone through a few contract transformations since the launch of the leaded gasoline futures contract on October 5, 1981.[21] This contract did not have a long life as a result of the EPA ban on leaded gasoline in the United States. Subsequently, the unleaded gasoline futures contract was launched on December 3, 1984.[22] This contract went through further refinement after passage of the Clean Air Act in 1990; the EPA required reformulated (RFG) gasoline to be used in the metropolitan New York City area. Since the NYMEX unleaded gasoline futures contract stipulates delivery to the New York Harbor, the specifications of the unleaded futures contract needed to be changed in order to comply with the new EPA regulations.

This change transformed the unleaded futures contract into an RFG unleaded futures contract starting in December 1994.[23] The RFG unleaded contract had its final day of trading on December 29, 2006, due to refiners dropping MTBE as an oxygenate and the EPA announcing in May 2006 that it was no longer requiring the oxygen requirement in gasoline,[24] This gave way to the current gasoline futures contract on the NYMEX, the RBOB (reformulated blendstock for oxygenate blending) gasoline futures contract.

The RBOB is made so that it can be blended with 10 percent fuel ethanol to meet the requirements for gasoline in the New York City metropolitan area. The RBOB contract began trading on October 3, 2005.[25] During 2006, both the RBOB futures and the RFG futures were traded on the NYMEX. The RFG contract was more actively traded for most of the year until the end of September 2006. At that time the RBOB futures contract became the active gasoline futures contract on the NYMEX.

All gasoline futures contracts are deliverable within the New York Harbor. This is why over time changes to the contract specifications have been necessary given that EPA regulations have changed the type of gasoline required in the New York City metro area. The gasoline futures contract trades in cents per gallon and one contract is equivalent to 42,000 gallons of gasoline. Similar to the heating oil market, a common trade with gasoline is the crack spread. This is the spread between one contract of gasoline and one contract of crude oil. Refiners will commonly use this spread to hedge both their input of crude oil and their output of gasoline.

Prices of products in the petroleum complex are highly correlated. This is discussed briefly in Chapter 5, "Heating Oil." Figure 6.3 shows prices of the prompt future (always shows the same future month for both on any given day) for WTI crude oil and NYH gasoline futures, along with the crack spread since 1985. Although the correlation is not perfect, the prices of these products do move together. In this chart gasoline exhibits more volatility

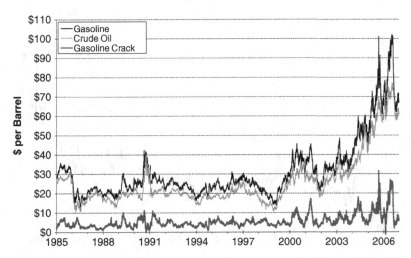

FIGURE 6.3 NYMEX WTI Crude Oil and NYH Gasoline Prices

than crude oil. It also has the highest price point (in $/barrel equivalents), reaching over $100 per barrel during the summer of 2006.

PRICE HISTORY AND MARKET REPORTS

As discussed in Chapter 5, "Heating Oil," major changes in the supply or demand for crude oil will affect the price of its refined products. If OPEC were to announce a large production cut, then down the line there may be less crude oil available to refine into gasoline. Figure 6.3 shows that of the three products, gasoline typically trades at the highest price. The higher price is caused by both the strong demand for gasoline and the high cost of production. Of all the finished products made from crude oil, demand for gasoline is the highest. In addition, the processing costs are higher since gasoline is one of the lightest products and it requires further refining and additives to meet various EPA, government, and state requirements. The peak demand for gasoline occurs during the summer months of July and August. Strong demand during this time can create sharp price spikes, as shown in Figure 6.4. Other large price increases for gasoline can occur during April and May if gasoline stocks are low for that time of year. This is necessary to increase the profit margin and entice refiners to produce as much gasoline as possible in order to build stocks before the summer demand season begins.

FIGURE 6.4 NYMEX Gasoline Futures Price

The *Weekly Petroleum Status Report* (*WPSR*) generated by the Energy Information Administration (EIA) has been discussed in both Chapter 4, "Crude Oil," and Chapter 5, "Heating Oil." As it is for those commodities, the *WPSR* is just as important in regard to the data it supplies to the gasoline market. The *WPSR* includes data on gasoline production, imports, stocks, and product supplied for the United States. Gasoline product supplied is the EIA's measure of consumption. This measure can be volatile from week to week, so it is beneficial to apply a four-week average or a similar measure when analyzing the data. Stocks for gasoline are broken down into two groups—finished gasoline and blending components. The blending component includes RBOB, the futures contract deliverable grade, as it is a blendstock.

As discussed previously in this chapter, different types of gasoline are required within different parts of the country, depending on both EPA and state regulations. The existence of these localized markets results in an inability to move finished gasoline stocks around the country to meet demand. This makes it important to focus on the amount of gasoline in storage within each Petroleum Administration for Defense Districts (PADD). High stocks in PADD V (West Coast) or PADD IV (Rockies) cannot suddenly help a low stock situation in PADD 1 (Northeast). Not only does gasoline from the West have different specifications, there is no easy way to transport it across the country.

SUBSTITUTES

Gasoline is facing competition from many other fuels. As the price of gasoline has increased dramatically since 2000, the world has been exploring other options in transportation. In the United States and Brazil the main alternative transportation fuel is a form of fuel ethanol, E85. This is discussed in length previously in this chapter. Of the two countries, Brazil has made more significant strides in the introduction of ethanol as a fuel source. In Europe diesel is the main transport fuel. The International Energy Agency (IEA) statistics show that the European Union-25 used over 50 percent more diesel than motor gasoline as a transport fuel in 2004.[26] In the United States diesel fuel is also an option, and with the introduction of cleaner burning diesel in 2006 along with the better mileage per gallon for diesel fuel this may become a stronger competitor in the future.

Still, in the United States gasoline will be the primary transportation fuel for the foreseeable future. A combination of factors in the United States, including urban sprawl and a lack of reliable public transportation has resulted in demand for gasoline growing each year even as prices have continued to increase. There are risks on the supply side from slow increases in refining capacity and further specification changes. Unless there are major changes made to refining capacity, public transportation, or a cheaper alternative fuel is discovered, gasoline prices are likely to rise over time.

ADDITIONAL SOURCES OF INFORMATION

Additional sources of information regarding the fundamentals of gasoline and other products in the petroleum complex can be found at the end of Chapter 4, "Crude Oil," and Chapter 5, "Heating Oil."

CHAPTER 7

Natural Gas

When people think of gas, usually the first thing that comes to mind is what they use to fuel their cars, gasoline. Natural gas sometimes gets overlooked, even though it is a critical part of the global energy supply. As oil deposits become harder to locate and the worldwide demand for hydrocarbons increases, a switch to natural gas has begun. Natural gas was formed during the same process that created petroleum. Plant and animal remains from millions of years ago formed organic material. Over time this organic material was trapped under rock and exposed to pressure and heat. The pressure and high temperatures changed the organic material into petroleum, coal, and natural gas. At low temperatures more oil was formed than natural gas, and at high temperatures more natural gas was formed. Natural gas is a combination of combustible hydrocarbons. It is composed primarily of methane, a gas compound that consists of one carbon and four hydrogen atoms, but it can also contain a variety of other compounds and gases. The purest form of natural gas is almost pure methane, which is called dry natural gas. When other hydrocarbons are also present, it is called wet natural gas.

Natural gas has a long history, although techniques to capture, process, and utilize it are more recent. In ancient history, natural gas would seep through the underground and could ignite. This would create what looked like a fire coming from the earth. One of the most famous instances of this occurred in Greece on Mount Parnassus around 1000 B.C. A flame rising from rock was discovered, and the Greeks believed it was of divine origin. They built a temple on the flame and in it housed the Oracle of Delphi. The Oracle gave out prophecies she claimed were inspired by the flame.

The natural gas industry in the United States began in the area surrounding Lake Erie. In 1821 William Hart dug the first well intended for natural gas in Fredonia, New York. He dug a 27-foot well into a creek after noticing gas bubbles on the surface. Hart is considered the father of natural gas. This initial well was the start of the Fredonia Gas Light Company, the first natural gas company in America.

Natural gas in the United States was first used as a form of light in the nineteenth century, but today it is used in many more ways, including heating, cooking, generating electricity, and as an industrial heat source. These new uses came about with advances in transporting natural gas from the wellhead to the consumer. Early pipelines for natural gas were not very efficient, but after World War II thousands of miles of reliable pipeline were built. Natural gas has many positive qualities when compared to other fossil fuels. When burned it gives off a great deal of energy, but emits fewer emissions than other fossil fuels, which makes it less harmful to the environment. Our appetite for energy, along with the clean burning characteristic of natural gas, has helped to increase its consumption in the United States. According to the *BP Annual Statistical Review of Energy*, in the decade from 1995 to 2005 natural gas consumption averaged 25.7 percent of total energy consumption.[1] This makes it the second most consumed fossil fuel in the United States, behind oil and ahead of coal.

PRODUCTION—CONVENTIONAL AND UNCONVENTIONAL

Like crude oil, natural gas is produced by drilling for a gas deposit and extracting the natural gas through a well. Natural gas produced through the basic drilling and well system is known as conventional natural gas because it is easy, feasible, and economic to produce. Natural gas can be found in deposits that contain gas and oil, gas and coal, or just gas. Deposits that contain gas and oil have the natural gas on the top since it is lighter. Natural gas deposits have been found both onshore, as in the Rocky Mountains, and offshore, as in the Gulf of Mexico. Unlike crude oil, most of the natural gas consumed in the United States is produced in the United States. This is because transportation of natural gas across the ocean on vessels is not a simple process. In order to be transported, for example, on a tanker from Qatar to the United States, natural gas must go through a liquefaction process, creating liquefied natural gas (LNG). The liquefaction process reduces volume and allows it to be shipped efficiently across oceans. LNG is discussed further on in this chapter. The United States does export and import natural gas through pipelines between Canada and Mexico. Of the natural gas consumed by the United States in 2005, 83 percent was produced within the United States and 16.5 percent was imported from Canada.[2] The remainder is largely from LNG imports.

Unconventional natural gas is much harder and more costly to produce than conventional gas. It may also use technological methods that are not fully developed. As these technologies become more advanced and the price received for natural gas production increases, then what is unconventional gas today may be considered conventional gas in the future. Coalbed methane is a good example of unconventional natural gas. Natural gas is found within the coal seams and surrounding rock underground. Historically the natural gas was released either intentionally or unintentionally during coal-mining activities. It was realized that this natural gas could be captured and either used to fuel mining activities or injected into a natural gas pipeline for resale. It has become a popular form of unconventional natural gas, and the Energy Information Administration (EIA) reports that there are 19.9 trillion cubic feet (tcf) of proven coalbed methane reserves in the United States.[3] Currently this is less than 10 percent of the natural gas proven reserves in the United States reported by the EIA, but don't count coalbed methane out just yet![4] There is a huge potential for future coalbed methane supplies according to the U.S. Geological Survey (USGS). The USGS's *2006 National Oil and Gas Assessment* reports that as of 2005, unproven coalbed methane reserves were as high as 132.7 tcf.[5]

The most recent and exciting discovery of unconventional natural gas is that of methane hydrates. Methane hydrates take the form of a cage-like web of ice that contains trapped methane. The discovery of methane hydrates is nothing new, but research into them is still in beginning stages. Methane hydrate deposits are usually found in two places. The first is in areas where cold temperatures persist, such as the Arctic and Siberia. The second is under the ocean floor at depths greater than 500 meters, where high pressure dominates. In the United States large deposits have been located in the Gulf of Mexico, offshore of both the East and West Coasts, and in Alaska. The USGS conservatively estimates that worldwide methane hydrates reserves contain twice the amount of carbon as all known fossil fuels on Earth.[6] In addition, mapping by the USGS has shown that conventional natural gas deposits appear to be located beneath methane hydrate deposits. The use of methane hydrates as an energy source is still being researched by many organizations, including the USGS and the U.S. Department of Energy (DOE). As yet, little is known about how methane hydrates form, evolve, and break down or about their potential effects on seabed stability and climate change. Still, their high concentration levels of methane give them a strong future in the worldwide energy mix.

LIQUEFIED NATURAL GAS

Each year natural gas becomes a more prominent energy source for both the United States and the entire world. In the United States, natural gas has become the second most consumed energy source after petroleum.[7] Yet, worldwide natural gas is a new energy source. In 2005, the United States accounted for 23 percent of the natural gas consumed globally.[8] This was more than South America, Central America, Africa, and the Asian Pacific combined! Most natural gas consumed by the United States comes from domestic production or is imported from Canada.[9] The rest of United States consumption is in the form of liquefied natural gas (LNG). Liquefied natural gas is formed by cooling natural gas to approximately −260°F.

LNG is costly to produce, but currently it is the best way to transport natural gas long distances across the seas. Not only does it occupy only one six hundredth of the volume of natural gas in gaseous form, but it is unlikely to explode in an unconfined environment. Once received by the importing country, the LNG must go through facilities in order to convert it back to gas form. This is done by warming the liquid above −260°F. In the United States there are five LNG import terminals. They are Cove Point in Maryland; Elba Island in Georgia; Everett in Massachusetts; Lake Charles in Louisiana; and the Gulf Gateway, which is offshore in the Gulf of Mexico. As of 2006, these five terminals have a deliverability capacity of 5,225 million cubic feet (MMcf) per day.[10] This is currently less than 10 percent of daily natural gas consumption in the United States.[11]

In both Japan and South Korea, LNG constitutes 90 percent of all natural gas supplies.[12] Both countries rely heavily on LNG to generate electricity. Strong demand worldwide can create bidding wars for LNG supplies, given that there are only so many vessels that have the ability to carry LNG. It is economical to store, taking up much less space than natural gas. This creates the possibility of natural gas storage through LNG in places where current storage facilities are unavailable. Most of all, LNG allows for the production of natural gas deposits in areas where it was previously uneconomical. For example, in 2005 Qatar produced 43.5 billion cubic meters (bcm) of natural gas, and it exported more than 62 percent of that production in the form of LNG.[13] Qatar is a large supplier of LNG to the Asian Pacific market. It is reasonable to assume that without the demand for its natural gas in the form of LNG, overall production in Qatar would be closer to its level of consumption.

NATURAL GAS PROCESSING

The natural gas that is produced directly underground is not the same form of natural gas that is used by the consumer. Pipelines require natural gas of a specific quality in order to operate properly. If the wellhead natural gas is not processed properly, it can cause the pipelines to deteriorate or rupture during transport. Natural gas at the wellhead contains additional natural gas liquids and gases that must be extracted before it enters the pipeline. Natural gas liquids (NGLs) are hydrocarbons in natural gas that are separated from the gas as liquid. These liquids consist of propane and heavier hydrocarbons.

After production, natural gas goes through a processing plant, where it is cleaned and brought to pipeline quality specifications. The goal is to make the natural gas able to meet British Thermal Unit (BTU) content range; free of harmful gases such as nitrogen, oxygen, or hydrogen sulfide; and free of solids and liquid water that could harm the pipeline. A BTU is the amount of energy (in this case natural gas) it takes to raise the temperature of one pound of water by one degree Fahrenheit. The processing of wellhead natural gas into pipeline quality natural gas is extremely complex and contains stages in which the natural gas liquids, gases, and water are extracted. Other solids and impurities, such as sand, are scrubbed out of the natural gas close to the wellhead. It is also important to keep the natural gas in a proper temperature range so it does not form hydrate crystals that can block the flow of natural gas from the wellhead to the processing plant. According the Energy Information Administration, the United States has more than 500 natural gas processing plants in operation. The majority of them are located in Texas, Louisiana, and Wyoming, near major production areas, Texas and Louisiana process natural gas produced in South Texas and the Gulf Coast basin, and Wyoming processes gas produced from the Rocky Mountains.[14]

Most of the time these solids, gases, liquids, and hydrocarbons are extracted at the processing plant in order to bring the wellhead natural gas to pipeline BTU content standards. At other times hydrocarbons are added into the gas stream to bring it to proper BTU content levels. For example, a blend of higher BTU content natural gas can help increase the BTU content of natural gas produced below pipeline grade. Producers continue to try to maximize the BTU content of the natural gas they put into the pipeline. This is because natural gas pricing has moved to a heat-content pricing system from a volume-based pricing system. Natural gas is bought and sold based on its BTU content, not on how many cubic feet it contains.

RESERVES

The real question is how much natural gas is there both in the United States and worldwide? Natural gas reserves are a supply of natural gas held underground. The energy industry classifies reserves as proven reserves or unproven reserves. Proven reserves of natural gas are reserve deposits that scientists know or strongly believe are recoverable given current natural gas prices and drilling technologies. Unproven reserves are natural gas reserve deposits that may be extracted in the future with the emergence of new technologies or a change in the price of natural gas. Unfortunately, unlike crude oil, there is no reliable data for total (proven and unproven) recoverable global natural gas reserves. The *Oil & Gas Journal* lists world natural gas proven reserves as of January 1, 2007 at 6,183 tcf.[15] This is equal to approximately 40 years of supply, given the global consumption reference case for natural gas by the EIA in the *International Energy Outlook 2006*.[16] Since exploration of global natural gas reserves has not been as extensive as exploration for crude oil reserves, this number can be viewed positively. In addition, this is only the amount of proven natural gas reserves, because there is no reliable data for unproven reserves. These unproven reserves can include future sources such as shale natural gas, tight sands natural gas, deep natural gas, coalbed methane, and methane hydrates.

Although there is no global data on total natural gas reserves, there is comprehensive data on total natural gas reserves in the United States. This data comes from the Potential Gas Committee, which is a nonprofit entity of the Potential Gas Agency. Both operate in conjunction with the Colorado School of Mines. The Potential Gas Committee estimates that total unproven reserves of natural gas for the lower 48 states and Alaska are 1,119 tcf as of December 31, 2004.[17] The Potential Gas Committee uses the mean of their reserve estimates and this estimate includes coalbed methane. Table 7.1 shows the reserve estimate broken down by region and whether

TABLE 7.1   U.S. Natural Gas Reserves (BCF)

	Probable	Possible	Speculative	Total Potential
Lower 48 States				
Onshore	154,755	244,893	182,959	582,958
Offshore	15,177	59,954	97,285	172,418
Alaska				
Onshore	31,717	22,300	40,417	94,432
Offshore	5,142	19,499	74,788	99,366
Coalbed Methane	17,570	56,780	94,948	169,298
Totals	224,335	402,988	491,576	1,119,255

Source: Potential Gas Committee Report, December 2004, Potential Gas Agency, Colorado School of Mines.
Notes: As of December 31, 2004. Excludes proven reserves. Mean values in BCF (May not total due to rounding and statistical aggregation of distributions).

it is onshore or offshore. Proven reserves of natural gas in the United States as of this date were 192.5 tcf according to the EIA.[18] Combining the two estimates yields a total natural gas reserve estimate for the United States as of December 31, 2004 of 1,312 tcf. With U.S. dry natural gas production averaging approximately 19 tcf/yr over the decade 1995–2005, there would be approximately 10 years of production left using proven reserves.[19] An additional 59 years of natural gas production in the United States may be available, given the Potential Gas Committee's estimate of total unproven natural gas reserves.[20]

These numbers may seem very small at first glance, but they do not include any reserves outside of the United States or any estimates involving methane hydrates. It is also important to mention that the EIA estimate of proven reserves in the United States has been increasing each year for at least the past decade. Proven reserves are increasing even as we continue to consume natural gas each year. In the future, the United States may consume more natural gas in the form of LNG. Further exploration for global natural gas reserves and technological advances in production of unconventional sources are likely to increase the total reserve base in the coming years. This increase is likely to lead to an increase in price also. The costs of research, new technology, and exploration continue to rise. If the prices paid to producers do not increase with these costs, production will be shut in when it becomes unprofitable and exploration will stop.

STORAGE

There are approximately 400 storage facilities operating in the United States that play an integral role in maintaining both supply and demand in the natural gas market.[21] Natural gas storage has both a withdrawal and an injection season. Natural gas consumption is dominated by its use to heat residential and commercial buildings. This results in the need to withdraw natural gas from storage during peak demand in the winter and inject it into storage during the spring, summer, and fall months. The injection season occurs from April through October and is associated with the non-heating season. The withdrawal period occurs between November and March during the heating season. Figure 7.1 illustrates how natural gas storage in the United States peaks sometime in early November and reaches its lowest point in early April, following the injection and withdrawal seasons.

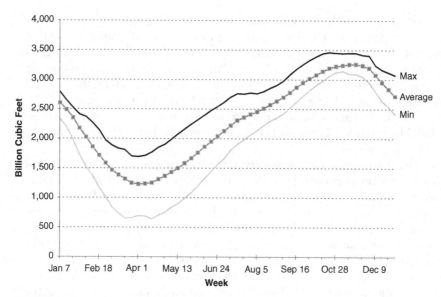

FIGURE 7.1   Weekly Natural Gas Storage: 2002–2006
Source: Energy Information Administration

Natural gas storage facilities contain two types of natural gas. The first is called base gas, which is the amount of natural gas necessary in the facility to allow enough pressure to extract the remaining natural gas. The second is called working gas, which is the natural gas that is injected and withdrawn from the storage facility in accordance with its operations. When we talk about how much natural gas is in storage or the capacity of a facility, we are referring to working gas. Sometimes storage operators will evaluate the operations of the facility and reclassify some base gas into working gas.

There are three main types of underground storage facilities: depleted gas reservoirs, aquifers, and salt caverns. Depleted gas reservoirs are the most common type of natural gas storage in the United States. Geographically they need to be near consuming regions. It is also important that they be highly permeable and porous. Permeability helps determine the flow of injection and withdrawal, and porosity determines how much gas can be held in the reservoir. Of all the storage facilities in the United States, 81 percent are depleted reservoirs, 11 percent are aquifers, and 8 percent are salt caverns.[22] Of these, 58 percent of all storage facilities are located in either the Northeast or Midwest consuming regions.[23] The Northeast region has the most depleted reservoirs, the Midwest has the most aquifers, and the Southwest has the most salt caverns.[24]

CONSUMPTION

Natural gas as an energy source is used in a variety of ways in the United States. It can heat homes and businesses, generate electricity, cook food, or serve as an industrial fuel or heat source. Figure 7.2 displays the seasonality of natural gas demand in the United States. Demand peaks in the winter months of January and February because of strong demand for residential and commercial heating. It rises again in the summer months of July and August on electrical generation demand driven by air conditioner use. The one thing in common in these two cases is the weather. Winter weather drives demand for natural gas as a heating fuel, whereas summer weather drives demand for natural gas as a generation fuel. These changes in demand from month to month in turn affect the price. The seasonality of natural gas consumption is exhibited in the futures curve, where the highest-priced months of January and February are also the two months with the highest demand. Storage is used in the winter to meet the strong demand for natural gas, because during that time domestic production and imports fall short of demand. This is why the natural gas storage withdrawal period extends from November to March. The lower demand time period of April to October coincides with injection of natural gas into storage as production exceeds demand.

Figure 7.3 shows natural gas consumption broken down by the percentage consumed in each sector. In terms of percentage of total consumption, the residential, commercial, and transportation sectors have been largely

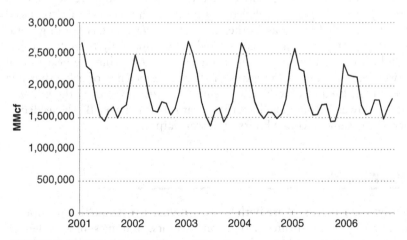

FIGURE 7.2 U.S. Monthly Natural Gas Consumption
Source: Energy Information Administration

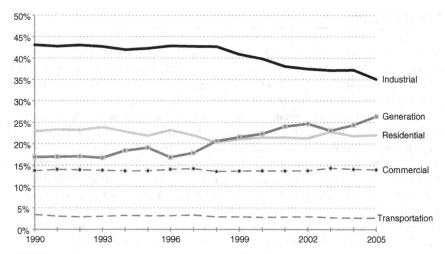

FIGURE 7.3   Percent Share of U.S. Natural Gas Consumption by Sector
Source: Energy Information Administration

unchanged since 1990. Figure 7.3 displays a consumption decline in the industrial sector coinciding with a consumption increase in electrical generation. The industrial sector decline occurred at the same time that prices of natural gas increased. Natural gas costs became too high to sustain profitability, and some industrial plants (such as in the aluminum smelter industry) were mothballed as a result. The electrical generation increase occurred as new generation plants fueled by natural gas came online and replaced older plants fueled by oil and other fossil fuels. Natural gas use in generation has grown as the fuel is considered environmentally friendly and has a high heat content, which is important when determining the heat rate of a power plant. The heat rate gives the thermal efficiency of a fuel-burning power plant. It equals the BTU content of the fuel divided by the kilowatt hours of power output. The lower the heat rate, the fewer BTUs needed to generate the same kilowatt hours of power output.

FUEL SWITCHING

Since natural gas and oil are both hydrocarbons, it is reasonable to suppose that they may be substitutes within some sectors. In homes and businesses, heating equipment is able to burn heating oil or natural gas as fuel, but not both. Homeowners cannot just flip a switch on the burner depending

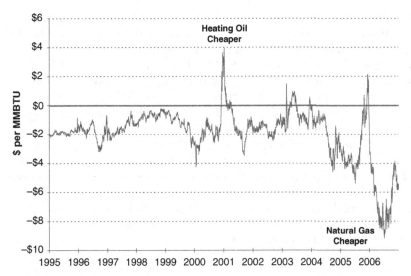

FIGURE 7.4 Natural Gas—Heating Oil Price Spread
Source: New York Mercantile Exchange.

on which fuel is cheaper to burn. One sector in which fuel switching does occur is electrical generation. Dual-fuel generators allow utilities to choose between an oil-based fuel (such as residual fuel oil, kerosene, or heating oil) and natural gas. Figure 7.4 shows a graph of the spread between heating oil futures and natural gas futures. Heating oil is priced under natural gas a few times during the winter when natural gas prices spiked due to heating demand. It is during these times that utilities may find it more profitable to burn heating oil in their dual-fuel power plants if they are able to switch. Keep in mind that utilities have other factors to consider when determining the economics of switching. These include the cost to switch the plant to a different fuel, taxes, and cost of extra emissions produced by burning a dirtier fuel. Utilities will not switch fuels if it is beneficial for just a day. They will look at the cost of either fuel over a medium to longer time frame to determine which fuel is more beneficial on a BTU basis.

FUTURES

In the United States natural gas futures trade on the New York Mercantile Exchange (NYMEX); they were launched in April 1990. Physical delivery is to the Henry Hub in Louisiana. The Henry Hub location was selected because of its proximity to the Gulf of Mexico (offshore production), and it has 16 interconnections with both interstate and intrastate pipelines.[25] These pipelines connect throughout the Midwest and East Coast. One futures contract is equal to 10,000 million British thermal units (MMBTU) of natural gas. The futures trade in $/MMBTU, with a minimum tick size of $.001 and a tick value of $10. That means for every tenth of a cent that the futures price moves, that equals a change in value of $10 on the future. So if the futures moves from $7.50 to $7.51 and you are long (own) one contract, you would have made $100. Natural gas futures are available to trade in the NYMEX floor pit and electronically through the CME Globex system.

There is also an E-mini NYMEX natural gas futures contract that is available for smaller investors. This contract trades electronically and is a quarter of the size of the natural gas futures contract, or 2,500 MMBTU. The natural gas E-mini future also trades in $/MMBTU. Its tick size is $.005, and the tick value is $12.50. It is financially settled to the NYMEX natural gas futures standard-sized contract.

PRICE HISTORY AND MARKET REPORTS

Natural gas price volatility has been very exciting in the twenty-first century. Natural gas futures trading began in 1990. As discussed previously, the use of natural gas as a heating fuel and to power air conditioners through electrical generation makes demand reliant on weather patterns in the United States. Figure 7.5 shows the prompt natural gas future price since inception. Many of the price spikes are the result of below-average winter temperatures in the natural gas consuming areas of the East and Midwest. For example, the winter of 2000 to 2001 began with a very cold December, resulting in a sharp increase in natural gas prices. January temperatures were close to normal and February temperatures were above normal, so the price spike for that winter lasted only through the cold month of December. The winter of 2002 to 2003 exhibited a short-lived price spike as temperatures in late February and early March were much colder than normal, which drew natural gas storage down to a low level of 642 BCF in April 2003. This left storage far under the 1,000 BCF end-of-winter comfort level that the market looks for. All of these weather anomalies led to dramatic movements in natural gas prices. For this reason natural gas traders are constantly focused on future weather patterns and developments.

As shown in Figure 7.5, hurricanes can also impact the price of natural gas. The Atlantic basin hurricane season runs from June to November with the peak occurring in mid-August to late October. Hurricanes can affect the natural gas market in terms of both production and demand. Hurricane

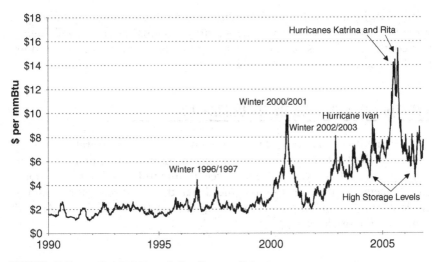

FIGURE 7.5 NYMEX Natural Gas Futures Price

destruction will cause industrial plants, homes, and businesses to shut down. This causes a decrease in demand until the region's utilities and industries get back up and running. Usually a hurricane's impact on the natural gas market is in the form of shut-in production in the Gulf of Mexico. Hurricanes Katrina and Rita in 2005 both had paths that lead them through the Gulf of Mexico and significantly affected both oil and natural gas production for months.

One of the most important fundamental reports for the natural gas market in the United States is the *Weekly Natural Gas Storage Report* published by the EIA. This report is usually released on Thursdays at 10:30 AM EST; it shows the net change in storage (withdrawal or injection) on a weekly basis. The report is broken down into three regions: consuming (Eastern/Midwestern areas), producing (South), and West. One way market participants look at storage numbers is with respect to their historical average for the same week. For example, if the EIA reported a large draw of natural gas during June, that would be abnormal compared to historical data because June falls within the injection season. Expectations would be for an injection during this time.

The future of natural gas looks bright. On the demand side, increased need for cleaner-burning fuel will help feed demand, along with strong growth in many emerging economies. Further exploration and production will continue as strong global demand from electrical generation and industrial sectors will support prices. Compared with oil, the natural gas market is still in its infancy. Many questions must be answered regarding the supply side of the market, specifically the amount of global reserves available. It will continue to be essential to watch how the prices of natural gas and its fossil fuel substitutes, oil and coal interact.

ADDITIONAL SOURCES OF INFORMATION

Additional information regarding the fundamentals of the natural gas futures market in the United States can be found through the EIA division of the Department of Energy. It produces weekly, monthly, and annual reports on all facets of natural gas supply and demand. Global natural gas data is available through the International Energy Agency (IEA) and the *BP Annual Statistical Energy Review*.

Three

Understanding Grains and Oilseeds

Corn

Corn is a unique grain with no close counterpart in the plant world. The origins of corn remain controversial. There is no historical evidence of wild corn as we know it today. Genetically its closest wild relative is teosinte. Teosinte looks more like a bunch of wild grasses, and its ears are smaller and simpler than those of corn. The name *teosinte* is derived from the Nahuatl Indian language *teotl,* meaning god, and *centil,* meaning dried ears of maize. This name, *God's corn,* is additional indication that corn was derived from teosinte. Scientists believe corn was developed in Central Mexico, thanks to aggressive breeders who searched for desired traits within the teosinte plant. This manmade plant transformation is a significant achievement, but in the process corn was significantly altered. It is not able to survive in the wild as it has no way of distributing its seeds, or kernels. It must be planted and cultivated each year by humans in order to produce a crop.

Corn started as a primary food source for humans, but today it's mainly used as animal feed. We consume corn as food in kernel form and in products such as corn flakes, tortillas, and popcorn. Corn also yields other products such as vegetable oil, high fructose corn syrup (HFCS), and ethanol. This versatility makes it one of the most important crops in the world. Corn is grown in more countries than any other crop and on all continents except Antarctica.[1] It can thrive in many climates. There are many types of corn grown, including flint corn, dent corn, waxy corn, and sweet corn. The majority of corn produced in the United States is dent corn, so called because the kernel typically forms a dent on the cap or crown at maturity. The dent occurs as the corn dries out to its ideal moisture level prior to harvest. This type of corn is used for livestock feed, industrial uses, sweeteners, and ethanol among other things. In the United States, sweet corn is also produced solely for human consumption.

CHAPTER **8**

PRODUCTION

Worldwide production of corn is dominated by the United States. During the 2005–2006 corn marketing year, the United States accounted for over 40 percent of world production.[2] The next largest producer of corn is China, with 20 percent of world production for 2005–2006. The European Union (EU-25) and Brazil follow with world production shares of 7 percent and 6 percent for 2005–2006. Figure 8.1 shows the percentage share of world production for these four countries since 1980. As the chart shows, corn production is not smooth from year to year. Corn production depends on two things—acreage harvested and yield per acre. The number of acres harvested is a function of the amount initially planted. If a farmer wants to increase his production of corn he has to plant more acres. When this choice is made, another crop such as soybeans, cotton, or wheat loses acreage. Some planted acreage may not be harvested due to poor performance of the crop, pest infestation, or extreme weather events that would destroy the crop. On average in the United States since 1980, 10 percent of the acreage planted for corn was not harvested.[3]

Crop yield is the main driver of production, and it is dependent on weather during the critical tasseling and pollination stages. Yet weather is

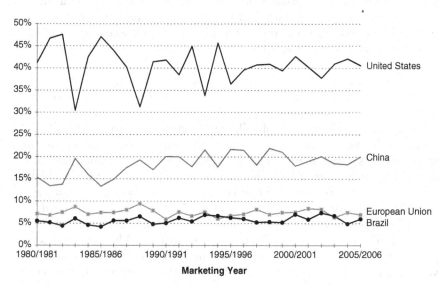

FIGURE 8.1   Percent Share of World Corn Production
Source: United States Department of Agriculture

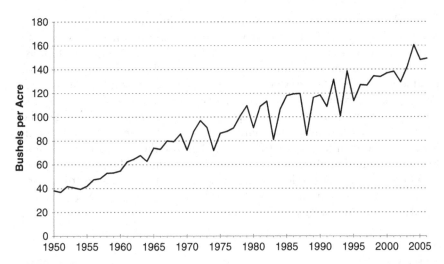

FIGURE 8.2 U.S. Corn Yield
Source: United States Department of Agriculture

anything but normal. Figure 8.2 exhibits the corn yield in the United States from 1950 to 2006. The yield is upward sloping as a result of technological advances in farm machinery, fertilizer, and genetically modified seed, among other things. It is noticeable that yield from year to year can be extremely volatile. The volatility in yield occurs because the crop is vulnerable to stress during the tasseling and pollination stages. In the United States, these two stages occur between the middle of July through August.

The two common stressors for agricultural plants are drought and heat. The lowest corn yield in the past 20 years occurred in 1988 as a result of a severe drought that dropped yields to 84.6 bushels/acre. Yield changes greater than ±10 percent from one year to the next are not uncommon. For this reason research in recent years has focused on creating drought-resistant corn seeds. The world's two largest seed producers, Monsanto and Pioneer Hi-Breed International, have seeds that are drought tolerant. Drought-tolerant seeds recover more quickly when moisture is lost. Research still continues on creating a truly drought-resistant seed. Additional weather stressors can occur during harvest of the corn in the fall. Excess moisture during the harvest can result in puddles in the fields, and as a result machinery can't get into the fields to harvest the crop. This causes the mature crop to sit in the field longer, exposing it to mold and mildew along with changing weather towards the winter season.

In the United States, corn is the largest crop in terms of planted acreage. Most of the crop is planted in the Corn Belt from April through May. The Corn Belt is an area in the Midwest that includes Ohio, Indiana, Illinois, and Iowa. Together, these four states account for almost 50 percent of corn production in the United States.[4] Harvesting of corn starts in September and can last through the middle of November. In the United States, the corn marketing year starts in September and ends in August. So the 2006–2007 marketing year would correspond to the interval between September 2006 and August 2007. This is because the new corn crop would begin to be marketed starting in September as harvest begins. Marketing years for other countries depend on when they plant and harvest their corn crop. For example, South Africa has a corn marketing year of May through April as most harvesting begins in May.

CONSUMPTION

Worldwide corn consumption is highest in the United States and is followed by China, the European Union, Brazil, and Mexico. Demand for corn is dominated by its use in livestock feed for animals such as cattle, hogs, and poultry. For the 2005–2006 marketing year the USDA estimates that 68 percent of corn produced will be used as feed worldwide.[5] As livestock feed, corn is important for its high energy value. It is fed in conjunction with a high protein source, such as soybean meal.

In some countries, corn is a staple for human consumption. Corn is the primary ingredient in foods such as polenta, tortillas, corn flakes, and grits. In addition, corn is widely used as a sweetener in the form of high fructose corn syrup (HFCS), dextrose, and corn syrup. These sweeteners replace sugar in some applications and are present in various products, including sodas, ice cream, and salad dressings. In fact, in the United States per capita yearly consumption of HFCS in 2005 was greater than 42 pounds, equating to about 200 calories a day.[6] Corn is also utilized in starch form in consumer and industrial products. Paper products, adhesives, and thickening agents are just a few of the ways we use corn starch.

Corn has been grabbing headlines since 2005 for its use as a fuel in the form of ethanol. Ethanol is an alcohol-based fuel made from the simple sugars and starches of various crops. In the United States ethanol is made primarily from corn. In Brazil it is produced from sugar cane. Current research is focused on producing ethanol from cellulose-based products such as farm waste, wood chips, and switch grass. Cellulose-based ethanol is ideal because it would allow ethanol production without taking away from current food supplies. Ethanol production in the United States is centered in the Midwest, since that is where most of its feedstock, corn, is grown. It is primarily used as a fuel additive in conjunction with gasoline. This mixture is called E10 because it contains 10 percent ethanol and 90 percent gasoline and is available is most major metropolitan areas in the United States. Ethanol is discussed extensively in Chapter 6, "Gasoline," since fuel is its primary application.

Demand for corn to make ethanol has begun to change the landscape of corn fundamentals in the United States. Figure 8.3 shows how ethanol demand is affecting the U.S. demand picture. As a percentage of total demand ethanol now consumes more corn than that used in the food and industrial sectors. Where has this extra corn supply come from? Some of it is coming from a decline in livestock feed use. When corn is used to produce ethanol, one of the byproducts is distillers' grains with solubles. These distillers' grains with solubles can come in either a wet (WDGS) or dry (DDGS) form. Both forms are marketed and used in livestock feed to replace some of the corn previously used in the feed sector. It is primarily used for animals with ruminant diets such as beef and dairy cattle but can also be used in small amounts for swine and poultry. Corn is fed to livestock as a source of energy,

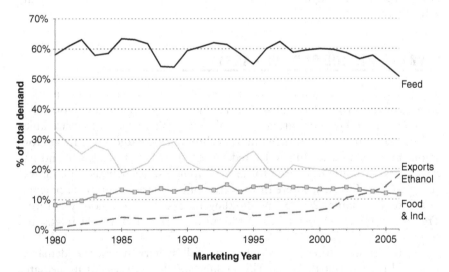

FIGURE 8.3 U.S. Corn Consumption by Sector
Source: United States Department of Agriculture

but since DGS is a byproduct of ethanol production, most of corn's original energy in the form of starch has already been used. The remaining elements of fiber, protein, and minerals are left in the DGS. This is why DGS can be used only in limited amounts as livestock feed; an energy source is still needed in the form of carbohydrates.

Exports are a significant part of the U.S. corn industry. Not only is the United States the largest worldwide producer of corn, it is also the largest exporter of corn. In the 2005–2006 marketing year the United States accounted for approximately 68 percent of the worldwide export market.[7] These exports equaled almost 20 percent of total production in the United States for that marketing year.[8] A greater portion of U.S. corn exports go to Japan, Taiwan, Egypt, and Mexico. Japan is by far the largest importer of corn followed by South Korea. Both countries do not produce many coarse grains. However, because they are large meat producers, it is necessary to import corn for feed use. Both Argentina and South Africa are large exporters of corn.

The corn market does compete with other grains for use in the feed sector. Other feed grains available to livestock producers are sorghum, barley, and oats. In addition, when corn is expensive as compared with wheat, livestock producers have the ability to feed wheat to their animals. Usually the wheat used is low-quality wheat, either soft white or soft red wheat. Corn also competes with sugar for its use in the sweetener market, especially in soft drinks.

STORAGE AND THE COST OF CARRY

Storage is an extremely important concern in the grain markets. Grains are largely stored in grain elevators located near major rivers and ports for shipping. Grain elevators are a series of bins, tanks, or silos that are able to store grain in bulk and then empty it into trucks, barges, or railcars for shipment to end users. In the United States, the Mississippi River and its tributaries are commonly used for grain shipments. The Mississippi allows access to New Orleans, where the majority of international grain shipments originate. In Chapter 20, "Some Building Blocks of a Commodity Futures Trading System," the dynamics of the futures curve and how it relates to storage costs are discussed in depth.

In the grain market, the supply comes all at harvest whereas demand is spread throughout the year. This creates supply in excess of immediate consumption. As discussed in Chapter 20, this market is a good candidate for futures prices to be determined by an arbitrage relationship. Let's look at an example. On November 30, 2006 the price of corn on the Chicago

Board of Trade for December 2006 delivery was 377.00 cents/bushel. The next delivery month is March 2007. If arbitrage theory held, what would the March 2007 price be on this date? You will need the daily storage cost, interest rate, and the number of days the corn will be stored. In this example we will assume that the grain will be held for 90 days in storage before being delivered against the March corn futures contract. We will also assume daily storage costs of 0.15 cents/bushel and an annual interest rate of 5.35 percent. So the cost is calculated as follows:

$$\text{cost} = (\text{cost of near future} * (\text{Interest}/360) + \text{daily storage cost})$$
$$* \text{days in storage}$$
$$= (377.00 * (.0535/360) + .15) * 90$$
$$= 18.54 \text{ cents/bushel}$$

So given that it would cost 18.54 cents to take December 2006 corn and deliver it to the March 2007 contract, the maximum expected price for the March 2007 would be

$$(377 + 18.54) = 395.54 \text{ cents/bushel for March 2007 corn}$$

If the actual March 2007 corn future was priced at 395.54 on November 30, 2006 grain traders would say the market is priced at full carry. Full carry is when the price difference between two different future months equals the full cost of carrying the commodity from the delivery month of the first contract to the next. If the actual March 2007 corn future was at a higher price, say 398.00 cents/bushel, an arbitrage would exist. In this case, an arbitrager would like to buy the December 2006 corn contract and sell the March 2007 contract. The arbitager would store the corn from December until the March delivery date and make a profit of

$$(377 + 18.54) - 398 = 2.46 \text{ cents/bushel}$$

In this case the futures market is pricing the March 2007 contract above the cost of storage or greater than 100 percent full carry. If this were to occur, the arbitrage would close quickly as those who could profit by storing the corn would do so immediately for a risk-free profit.

The actual price for March 2007 corn on November 30, 2006 was 390.50 cents/bushel. The future spread between the December 2006 and March 2007 contracts on this date is 13.50 cents/bushel with March over. This means that if you bought December corn futures and took delivery, the market would pay you 13.50 cents/bushel of the storage cost to redeliver the physical corn in March. You already know the true cost to store corn until the future delivery in March is 18.54 cents/bushel. Since the spread between the December and March corn futures contracts is 13.50, the market is said to be at 73 percent (13.50/18.54) of full carry. Why is the market pricing less than 100 percent full carry? In this case, an arbitrager would like to sell short the physical corn and buy the March contract. One reason the market is less than 100 percent full carry is that it is extremely difficult to go short the physical corn. In addition, even if the arbitrager were able to short the physical corn, he would not receive the storage costs.

In the corn market, when the futures contracts are pricing in some percentage of full carry, as in the previous example, it is called a normal futures curve. It is normal because this is how the futures curve is shaped most of the time in the grain markets. This is also called contango, when the far future price is higher than the near future price. What happens if the futures curve is inverted, or the price of the near future is higher than the price of the far future? This is called backwardation or an inverted curve in the grain markets. An inverted curve shows a negative percent of full carry, suggesting that consumers are unwilling to pay the farmer part of the cost to store the corn for future consumption. An inverted curve in the grain markets implies there may be a short-term shortage in the market and consumers would rather have the grain now than later.

FUTURES

Different corn futures trade in many different countries. The most liquid corn future trades on the Chicago Board of Trade (CBOT). The CBOT corn future has a contract size of 5,000 bushels. It trades in cents/bushel and has a minimum tick size of .25 cents/bushel. This tick size is equal to a value of $12.50. That means if you own one futures contract at a price of 400.00 cents/bushel and you sell it at 400.25 cents/bushel, you have made $12.50, minus transaction costs. The CBOT corn future contract trades futures months of December, March, May, and July for each marketing year. The September futures contract is active for a small period of time, and many market participants elect to skip this future and trade the December instead.

For smaller investors the CBOT has an E-mini corn futures contract. This contract is one-fifth of the size of the regular CBOT corn futures contract. Each E-mini corn future has a contract size of 1,000 bushel, a tick size of 0.125 cents/bushel, and a tick value of $1.25. The E-mini corn future can be physically delivered. The delivery specifications are the same as those on the full-size corn future.

Corn futures are deliverable from select shipping stations and warehouses around Chicago. Delivery of corn futures and other grain futures is a little different from that of other commodities such as energies. Deliveries of corn futures are made by delivery of shipping certificates issued by shippers designated by the CBOT Exchange. The shipping certificates represent the physical commodity exchanging hands. These corn shipping certificates specify shipment from one of the registered shipping stations or warehouses in the Chicago delivery area.

Various other corn futures trade on different exchanges worldwide, but none is as liquid as the one on the CBOT. Both the Tokyo Grain Exchange and the Dalian Commodity Exchange in China also trade fairly liquid corn future contracts.

PRICE HISTORY AND MARKET REPORTS

Corn has a long-term price history that is remarkably range bound. Figure 8.4 shows the price history of the prompt month CBOT corn future from 1975 through 2006. You can see there are price spikes that occur such as in 1980, 1988, and 1996. Yet, overall the price of corn stayed between 200 cents/bushel and 300 cents/bushel for most of this time period. Why do the price spikes last for only a short time? The answer is economics. When prices for corn get extremely high, farmers react accordingly to supply the market. They may plant more corn than soybeans that year, or they may take livestock pasture and plant corn for a year. They may spend a little extra to get high-quality seeds or fertilizer because they expect a great year based on futures prices. When that crop finally comes to harvest in the fall, prices may decline when the new supply finally hits the market. Now why is the price range bound for so much of the time? Again, the answer is economics. Common sense would tell you that if the foregoing was true, then when the corn price was low and profit margins small less corn would be planted for the next year. While this concept does hold to a small degree, there is also the issue of government subsidies to farmers. The extra money that farmers receive from subsidies allows them to continue to plant corn each year regardless of how low the price is.

Government subsidies for corn come mainly in three forms: direct payments, counter-cyclical payments, and subsidized insurance. Eligible corn producers are able to receive direct payments as a function of the yield and their base acres planted. Counter-cyclical payments give the farmers a floor price of corn and issue payments if the market price for corn falls below the government floor price. There is also a loan program that gives no-recourse loans to farmers with their crop as collateral. At the end of the loan terms,

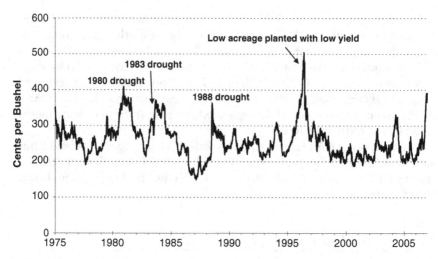

FIGURE 8.4   CBOT Corn Futures Price

they can pay the loan or just hand over the crop. At the end of 2005, total
U.S. Department of Agriculture (USDA) subsidies payments amounted to
over $21 billion dollars to more than 1.5 million recipients.[9]

Still, price spikes for corn do occur, and they are usually a result of poor
crop yields due to weather. Figure 8.4 shows the largest price spikes in corn
since 1975; they all occurred because of severe drought and heat waves in the
major corn-producing states. When drought occurred in 1980, 1983, and
1988, yields all came in significantly below 100 bushels/acre. The large price
spike of 1995–1996 was as much a result of weather conditions affecting
crop yields as it was of an extremely low amount of acreage planted. This
combination resulted in low corn supply for the 1995–1996 year, and the
price increase was necessary to ration demand and entice farmers to plant
more corn in 1996–1997. They responded by planting over 10 percent more
corn acreage in the 1996–1997 crop year, resulting in an easing of prices.

The USDA publishes a variety of weekly, monthly, and yearly reports
that are helpful in determining the fundamental picture of the corn market. On a weekly basis, the Foreign Agricultural Service (FAS) division of
the USDA publishes export sales for corn and other agricultural products.
Export sales are usually published on Thursday mornings at 8:30 AM EST
before the CBOT market opening. Exports for corn are spoken about in
terms of net sales for the week along with their destination. Net sales are
sales negotiated and reported for that specific week, but they have not necessarily been exported yet. Weekly exports, which have actually occurred for
the reported week, and accumulated exports for the current marketing year

are also reported. Possibly the most important publication from the USDA is the monthly *World Agricultural Supply and Demand Estimates* (WASDE). In this report the USDA gives supply and demand estimates for the current or upcoming marketing year on corn and other agricultural crops. In the WASDE, each May marks the beginning of the USDA estimates for the upcoming marketing year. For example, when the May 2007 WASDE is released, it will contain the first USDA published estimates for the 2007–2008 corn crop (harvest beginning in September 2007). The WASDE includes a section on corn supply and demand in the United States along with a separate section on world corn supply and demand.

The USDA makes estimates for many categories including domestic demand, acreage harvested, crop yield, production, exports, and ending stock totals. The ending stocks total is often discussed as a percent of total usage or consumption. This is called stocks usage. For example, if the USDA estimated ending stocks of 1,900 million bushels of corn for the 2005–2006 marketing year and total usage for the marketing year was 11,000 million bushels the 2005– 2006 corn stocks usage would be 17.27 percent.

Another USDA publication that is important for the corn market is the yearly Prospective Planting report published at the end of March. This report gives an estimate of the acreage farmers will plant for corn and other crops that spring. This report is updated again in June when the USDA Acreage report shows new estimates of acres planted for corn and other crops. At this point in June, most of the acres have already been planted.

The future outlook for corn demand looks strong with increasing use of corn to make ethanol for fuel. The demand for corn from ethanol production will not change until additional and cheaper sources of ethanol are established. In addition, the demand for meat, and thus livestock feed, will increase as strong global economies create new wealth. On the supply side, each year's harvest will be dependent on weather for final yields. In some countries, additional acreage will have to come at the expense of other crops, but expect farmers to continue to chase the highest-return crop for the next season. Other countries, such as Brazil, have arable land available for expansion and their percentage of world production of corn will grow. Corn prices will continue to be volatile depending on yield, but over the long run they should continue to be steady.

ADDITIONAL SOURCES OF INFORMATION

The USDA is the best source for fundamental market information on corn and other agricultural crops. The Economic Research Service (ERS) section of the USDA has numerous research reports along with a corn briefing room on its website www.ers.usda.gov. The National Agricultural Statistics Service (NASS) section of the USDA provides useful corn statistics with regard to both supply and demand. The USDA's Office of the Chief Economist is the area that puts together the WASDE; it also has a wealth of information on long-term corn projections, the farm bill, and ethanol subsidies, among other things.

CHAPTER 9

Wheat

Wheat is the staple food of mankind. It is a cereal grain and globally the most important grain for human consumption. Cereal grains are grasses cultivated for their grains or seeds, and they provide more food energy to humans than any other crop. Other cereal grains include corn, rice, barley, oats, and rye. The calories that have fed the population boom of the world have largely come from these grains. Wheat is the first known cereal grain to be domesticated. Its origins go back as early as 6500 B.C. to Mesopotamia. From there wheat cultivation spread to the rest of the world. Currently wheat is grown on all continents except Antarctica and in more than 80 countries.[1]

Wheat is grouped into two categories based on its growing season: winter wheat and spring wheat. Winter wheat is planted in the fall and becomes established before a period of dormancy during the winter. When spring comes, the winter wheat resumes its growth until an early summertime harvest. In areas where the winter is harsh, spring wheat is planted during the spring. It then is harvested in the late summer or early fall. In the United States the wheat industry classifies the many varieties of wheat according to six classes. These classes are defined by the wheat's growing season and percent of protein. The winter wheat classes are hard red winter (HRW) and soft red winter (SRW). Spring wheat classes are hard red spring (HRS), durum, hard white, and soft white. Each wheat class is important as it has characteristics that are important to food manufacturers for specific products. Worldwide there are different classes (dependent on the country it is grown in) and varieties of wheat, but any wheat produced can be classified as either winter wheat or spring wheat.

PRODUCTION

The majority of the world's wheat production is grown as winter wheat in the Northern Hemisphere. Large spring wheat crops do occur in Canada,

Russia, and the United States. In the Southern Hemisphere wheat producers plant after the spring wheat crop in the Northern Hemisphere. This creates a smooth supply of wheat year round.

Worldwide production of wheat has begun to take a back seat to production of corn and soybeans. Figure 9.1 shows that in terms of worldwide area harvested, wheat still dominates but over the last decade its area harvested has declined by more than 7 percent.[2] During this same time the area harvested for corn has increased over 7 percent and soybeans area harvested has increased over 36 percent.[3] In addition, the physical quantity of corn produced worldwide has exceeded that of wheat each year since the 1998–1999 marketing year.[4] Wheat production has lost its luster as demand for corn and soybeans has increased at a faster pace than demand for wheat. In addition, declining returns relative to other crops have helped entice farmers to switch away from planting wheat.

The European Union (EU-25) leads the worldwide production of wheat with approximately 20 percent of the market during the 2005–2006 marketing year.[5] Other countries that produce a large quantity of wheat are China, the Former Soviet Union (FSU-12), India, the United States, and Russia. Combined, they accounted for almost 80 percent of world wheat production in the 2005–2006 marketing year.[6] Other countries, such as Australia and Canada, are also important with regard to their levels of wheat production. Although they may not be the largest producers, these two

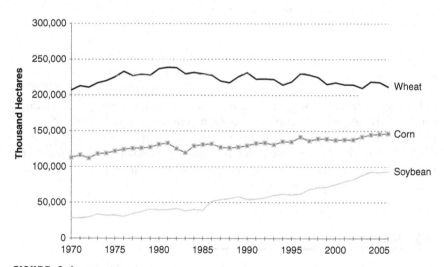

FIGURE 9.1 Worldwide Area Harvested
Source: United States Department of Agriculture

countries are large exporters of wheat; historically, they export more than half of their production each year.

The production of wheat in the United States is extremely important to the worldwide market. This is because the United States is the largest exporter of wheat. Approximately half of the country's production is exported each year. In the United States, production of wheat is region specific, and each class has a different end use. Hard red winter wheat (HRW wheat) accounts for approximately 40 percent of U.S. production.[7] HRW wheat is grown north of Texas through the Great Plains. It is best used as bread flour and has a higher shelf life than lower-protein wheat such as white wheat. Hard red spring wheat (HRS wheat) is valued for its high protein content and comprises about 25 percent of production.[8] HRS wheat is grown in the Northern plains of Minnesota, Montana, and the Dakotas. Its high protein content makes it suitable for specialty breads and for blending with lower-protein wheat. Soft red winter wheat (SRW wheat) accounts for between 15 percent and 20 percent of production and is grown along the Mississippi River and some Eastern states.[9] SRW wheat is good for cookies, crackers, and cakes. White wheat accounts for 10 percent to 15 percent of production.[10] It is grown in Washington, Oregon, Idaho, Michigan, and New York. White wheat is best used for items such as rich cakes and doughnuts. Durum wheat accounts for approximately 5 percent of production and is primarily used for pasta.[11] It is grown in both Montana and North Dakota.

As with other agricultural crops, the weather is an important factor in the final crop yield for wheat. Some damage can occur during the pollination stage, when high temperatures and severe drought will reduce the number of grains set. With regard to winter wheat, the market is primarily concerned about winter kill. Winter kill results when there is no snow to cover the winter wheat and to allow it to lie dormant and protected during the winter season. When there is no snow cover to provide moisture and protection, the cold can have an adverse affect on exposed wheat. In addition, repeated freezes and thaws during the winter can cause the soil to heave and lift the wheat plants out of the ground. Otherwise, of all the grains wheat is the best in making adjustments to adverse weather conditions. It takes a lot to actually kill it. In both corn and soybeans, genetically modified seeds (GMO) have enabled those crops to become more resistant to adverse conditions. In the case of wheat, genetic improvements have been slow because of the genetic complexity of wheat. In addition, as farmers are moving cropland away from wheat, research into wheat genetics is discouraged by companies. While corn farmers tend to buy their seed from dealers each year, wheat farmers use saved seeds from prior production.

CONSUMPTION

Wheat consumption per capita has been in decline for almost 20 years. This is shown in Figure 9.2, where you can see that per capita consumption of wheat peaked in 1987. This is in comparison with corn, where per capita consumption has been rising during the same period of time. Why is this? One of the reasons is that as diets become more diversified and disposable income rises, demand for more expensive foods such as meats, fruits, and vegetables replaces demand for wheat. Keep in mind that wheat is still primarily consumed as a food source. On the other hand, corn is used in a variety of applications outside of food such as industrial uses and ethanol. The lack of additional uses for wheat results in slower growth in demand over time. Wheat is primarily consumed in the form of flour used to bake breads, cakes, crackers, pasta, and other edibles. The flour is made by putting wheat kernels through the milling process. The wheat milling byproducts bran, germ, middling, and shorts are also produced. These milling byproducts are used by feed manufacturers in the production of livestock feeds.

Worldwide consumption of wheat is dominated by China. This is not surprising considering that it is the most populated country in the world. In the period 2005–2006 China consumed more than 15 percent of worldwide production.[12] Most of the wheat consumed in China is produced within

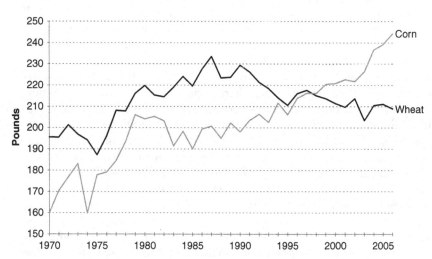

FIGURE 9.2   World Wheat and Corn Consumption per Capita
Sources: U.S. Census Bureau and United States Department of Agriculture

the country; China imports only a small amount of wheat. Other large consumers of wheat include the EU-25, FSU-12, India, Russia, and the United States. Together they constituted almost 70 percent of worldwide wheat consumption in the 2005–2006 marketing year,[13] Not surprisingly, all of these countries are also the ones with the highest levels of production. They do not rely on imports for their domestic consumption needs. Instead, with the exception of China, they are also some of the market's largest exporters.

Unlike the corn export market, which is dominated by one player—the United States—the wheat market has a number of exporters. The United States happens to be the largest wheat exporter, but it faces competition from the FSU-12, Canada, Russia, Argentina, and Australia. This competition is healthy for the market and allows importers several choices from which to buy their wheat. In addition, since wheat is planted and harvested at different times during the year, a production shortfall in one region may be made up easily by upcoming harvests in other regions. This diversity of exporting countries provides stability to wheat trade and prices. The result is lower price volatility for wheat than in the corn market, because the corn market relies on one country's production for the majority of the world export market.

Since wheat is primarily consumed in the form of flour, other cereal grains and starchy food substances can be considered substitutes. Besides wheat, flour can be made from many other crops such as corn, barley, rye, and rice. Wheat flour is considered superior because of its gluten content. Gluten is a protein in wheat and other cereal grains that gives kneaded dough its elasticity and allows it to be leavened. Other cereal grains such as barley and rye contain gluten, but in lower levels than wheat. Other flour alternatives such as corn flour, bean flour, and rice flour are important because of their use in specific cultures. Rice flour is very important in Southeast Asian cuisine. Corn flour is widely used in Mexico in tamales and tortillas. These region-specific cuisines would not be the same if wheat flour were used. This limits the extent to which different types of flours may be substituted for each other. Wheat and wheat milling byproducts may also be utilized in livestock feed. In this case, wheat would be substituted for corn in livestock feed.

STORAGE

In the United States, the wheat marketing year runs from June through May. So the 2006–2007 wheat marketing year is from June 2006 through May 2007. Countries have different marketing years depending on when they begin to harvest the new crop. In wheat, the international marketing year is from July through June. In the United States, winter wheat is harvested starting in June. Much of this harvest is put into storage to ensure supply throughout the marketing year. The normal market futures curve for wheat entices the farmer or storage operator to store grain for later by paying for some of the storage costs. This normal futures curve for wheat is also called contango, when the near future month is cheaper than the further out future. If the price of the near future is higher than the further out future, the curve is inverted, or backwardated. An inverted curve implies that the market wants the wheat now and is not willing to pay the cost to store it for later. Storage and the cost of carry, as they apply to the grain markets, are discussed in Chapter 20, "Some Building Blocks of a Commodity Futures Trading System" and Chapter 8, "Corn."

FUTURES

The benchmark wheat future is the Chicago Board of Trade (CBOT) wheat future. The CBOT wheat future has a contract size of 5,000 bushels and trades in cents per bushel. It has a tick size of $0.25, which means its minimum fluctuation can be a quarter of a cent. Each tick has a tick value of $12.50. This means that if you were long one contract of wheat at 460.00 cts/bu and you sold it at 460.25 cts/bu your profit before commission would be $12.50. The CBOT wheat contract trades future months July, September, December, March, and May of each marketing year.

For smaller investors the CBOT has an E-mini wheat futures contract. This contract is one-fifth of the size of the regular CBOT corn futures contract. Each E-mini soybean future has a contract size of 1,000 bushel, a tick size of 0.125 cents/bushel, and a tick value of $1.25. The E-mini wheat future can be physically delivered. The delivery specifications are the same as those of the full-size wheat future.

Given that there are many classes of wheat in the United States, which one is deliverable to the CBOT wheat future contract? The CBOT lists these varieties as deliverable (at par) to the CBOT wheat future: No. 2 grades of Soft Red Winter, Hard Red Winter, Dark Northern Spring, and Northern Spring. The problem is that these four wheat varieties are extremely different in their content, use, and price. In this case, delivery against a short wheat future position would be made with the cheapest wheat of these grades to deliver, which is the Soft Red Winter. For this reason the grain industry considers the CBOT wheat future contract a Soft Red Winter (SRW) wheat future contract. The rules regarding delivery of wheat futures are outlined in depth in the *CBOT Rules and Regulations Handbook.* Delivery locations for wheat include the Chicago area; Burns Harbor, Indiana area;

and the Toledo, Ohio area. Deliveries of wheat are made by exchange of warehouse depository receipts (WDRs). Each WDR represents stocks of wheat in warehouses that have been declared regular for delivery of wheat by the Exchange. The WDR will specify the warehouse in which the wheat is held for delivery.

In the United States there are two additional wheat future contracts that are fairly liquid. One trades on the Kansas City Board of Trade (KCBT), and the other trades on the Minneapolis Grain Exchange (MGE). The KCBT and MGE wheat futures have the same traded months, contract size, tick size, and tick value as the CBOT wheat future. The difference is the type of wheat deliverable and the location of delivery. The KCBT wheat future allows delivery of Hard Red Winter wheat (HRW wheat) within Kansas City, Missouri. The MGE wheat future allows delivery of Northern Spring Wheat (also called Hard Red Spring wheat) to grain elevators in the Minneapolis and Duluth, Minnesota regions. Figure 9.3 shows the prices of each wheat future in the United States. As you would expect, the prices are highly correlated. Since each future pertains to a specific wheat class, you can see that although the prices are very close at times, there are a few disconnects in price. The spreads between each future can widen if there are production surpluses or deficits in a particular wheat class. In addition, each wheat class

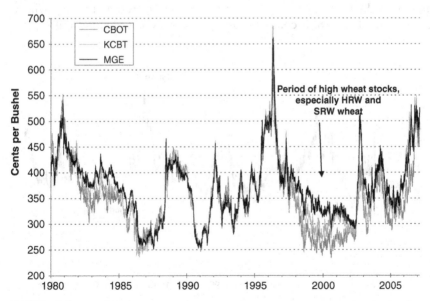

FIGURE 9.3 U.S. Wheat Futures by Exchange

has a specific value to the consumer. The MGE HRS wheat is usually the most expensive wheat of the three futures because of its high protein content and use in specialty breads. The cheapest future is usually the CBOT SRW future because it has the lowest protein content of the three futures. An example of widening between the wheat futures occurred between 1998 and 2001, when wheat stocks were very high. Then, most of the wheat in storage consisted of HRW and SRW wheat. This resulted in the spreads between CBOT SRW wheat futures, KCBT HRW wheat futures, and MGE HRS wheat futures widening, as shown in Figure 9.3.

Worldwide there are additional wheat future contracts, but none are as liquid as the three in the United States. The most liquid global wheat futures are listed on the Winnipeg Commodity Exchange in Canada, The Australian Stock Exchange, and the LIFFE exchange in Europe. Information regarding these future contracts can be found through the exchanges.

PRICE HISTORY AND MARKET REPORTS

As with corn, the price history for the CBOT wheat future is remarkably range bound. Figure 9.4 shows the wheat price in a range of 200–400 cents per bushel most of the time since 1975. Significant price spikes that resulted in wheat prices above the 500 cents per bushel level did occur in 1980, 1996, and 2006. In 1980, unfavorable weather conditions resulted in low wheat crop yields. In 1996, a combination of strong export demand during the

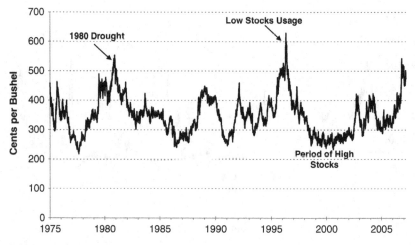

FIGURE 9.4   CBOT Wheat Futures Price

1995–1996 marketing year and concern over the winter wheat production resulted in low stocks for wheat. This marked the lowest stocks usage level for wheat in more than 20 years, reaching a low of near 10 percent during the year. Stocks usage is the expected ending stocks for a given marketing year divided by the total demand for the same marketing year. Not long after the low stocks usage situation in 1996 there occurred a long period of low prices and high stocks usage beginning with the 1997–1998 marketing year. This occurred because farmers reacted to the high prices in 1996 and planted extra wheat accordingly as their profit margins increased.

The monthly *World Agricultural Supply and Demand Estimates* (WASDE) published by the USDA is a great source of fundamental information on the wheat market. In this report, the USDA publishes production, demand, and stock estimates for wheat as a whole and separated by classes. In addition, supply and demand estimates for the world wheat market are made. This report is closely watched by the grain market community. For information regarding wheat exports, the Foreign Agricultural Service (FAS) division of the USDA publishes export sales for wheat and other agricultural products. Export sales are usually published on Thursday mornings at 8:30 AM EST prior to the CBOT market opening.

The future outlook for wheat prices is mixed. Demand should remain steady, yet the supply side could have many changes. The most likely change comes from increasing competition for acreage from other crops such as corn and soybeans. Farmers that have the ability to plant multiple crops on their land will choose the crop with the highest profit margin. This battle for acreage will result in more competition between products for land and the potential for higher price correlation among crops. Overall wheat prices should lag gains in other crops as demand growth will be slower. As with other crops, the weather will play an important part in determining yields and thus production for each year's harvest. Poor weather will lead to price spikes similar to those seen in the past.

ADDITIONAL SOURCES OF INFORMATION

The USDA is the best source for fundamental market information on wheat and other agricultural crops. The Economic Research Service (ERS) section of the USDA has a variety of research reports along with a wheat briefing room on its website (www.ers.usda.gov). This briefing room will give you an overview of the United States and world wheat markets in terms of supply and demand, trade, and policy. The National Agricultural Statistics Service (NASS) section of the USDA provides useful statistics with regard to both supply and demand.

CHAPTER 10

Soybeans

Soybeans date back nearly 5,000 years; they were first created in China where they were considered the most important cultivated legume. The Chinese called them *dadou*, literally meaning *great bean*. In Mandarin this is still the term used today. Soybeans are part of the oilseed family of legumes. This is unlike dry peas, lentils, kidney beans, and other food legumes, which are pulses. The Food and Agricultural Organization (FAO) of the United Nations uses the term *pulses* to describe legume crops that are harvested solely for the dry grain. Oilseeds are crops that are grown mainly for their vegetable oil and protein meal content. Other oilseeds crops include canola (rapeseed), cottonseed, sunflower, and peanuts. Within the oilseeds complex, soybeans are the most important in terms of world production and trade.

The climate, soil, and topography in the Midwest and in the southeastern parts of the United States are ideal for soybean production. This has allowed it to become the world's largest soybean producer and exporter. This is quite an achievement when you realize that soybeans are a relatively new crop in the United States compared with corn and wheat. It was during the 1920s that soybeans became a crop of major importance in the United States. Originally, soybeans were first planted in the United States as a high-protein forage crop for livestock and for its nitrogen-fixing qualities. Nitrogen-fixing crops put nitrogen back into the soil, which enriches it for other, nitrogen-depleting crops such as corn or winter wheat. Farmers utilize a crop rotation of soybeans and corn, planting one of the crops every other year. Another way farmers rotate crops is to plant half their acreage with corn and half with soybeans and switch the area in which each is planted the next year. Crop rotation increases soil productivity and reduces the need for farmers to purchase commercial nitrogen fertilizer. Before the 1920s most farmers in the United States used soybeans for this purpose. The soybean expansion started with the creation of the American Soybean Association (ASA), which began promoting soybean production in the early 1920s. In 1922, the first soybean processing plant opened in the United States, creating additional demand for soybeans to process into protein meal and vegetable oil.

Soybeans are a raw product that must be processed to create protein meal and vegetable oil. The protein meal, soymeal, is used as a protein source in animal feed. The vegetable oil is called soybean oil, soyoil, or bean oil and is used primarily for human consumption. Bean oil also has some industrial applications, and more recently it has been used as a fuel in the form of biodiesel. Soymeal and bean oil are created by processing the raw soybeans, a process called crushing. These products along with soybeans make up the soy complex.

PRODUCTION

Within the soy complex there are two separate production stages. The first stage is the production of soybeans. Worldwide, there are four large soybean producers: Argentina, Brazil, China, and the United States. These countries account for approximately 90 percent of world soybean production.[1] Figure 10.1 displays how production for each country has changed during

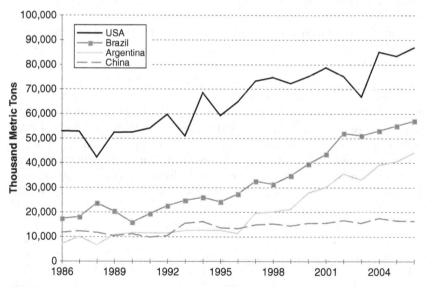

FIGURE 10.1 World Soybean Production
Source: United States Department of Agriculture

the past 20 years. It is impressive to see how Brazil and Argentina have ramped up production. Recently, in 2002, their combined production began to surpass the production of the United States. Since these four countries account for the majority of worldwide soybean production, they must also be responsible for the soybean export market. This is true with the exception of China, whose vast population still consumes more than China can produce. This leaves Argentina, Brazil, and the United States with the bulk of the export market.

In Brazil, soybeans are planted in November and December, and they are harvested in March through May. Argentina follows a similar planting and harvesting schedule for its main soybean crop. Some farmers in Argentina plant soybeans double cropped with winter wheat. These farmers plant in January after the winter wheat harvest, and they harvest the soybeans in May and June. This double crop represents a small amount of soybean production in Argentina. The crop marketing year for soybeans in Brazil extends from February through January. This means the 2006–2007 soybean marketing year for Brazil is from February 2006 through January 2007. In the U.S., the soybean marketing year is September through August with planting in May and June, and harvest in September through October. Since harvests in these large producing countries do not occur at the same time, this creates a more stable soybean supply year round. In the United States, the crop marketing years for soymeal and bean oil are from October through September. This lags the soybean marketing year by one month to allow for the time it takes to put the new soybean harvest through the crushing process.

As with other agricultural crops, the amount of soybean production relies on the acreage harvested and the yield. Yields can vary depending on the weather during the growing season. The critical period for soybeans occurs during the flowering or pod-set stage. In South America, this occurs during January through February; in the United States, this occurs in July through early August. During this pod-setting period drought-induced stress can result in low yields as the pods fall off. Fortunately for soybeans, the pod-setting period is longer than the similarly critical pollination period for corn. Usually, the pod-setting period lasts between three to four weeks. This means that if drought-induced stress occurs early in the pod-setting period, there is still potential for normal yields if favorable weather resumes in time, because the soybean bush will set pods then.

Early farmers recognized that soybeans were more drought resistant than corn, and this helped to entice them to plant more soybeans in the early 1900s in the United States. Other weather-induced stress that can lower yield is extreme heat at the end of the flowering period. In addition, in the United States it is thought that frost may seriously reduce yields, but this is false. Nighttime temperatures prior to harvest must be sustained below

28°F to seriously reduce yield.[2] Over time, higher yields have occurred as a result of technological advances in farming and the emergence of genetically modified (GMO) seed for soybeans. Soybeans are one of the first bioengineered crops to have commercial success. Most GMO soybeans are pest resistant and herbicide tolerant. In the United States, genetically modified soybeans account for the largest share of biotech acreage.[3]

The second stage of production occurs when the soybeans are processed into soymeal and bean oil. This occurs at a soybean processing plant and is called crushing. The soybeans are crushed, resulting in approximately 11 pounds of bean oil, 44 pounds of 48 percent protein soymeal, and 5 pounds of hull per each bushel crushed. The hulls can be combined with the soymeal to lower its protein content or put into pellets to be used for feed. Crushing occurs year round, as the soybeans are stored at harvest and processors buy supply as needed throughout the year. In the United States, nearly all soybeans are crushed. Worldwide, soybean crush has been growing since the 1990s, but its regional mix has undergone changes.[4] Both the U.S. and the European Union shares of worldwide soybean crush has declined since 1991–1992 while the soybean crush shares of Brazil, Argentina, and China have increased.[5] This pattern follows the emergence of Argentina and Brazil as large soybean-producing countries whose crushing capacity has increased with their soybean production. In addition, China's large population continues to require additional crushing to meet demand. Crushing facilities are often located near production regions and major transportation areas. This allows countries to import soybeans and process them as soon as they are received and then send the soymeal and bean oil to various other regions. Logistically, many countries find it is easier to import soybeans and do the crushing themselves instead of importing soymeal and bean oil. For example, in Europe the major transportation hub in Rotterdam, Netherlands has oilseed crushing facilities. Soybeans are imported to Rotterdam and then processed, and the meal and oil are shipped throughout Europe.

The soybean processing decision is determined by the gross soybean processing margin (GPM). The GPM is the gross return for each bushel of soybeans processed. Processors need to decide when and if to make binding commitments to purchase and process soybeans in the future. The GPM is also referred to as the crushing margin. The soybean processor can elect to keep the capacity idle or to utilize it on any given date. The GPM can be locked in prior to the processing date by using futures. The processor would buy soybean futures and sell the corresponding amount of soymeal and bean oil futures. The Chicago Board of Trade (CBOT) publishes a soybean synthetic crush spread index that is used to trade the corresponding

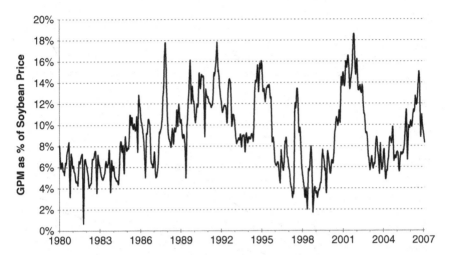

FIGURE 10.2 Soybean Gross Processing Margin: 20 Day Moving Average
Source: Chicago Board of Trade prices, calculation done by authors

options. This synthetic crush is derived off the futures of soybeans, soymeal, and bean oil; this is also referred to as the board crush. Figure 10.2 shows the futures market GPM as a percentage of the input cost, one bushel of soybeans. The chart shows that when the GPM gets to extremes it stays there for only a short time. This suggests the processors are able to react quickly to changes in the GPM. The processor will try to maximize the crush if the GPM is extremely high, and they will limit the crush when the GPM is very low.

CONSUMPTION

A small amount of whole soybeans are used for seed and human consumption. The majority of soybeans are crushed for the meal and oil. Demand for soybeans in the form of soymeal and bean oil has grown excessively during the past 25 years. Figure 10.3 displays the cumulative increase in consumption since 1980 for the major agricultural products. Worldwide demand for soybeans and thus soymeal and bean oil has grown at a rate of 8 percent a year since 1980.[6] This is three times greater than the demand growth in corn, and five times greater than the demand growth in wheat during the same time period.[7] Why is demand for the soy complex so strong? One reason is

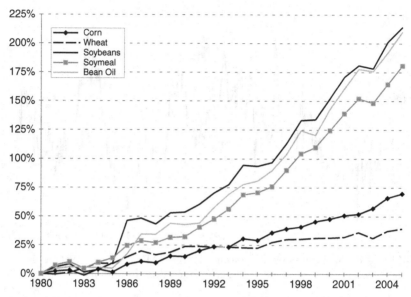

FIGURE 10.3 Cumulative World Demand Growth in Major Agricultural Products
Source: United States Department of Agriculture

that the increase in world wealth can cause a diet change that incorporates more meat. This results in more livestock being raised and a correspondingly higher demand for soymeal to feed them. In addition, given that soybeans are a new crop as compared with corn and wheat, there has been demand from new products that use soymeal and bean oil in the food and industrial sectors.

Of the two soy products, soymeal is considered the more valuable and is the most significant protein meal produced in the world. It has the highest percentage of protein meal produced from any of the major oilseeds. In 2005–2006, consumption of soymeal was approximately 70 percent of all protein meal consumed worldwide.[8] Its closest competitor in the protein meal market is rapeseed meal (also known as canola meal), which accounts for slightly more than 10 percent of worldwide protein meal consumption.[9] Another protein meal, fish meal, can also be a significant competitor as it has protein content comparable to soymeal. The largest consumers of soymeal are the European Union (EU-25), the United States, and China. Soymeal is an excellent source of protein and is used extensively in the feed industry for cattle, hogs, poultry, and aquaculture.

More recently, soymeal has had to compete with distillers dried grains (DDG) in the United States feed market. DDG is a byproduct of corn-based ethanol production and is used as the protein feed for beef and dairy cattle in the United States. DDG can also be fed to poultry and hogs, but digestion of DDG is an issue for these animals. Cattle do not seem to have the same digestion problem with DDG because of their ruminant digestive systems. On a protein equivalent basis, for every ton of DDG used in livestock rations about two-fifths of a ton of soymeal is displaced.[10] This shows that as a livestock feed soymeal is a more stable product than DDG and has higher energy, protein, and critical amino acids. Both the cost and feasibility of use will be the drivers to choose one product over the other.

Bean oil is mainly consumed by humans in a number of foods such as cooking oils, salad dressing, margarine, and various bakery products and food spreads. More than 90 percent of total use comes from human consumption.[11] Bean oil does have some industrial applications in products such as paints, putty, epoxy, and adhesives. Unlike soymeal, bean oil has more direct competition with a variety of vegetable oils such as palm oil, canola/rapeseed oil, and sunflower oil. Figure 10.4 displays world consumption of the four major vegetable oils. Palm oil world consumption surpassed bean oil world consumption in 2004. Palm oil is primarily produced in Southeast Asia, and production increases in the region have made palm oil very competitive with soybean oil on a global scale. The two products are

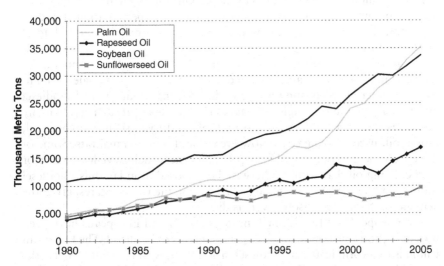

FIGURE 10.4 World Vegetable Oil Consumption
Source: United States Department of Agriculture

direct competitors in the marketplace in Asia and Europe. In North America, there is more competition between soybean oil and canola oil, because canola oil is produced in Canada making it easily accessible to the United States market. In fact the name *Canola* is derived from the terms *Canada oil* and *low acid*, as this oil was initially bred in Canada. Canola is just a variety of the oilseed rapeseed.

Vegetable oil demand has increased in the industrial sector in the form of biodiesel. Biodiesel is a diesel fuel made from vegetable oils such as soybean oil, palm oil, and rapeseed oil. In some cases, used vegetable oil (old cooking oil) can be used as feedstock for biodiesel. Even though diesel is part of its name, there are no petroleum-based products mixed into biodiesel—it is 100 percent vegetable oil. One of the important features of biodiesel is that it emits far less unburned hydrocarbons and carbon monoxide into the air than petroleum-based diesel. Blends of biodiesel with diesel such as B20 (20 percent biodiesel, 80 percent diesel) are more common than 100 percent biodiesel. In terms of efficiency, the miles per gallon (MPG) rating is very similar to petroleum-based diesel. In the United States, approximately 75 million gallons of biodiesel was produced in 2005.[12] This number is expected to triple to approximately 225 million gallons of production in 2006.[13] Due to ever-growing expansion of biodiesel capacity in the U.S, the National Biodiesel Board finds it difficult to estimate production into 2007. As of September 2007 the National Biodiesel Board lists 165 operating plants in the United States with a capacity to produce over 1.8 billion gallons a year. Given the current estimates for biodiesel production in 2006, and even if production is expected to increase at an exponential pace, the U.S. is utilizing only a small amount of total production capacity.[14]

Why is capacity so much greater than production? First, demand for biodiesel in the United States is limited, as diesel consumption pales as compared with gasoline consumption. In addition, the production of biodiesel may not be profitable enough for plants to be producing at capacity. In many cases these plants are able to process multiple feedstocks such as soybean oil, canola oil, used cooking oil, yellow grease, and other animal fats. Some of these feedstocks may be much cheaper than others such as yellow grease or used cooking oil that would otherwise be disposed of in landfills. Biodiesel should not have as large an impact as ethanol in the United States, given the demand preference of gasoline versus diesel.

In Europe diesel fuel is much more common and Europeans have been producing and consuming much larger quantities of biodiesel. The European Union is the world leader in biodiesel production, with the United States the second largest producer. Europe has approximately 185 biodiesel plants (as of September 2007) and produced 4.89 million metric tons (about 1.5 billion gallons) of biodiesel in 2006.[15] Biodiesel production in Europe is much closer to capacity, with 2006 plant utilization at 80 percent.[16] Europe biodiesel plants primarily use rapeseed oil that is grown in Europe as feedstock. The USDA estimates that 80 percent of European biodiesel is produced using rapeseed oil and that this consumes approximately half of Europe's rapeseed production.[17] As biodiesel production grows it will become necessary for European biodiesel plants to import more palm oil from Southeast Asia or bean oil from South America and the United States to use as feedstock.

FUTURES

Like the other major agricultural products corn and wheat, the benchmark future contracts for soybeans, soymeal, and bean oil all trade on the Chicago Board of Trade (CBOT). Each contract has different specifications with regard to contract size, tick size, value, and delivery specifications.

The CBOT Soybean future trades in cents per bushel with one future contract equal to 5,000 bushels of soybeans. The minimum price fluctuation of the contract, or its tick size, is .25 cents per bushel. This tick size has a value of $12.50, which means that for every .25 cents per bushel change in price the value of one soybean future goes up or down $12.50. Soybean futures are deliverable to six separate regions, including areas around Chicago and St. Louis. Soybean futures are delivered using soybean shipping certificates that have been registered with the CBOT. These shipping certificates specify shipment from warehouses or shipping stations within the six specified delivery regions.

For smaller investors the CBOT has an E-mini soybean futures contract. This contract is one-fifth of the size of the regular CBOT corn futures contract. Each E-mini soybean future has a contract size of 1,000 bushel, a tick size of 0.125 cents/bushel, and a tick value of $1.25. The E-mini soybean future can be physically delivered. The delivery specifications are the same as those on the full-size soybean future, but they use mini-sized soybean certificates.

The CBOT soybean meal future trades in dollars per ton, with one future contract equal to 100 short tons (1 short ton = 2,000 pounds). The minimum price fluctuation, or its tick size, is $0.10 with a tick value of $10.00. The CBOT soybean oil future trades in cents per pound with one future contract equal to 60,000 pounds. The tick size of the soybean future is $0.01, with a tick value of $6.00. Like soybean futures, deliveries of soybean oil and soybean meal futures are made with warehouse receipts or shipping certificates. Soybean oil deliveries are made using warehouse receipts issued by designated CBOT warehouses to areas within the Illinois territory. Soybean meal deliveries are made using shipping certificates by designated CBOT shippers within the Central Territory (shipping plants in Illinois and Kentucky). Neither the soybean oil future nor the soybean meal future has a mini-sized contract.

Different soybean, soymeal and bean oil futures contracts are traded on global exchanges, but none are as liquid as those on the CBOT. Other exchanges with futures on soy complex products include the Dalian Commodity Exchange in China, the Kansai Commodity and Tokyo Grain Exchanges in Japan, and the Brazilian Mercantile and Futures Exchange.

PRICE HISTORY AND MARKET REPORTS

The soy complex has a more volatile price history than corn or wheat. In soybean futures the price spiked to over 800 cents per bushel eight times during the past 25 years. These dramatic price movements are very different from the more range-bound price movements in corn and wheat. This resulted in price spikes for soymeal and bean oil during the same time frames, because the three products are highly correlated. If there is a shortage of soybeans, there will be a resulting shortage of meal and oil, since there will be a smaller amount of soybeans available to crush. Figures 10.5, 10.6, and 10.7 show the price history for soybean, soymeal, and bean oil futures. You can

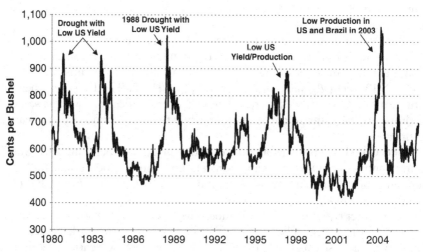

FIGURE 10.5   CBOT Soybean Futures Price

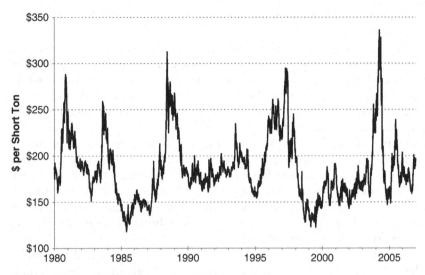

FIGURE 10.6   CBOT Soybean Meal Futures Price

see that they all exhibit a similar pattern. Of the two products, bean oil has the lower correlation with soybeans, which is shown by the lack of price volatility as compared with soybeans in the 1990s. This is consistent with the fact that soymeal is the main product from soybeans in both volume and demand. In addition, bean oil has a large amount of substitutable

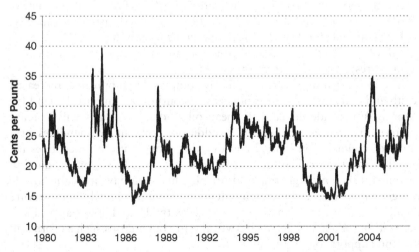

FIGURE 10.7   CBOT Soybean Oil Futures Price

commodities, unlike soymeal, so its price may respond to be competitive with those oils.

What caused all these price spikes in soybeans, soymeal, and bean oil during the past 25 years? The major culprit is a low stocks usage level in soybeans during those times. The majority of the price spikes occur when the stocks usage level for soybeans is less than 10 percent. Stocks usage is the ending stocks for the marketing year divided by the usage for the same marketing year. In the case of the price increase to 1,000 cents per bushel in 1988 and 2004, the stocks usage at those times was at or below 5 percent.[18] The low stocks usage is often a result of different factors. In some years a drought can lead to low yield and low production levels, reducing ending stocks. In other years a surge in feed demand can lower stocks of soybeans through high demand for soymeal. The stocks usage figure is a key fundamental factor not just in the soy complex but also in the other major grain markets of corn and wheat.

The *World Agricultural Supply and Demand Estimates* (WASDE) published by the USDA is a good source of fundamental data for both supply and demand of the soy complex. This monthly report has detailed data regarding the United States soybean, soymeal, and bean oil markets. It also contains important information regarding soybean production and trade from Brazil and Argentina, the two major competitors to the United States in the soybean market. The pace of U.S. exports for the soy complex is reported during each marketing year in the weekly Export Sales report from the Foreign Agricultural Service (FAS) division of the USDA. A good fundamental report that focuses on the quantity of soybeans crushed in the United States is the monthly report from the National Oilseed Processor Association (NOPA). This report is released midmonth and shows statistics for capacity, crushings, and bean oil stocks for the previous month. It also publishes the amount of meal and oil produced from that month's crush along with each product's respective yield from one soybean.

The long-term prospects for the soy complex are supportive. Increased wealth and demand for meat products will continue to support demand for soymeal. Worldwide demand for bean oil to create biofuels will increase as interest rises in greener fuels. In addition, government mandates in a variety of countries on biofuel consumption along with tax incentives for biofuel production will continue to support this specific sector. Production in countries such as Argentina and Brazil, which still have available arable acreage, will increase. This increase in acreage will be needed to meet future demand increases. In other countries such as the United States and China, competition for acreage between soybeans and other crops such as corn will also lend support to the soy complex.

ADDITIONAL SOURCES OF INFORMATION

The USDA is the best source for fundamental market information on soybeans, soymeal, and bean oil. The Economic Research Service (ERS) section of the USDA has a variety of research reports along with a briefing room on soybeans and oilseeds on its website (www.ers.usda.gov). This briefing room gives an overview of the U.S. and world oilseeds markets in terms of supply, demand, trade, and policy. The National Agricultural Statistics Service (NASS) section of the USDA provides useful statistics with regard to both supply and demand for the soy complex in the United States.

The USDA does publish some data regarding the South American soybean markets, and organizations within Brazil and Argentina are beginning to report more consistent data regarding their soybean production, demand, and trade. Brazil's Association of Vegetable Oil Industries (ABIOVE) reports soybean complex fundamental data monthly for each marketing year.

Understanding Livestock

CHAPTER 11

Hogs

Hogs, along with goats and sheep, are the oldest known domesticated animal food source, with evidence of domestication dating back 10,000 years. Since the time of domestication, hog-raising has taken many forms, from forest pasturing and mast feeding in Europe to garbage scavenging in Asia and industrial farming in the modern era. The greatest changes (other than the original domestication, of course!) have certainly been made in the past 50 years. Today's hog farming is high-tech big business. Long gone are most of the small family farms. In their place are massive buildings containing thousands of hogs under a common roof. The rigorous application of scientific and management principles has driven a spectacular leap forward in pork production productivity.

RAISING HOGS

For most of us, our interest in hogs peaks at the kitchen table when we are contemplating the bacon, pork chops, or underappreciated scrapple on our plates. The following two sections lay out how your friendly neighborhood hog transforms into our favorite foods, how this has changed over time, and what this has meant for prices. This transformation is demonstrated in Figure 11.1.

Gestation for sows lasts approximately 16 weeks and yields on average 9 piglets. After farrowing, the piglets nurse for two to three weeks, and they are then weaned. Sows are ready to be inseminated again within a week of weaning, and the reproductive cycle for them is restarted. Meanwhile, weaned piglets are fed a diet consisting predominantly of carbohydrates (commonly corn) and protein (commonly soybean meal). By 26 weeks of age, the piglet has grown into a 260 pound hog and is ready for slaughter. Roughly 25 percent of hog weight is lost during the slaughter process, leaving

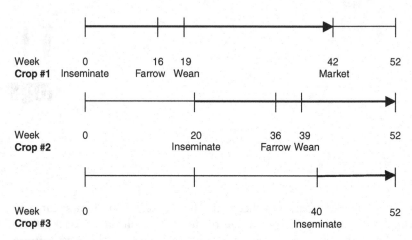

FIGURE 11.1 Hog Production

a carcass weight of about 200 pounds. In addition, 10 percent of the pig crop is commonly lost to death and disease before slaughter.[1,2]

That was a lot of information. What have we learned? Putting these numbers together, each batch of hogs requires about 42 weeks to progress from previous crop weaning to current crop slaughter, and each sow spends about 20 weeks between successive farrowings. Thus, an efficient operation could see a sow produce three litters per year. If we begin in the first week of the year, by the end of the year the first litter would have reached the supermarket, the second litter would be nearly 16 weeks old, and the third litter would be 4 weeks shy of birth. If we linearly interpolate the pounds of pork produced on a 42-week cycle basis, each sow generates 3,300 pound of pork per year.[a] Since the average American consumes 200 pounds of meat per year, each sow produces enough meat to satisfy a whopping 16 people.[b,3]

---

[a] The first crop has been sold, yielding 1620 (42/42*9*0.9*200) pounds. The second crop has passed through 32 of the 42 weeks of the cycle, yielding 1230 (32/42*9*0.9*200) pounds. The third crop has passed through 12 of the 42 weeks of the cycle, yielding 460 (12/42*9*0.9*200) pounds of pork. Admittedly, weight gain in hogs is biased towards the end of the life cycle, but if sows are bred uniformly throughout the year, this does not matter on average.

[b] This simple back-of-the-envelope calculation comes quite close to the actual average productivity of 3,000 pounds per year. The differences likely arise from some combination of modeling an efficient rather than an average hog operation, ignoring the time required to get hogs from the farm to the plate, and ignoring the fact that sows do not last forever and need to be replaced. Even the lower actual number of 15 people fed per sow is a remarkable figure.

We next turn to an interesting conundrum: During the past 30 years annual per capita pork consumption has increased by 20 percent while the U.S. population has increased by more than 35 percent, and yet the domestic sow herd has fallen by 20 percent. Figure 11.2 illustrates the extreme differences between consumption and the breeding herd (capital stock) evident in the history. How can this be?

Well, one possibility would be that the United States has become an importer of pork. This is not the case. In fact, it is precisely backwards, as the United States has gone from a position of rough external balance in pork to becoming an exporter of 10 percent of domestic production.[4] Another possibility would be that the United States has become an importer of hogs which are then slaughtered and consumed domestically. This is indeed the case. The United States imports nearly 10 percent of all domestically slaughtered hogs from Canada.[5] Yet hog imports can not be the primary answer either: 10 percent is much too small a number to resolve the apparent supply–demand imbalance. Instead, the answer is that sow productivity, measured in pounds of pork per sow per year, has increased by more than 70 percent over this period.[6] While this is interesting to know in and of itself, it also helps to explain why the unadjusted size of the sow herd does not help forecast hog prices (our main interest after all).

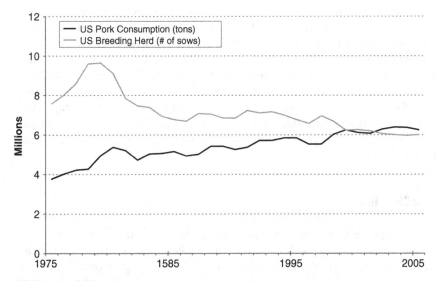

FIGURE 11.2 Pork Consumption and Capital Stock
Sources: Economic Report of the President, 2007; National Agricultural Statistics Service, USDA; Economic Research Service, USDA

This productivity growth has come from a handful of key drivers: increases in pigs per litter, litters per year and rates of weight gain for feeder pigs, and decreases in farrow-to-slaughter mortality rates for feeder pigs. These drivers in turn have been improved via innovations in areas such as hog genetics, hog healthcare, feed efficiency, climate control, and barn management.

Facilitating this process has been the rise of specialized operations and the increase in average hog farm size. Fifty years ago, the hog industry consisted of a large number of small, independent hog producers. Today's massive, efficient, specialized hog farms have supplanted the traditional, full-cycle, lovable, but inefficient family farm. Modern large operations frequently specialize in stages of the pig's life (farrow to feeder, farrow to wean, or feeder to slaughter) rather than covering the full life cycle historically favored by small farms.

Alongside the move to larger-scale farms has been the migration of much of the industry out of its traditional home, the Corn Belt. As the primary growers of corn and soybeans, states such as Iowa, Illinois, Indiana, Minnesota, and Nebraska had a ready source of food for home grown hogs. Consequently, these states played principal host to the nation's hog farmers from the mid-nineteenth century though the 1980s. Since that time, however, large hog farmers have discovered that the Corn Belt's feed cost advantage could be overcome by other efficiencies arising from scale economies, differences in local environmental regulations, and proximity to the end consumer. Smithfield, in particular, led the charge into North Carolina, which has gone from off the map to the number two hog state behind Iowa. This movement of the herd is particularly surprising, because many of the hog farmers outside the Corn Belt still ship their hogs back to the large packing houses in the Corn Belt for slaughter. Thus, it would appear that they suffer a feed cost disadvantage as well as a final transport cost disadvantage. Yet the trend continues, as Oklahoma, Utah, and other Western states see their share of the herd grow while shares in the Corn Belt continue to fall or at best stabilize.

PROCESSING HOGS

Any discussion of the pork industry would be remiss without a discussion of the gorillas of the pork industry, the packers. These firms process the hogs from the nation's farms and convert them into portions fit for our tables, earning profits by buying hogs from farmers and selling the processed ensemble, known as the pork cutout, to wholesalers and retailers. The packer industry has undergone substantial consolidation over the last 20 years with more than 50 plants closing and the top 3 packers increasing their share of total slaughter capacity from 35 percent to 55 percent. This consolidation has seen the scale of individual packing plants grow dramatically and has seen substantial improvements in productivity, such that processing is now seen as a distinctive source of comparative advantage for the U.S. pork industry.[7]

At the same time, in order to secure consistent supplies for their plants, packers have changed the way they source market hogs by integrating backward into hog production and developing long-term contracting relationships with independent producers. In fact, less than 20 percent of hogs today are sold in cash markets, compared with 87 percent 15 years ago.[8,9] The move from cash markets to long-term contracts has led to the practice of merit pricing, a pricing scheme by which farmers receive price incentives to produce the leaner, darker pork preferred by the average end consumer. This in turn has hastened genetic and other technological improvements to take advantage of contract terms.

FUTURES PRICE, THE HOG CYCLE, AND MARKET-MOVING EVENTS

In December 1998, cash live hog prices hit $10 per hundred pounds. Just six months earlier they had been over $40 per hundred pounds, and within eight months they were back near $40 per hundred pounds. Is this market manipulation? What is going on?

Hog markets have a long history of cyclical prices, commonly known as the hog cycle, and distinguished from Harleys by the lower case 'h.' These cycles are evident in the price series depicted in Figure 11.3, with successive peaks following each other every four to six years. The source of these manmade cycles is the 10-month delay between the decision to invest by breeding a sow rather than sending it to the slaughterhouse and the return on the investment in the form of a marketable pig crop. Suppose hog prices are high when the decision is made. Then, an individually optimizing farmer will keep his sow in expectation of reaping a windfall when her piglets are sent to the packers. Having 9 hogs in 10 months is certainly better than having a single hog today. But, if all farmers do this, then in 10 months, when the piglets-cum-hogs are ready for slaughter, the price will collapse devastatingly. This is what happened in 1998. Of course, once the price has collapsed, the farmers would no longer want hogs, because the cost of feed is too high to generate profits on new piglets. Therefore, they cull the sows and sell their excess corn on the market. In another 10 months, the lack of piglets sends prices sky high and the process repeats. Of course, hog farmers are more sophisticated than this. But the basic principle still applies, even if the timing of actual cycles is complicated by similar, partially correlated price cycles in broilers (chicken) and cattle and by the opening and closing of export markets.

The dramatic increase in the size of hog farms and packers as well as the rise of long-term contract pricing have, in part, been institutional responses to attempt to mitigate these cycles through implicit coordination of decision making. As of 2006, many argue that the industry participants have been largely successful and the amplitude of market price swings has diminished. But don't hold your breath—a cyclical low occurred as recently as 2002.

If you stare closely at Figure 11.3, you will also notice a high degree of seasonality in hog prices. In fact, lean hogs are one of the most seasonal of all futures contracts. This is at least partially due to natural seasonal variation in reproductive fitness and weight gain. Farrowings are lowest during the heart of winter and highest in mid to late spring, yielding low supplies of marketable hogs in early summer and high supplies just before the holiday season. Natural patterns of weight gain reinforce the reproductive cycle as hogs grow fastest in the spring and fall.[10] Enclosed, temperature-controlled barns have mitigated but not eliminated nature's own hog production cycle.

As for future trends, if ethanol from corn or biodiesel from soybeans develop into significant sources of energy for fueling cars, the price of these

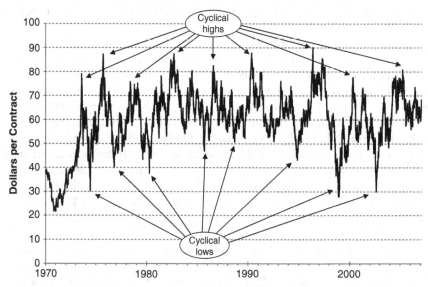

FIGURE 11.3 Lean Hog Futures Price—Lean Equivalent

two commodities may be expected to rise. Since feed composed of corn and beans constitutes the largest component of hog costs, the price of hogs ought to rise as well. This applies to broilers and cattle as well, however. Relative shifts in feed costs across meats ought, therefore, to be small, although the proportional impact would probably be smallest on cattle, which feed on grass when young and can better digest DDGS (dried distillers grains), the fibrous plant residue from ethanol production. Demand for meat tends to be relatively inelastic, so an increase in the price of hogs driven by feed cost would have a moderate downward impact on overall meat consumption and production.[c]

Another upward price risk would be stricter enforcement of environmental regulations. While the pork industry has made impressive productivity improvements, there have been local environmental consequences, including odor and ground and water pollution. These concerns even led the state of North Carolina to impose a moratorium on hog farm expansion. If this sentiment were to expand, it would likely send more hog production to less dense parts of the country. This already appears to be happening. Because the United States still has ample low-density land, the impact on price of local environmental regulations would likely be small. Finally, as unlikely as it seems currently, an outbreak of mad cow disease would also generate an increase in pork prices as consumers switch from beef to pork.

Combating these drivers of price increase are the aforementioned productivity improvements and the potential for international competition from low-priced producers such as Brazil and Argentina.

Many of the most important public sources of information come from the U.S. Department of Agriculture (USDA). These include daily slaughter reports, quarterly hogs and pigs reports, and weekly import reports, among other things. To get up to speed on the hog industry, the USDA's website is a good source of information, as is the *Daily Livestock Report* put out by Steve Meyer and Len Steiner for the Chicago Mercantile Exchange (CME). For high-quality data and market insight, Informa based in Louisville, Kentucky, is an excellent source for paying customers.

CONTRACT DETAILS

The move from a predominantly spot market to a long-term merit-based contract market and the backward integration of packers into hog production might have raised some issues for the lean hogs futures contract. If the

---

[c] An elasticity of -0.75 is commonly employed for meat demand. See, for example, various issues of the *Daily Livestock Report* by Steve Meyer and Len Steiner.

hog futures contract were to settle to the average price of hogs in the spot market and the number of hogs transacted in the spot market were to fall, the representativeness of the cash price could be questioned. This is important because a nonrepresentative price becomes less valuable for hedging and could potentially lead to the demise of the contract. In addition, with such a small number of hogs determining cash settlement, the temptation of firms to strategically influence market prices rises. This is made all the more worrisome by the backward integration of packers. Suppose the extreme case: that one firm controls all hog farming and packing. Then the lean hog price would not have any real meaning. It would be a transfer price internal to that integrated firm. All that would matter for the integrated firm's profits would be the value of the cutout and the cost of the feed and grain to raise the hogs. The solitary firm could set the lean hog price anywhere it liked to maximize trading profits. Of course, there would not be any need for hedging the price of lean hogs in this case, but this polar example illustrates the potential for opportunistic behavior on the behalf of large market participants.

The CME has thoughtfully incorporated three provisions into the lean hogs futures contract to mitigate these risks. First, the contract settles to cash rather than uniquely to delivery of actual hogs, encouraging the participation of a broader trading audience. Second, the average price from two days rather than just one day is used in calculating the final settlement price. Third, the scope of hogs eligible for inclusion in the index includes hogs priced in the spot markets and those priced according to market formulas (pricing schedules). Together, these yield a high percentage of all hogs transacted. Eligible hogs are barrows and gilts (young males and females) delivered to packers and reported to the USDA. See the CME Rulebook for more details.

The lean (i.e., dead) hogs contract trades on the Chicago Mercantile Exchange from 9:10 AM to 1:00 PM CST. Each contract is for 40,000 pounds, with a tick size of 0.025. One point =$0.01 per hundred pounds and is worth $4. Daily price limits are $0.03 per pound above or below the previous day's settlement. Primary monthly contracts are G, J, M, N, Q, V, and Z with limited liquidity for other contracts. The contract trades on Globex as well as on the floor, but current electronic volumes are not very attractive.

Anyone looking at historical data should be aware that prior to 1997 the current lean hog contract was a live hog contract. As lean hogs weighed 74 percent of live hogs at that time, market prices for older contracts should be adjusted upward by about 35 percent (1/0.74) for earlier periods to ensure consistency throughout the sample.

CHAPTER 12

Cattle

Perhaps the cow ought to be considered man's best friend. Cattle provide meat and dairy for food, leather for clothing, raw muscle power for transportation and farm work, and, in many poorer countries, serve as a store of wealth. And, unlike the dog, you can send cattle outside to feed themselves. This is because cattle are ruminants, a term that refers not to their capacity for deep thought but rather to their distinctive ability to digest plant fibers. Remarkably, the cow can convert the plant fibers cellulose, hemicellulose, and lignin into usable energy, a feat that modern ethanol producers are also working hard to achieve. (See Chapter 8, "Corn," for further information on ethanol.) In the cow, this process is achieved by microorganisms that live in the rumen, the largest of the cow's four stomachs. When cows ruminate, they regurgitate and chew partially digested food so that the microbes in their rumen are better able to process it. Somewhat coarsely, cows could be described as small biofuel plants that produce beef rather than ethanol.

RAISING CATTLE

Raising cattle is a more complicated process than raising hogs. First, the time from gestation to slaughter in cattle runs 30 months, whereas the life cycle for slaughter hogs runs 10 months. Thus, cattle production requires more long-term planning and, consequently, one might expect longer cattle cycles and more financial hedging on the part of farmers. Second, the life cycle of fed cattle typically comprises four stages: 9 months in utero, 7 to 9 months nursing, 7 to 10 months in backgrounding or on pasture, and 5 to 6 months in a feedlot.[a]

---

[a] Simple average of typical cattle timelines for spring-born and fall-born animals. Some animals may enter a feedlot earlier, progressing to fed status more quickly at the cost of more grain.

A typical calf will be weaned at 500 pounds and sent to a backgrounding lot or out to pasture. Backgrounded calves are commonly confined and receive a combination of forages and supplements. Pastured calves graze freely and may receive limited supplements. At 600 to 800 pounds, the calf becomes feeder cattle and is ready to be placed in a feedlot. Placements refers to the number of feeder cattle placed in feedlots. Feeder cattle are fed a combination of grains, protein, and forages in confinement. At 1,100 to 1,350 pounds, the animals become fed cattle and are marketed to a packer. Marketings refers to the number of live cattle sold to packers.[1]

Depending upon economics, the backgrounding/pasturing and feedlot stages may be expanded or compressed. For example, if pastures and range-land are poor as a result of drought, as in the spring of 2006, young cattle may be brought to the feedlots early. Alternatively, if grain prices are particularly high, as in the fall of 2006, ranchers may keep cattle longer, holding them to higher weights on their farms before sending them off to feedlots. Feedlots would also likely market lighter-weight cattle to the packers.

Per pound, feeder cattle trade at a premium to fed cattle. This differential arises because the dollar cost per pound of gain is typically higher for raising feeder cattle than for converting feeder cattle to fed cattle. To understand why this is, notice that it takes 24 months to get the calf to 700 pounds and then only 6 months to gain the final 400 to 500 pounds. During the first year and a half from conception, the mother must be fed as well.

Feeder steer typically consume about 25 pounds of grain per day. With a conversion rate of 8.3 pounds of grain per pound of gain in the Great Plains, the typical animal puts on roughly 3.2 pounds of weight per day.[2] Weather can affect this equation, however. With cold temperatures, gain may be sacrificed by the animal to keep itself warm, and with hot temperatures, appetite may be suppressed. The carbohydrates come from corn, distillers' grains, barley or sorghum.[b] Soybean or some other oilseed meal provides the required protein, and roughage comes from forages such as alfalfa or timothy hay. Since feed is the primary driver of feedlot costs, the price of feeder cattle should equal, on average, the price of fed cattle net of grain costs after allowing reasonable profits for feedlot operators.

U.S. cattle are awarded one of eight grade designations based on age, the degree of fatness, and the firmness of muscling. The top grades, the grades most commonly encountered in the supermarket are, from highest to lowest, Prime, Choice, and Select. Most young U.S. and Canadian cattle are

[b] Distillers' grains are the main byproduct of ethanol production from corn and may be substituted for corn pound for pound on a dry matter basis. *USDA Agricultural Projections to 2016*, Office of the Chief Economist, February 2007, p. 52.

Choice or Select, with the lower, processing quality beef coming from older animals or animals imported from abroad. Quoted cash prices are based on the proportion of these grades, a common variant being 35 to 65 percent Choice. Quotes may be for either steers or heifers and for live or dressed animals. Ironically, dressed means hide removed (rather than clothed). To convert dressed to live, multiply dressed prices by 0.63.

The Livestock Mandatory Reporting Act of 1999 dictated that large packers must report price, volume, and grade purchasing and processing information to the USDA on a daily basis. In practice, solid daily national cash data have been available since April 2001. Prior to mandatory reporting, so called five-area prices must be used. These five-area prices refer to prices in eight states: Texas/Oklahoma/New Mexico, Kansas, Nebraska, Colorado, and Iowa/Minnesota.

For farmers and feedlots the Choice to Select price spread has a strong bearing on feeding decisions. The larger the spread, the more attractive it is to feed cattle longer to achieve a higher grade. For traders the ratio of Choice to Select slaughter can be informative, inasmuch as a higher ratio of Choice to Select suggests less current (older) supplies of fed cattle and more pressure for slaughter.

As with hogs, fewer and fewer cattle are being sold in cash markets. In 1996, more than 80 percent of fed cattle were sold through cash markets; as of 2006, this had fallen to less than 60 percent. The decline in cash markets has been mostly offset by the growth of grid-pricing schemes. Grid-pricing schemes specify premiums and discounts for different qualities and yields and have encouraged producers to raise animals that conform more tightly to consumer tastes and processor needs.[3,4]

Simultaneously, marketing agreements and alliances between producers and packers have grown substantially. These longer-term arrangements guarantee steady, consistent quality throughput for packers while lowering price risk and providing access to quality premiums for producers. Some in the industry are concerned that these new pricing arrangements are reflective of increasing monopsony power amongst the packers. The four major cattle packers—Tyson (IBP), Cargill (Excel), Swift, and National Beef—slaughter 70 percent of all cattle in the United States.[5] In 1980, the top four accounted for only 28 percent.[6]

It is not clear that increased concentration is bad. The packers have made substantial productivity improvements on the processing side by increasing economies of scale and adopting new technologies to improve throughput, quality, and safety. They have also increased their value-added in the beef production chain by internalizing tasks further downstream, moving from boxed beef to case-ready, convenience, and precooked beef. All of this could well be beneficial for the consumer.[7]

Some of the critical evidence for increased packer power comes from the evolution of price spreads. The spread between the retail price faced by consumers and the farm price received by producers can be decomposed into two parts: the farm-to-wholesale spread and the wholesale-to-retail spread. If packers wield increasing market power, the farm-to-wholesale spread would likely increase, and the wholesale-to-retail spread would likely fall. A few researchers have indeed documented an increase in the appropriately deflated farm to wholesale price spread since 1998. This is certainly consistent with increased packer market power. On the other hand, there is little if any movement in the wholesale-to-retail margin. This may be because retail grocers have also become more concentrated during this period.[c,8,9]

PRODUCTION, CONSUMPTION, AND TRADE

The United States is the major producer of beef, accounting for nearly one-quarter of world production during the past 10 years (see Figure 12.1). Other major producers include Argentina and Brazil (together about as large as the United States), Europe, and China. Unlike the case with hogs, the location of beef cattle production in the United States has remained relatively constant over time. The five states with the most beef cows have not changed from 1975 to 2005; they are Texas, Missouri, Oklahoma, Nebraska, and South Dakota. If anything, beef cows have become more concentrated geographically as the share of these states has risen from 37 percent to 40 percent during this period. A few states have seen significant declines, notably Iowa and Florida. Large feedlots are concentrated in Texas, Kansas, and Nebraska, which together account for 70 percent of all marketings and placements in feedlots with more than 1,000 head of cattle.[10]

Physical live cattle trade is mostly very local, with U.S. live exports and imports going to and from Canada and Mexico. Historically, imports from Canada consist of feeder cattle destined for feedlots and live cattle destined for packing plants. Mexico exports primarily lighter cattle for finishing in U.S. feedlots or stocking/pasturing operations. Ultimately the major players drawing cattle into the United States are the large, efficient packing facilities that need a continual supply of live animals.[11]

As cattle are far more expensive to transport than beef, most of the movement of meat occurs after processing. The major exporters of beef are

---

[c] As Hahn (2004) notes, these movements in spreads are not a reflection of changes in packer value-added because the spreads are measured using standard cuts and standard animals over time. The use of standard measures controls for changes in packer value-added.

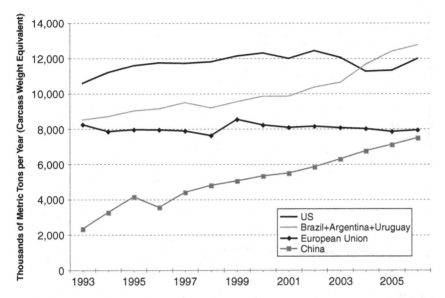

FIGURE 12.1 Major Producers of Beef and Veal
Source: Livestock and Poultry: World Market and Trade Circular (Foreign
Agricultural Service, USDA)
Note: EU-15 through 1999; EU-25 afterwards

the Brazil–Argentina–Uruguay axis, the Australia–New Zealand axis, the
United States and Canada, and India (see Figure 12.2). Of this group,
the United States and Canada typically export the highest quality beef. The
most salient feature of the graph is certainly the divergence in North and
South American beef exports fortunes over the last five years and, in particular, the massive plunge in North American beef exports from 2002 to
2004. Clearly something major happened. We will return to this development shortly.

Perhaps surprisingly given its dominant production position and its
massive exports, the United States on its own has been a net importer of
beef for more than 25 years. In fact, the United States is the world's largest
importer of beef (see Figure 12.3). This is partly because many of these
imports are re-exported, as the United States imports low-quality beef for
processing and then sends it back out again. Russia, the European Union,
and East Asia are the other major importers worldwide. China imports
virtually no beef, probably a political rather than an economic outcome.

U.S. per capita consumption patterns have changed quite dramatically
as depicted in Figure 12.4. In the late 1970s, Americans ate more beef than
pork and chicken combined, about 85 lbs per capita. Today, the average

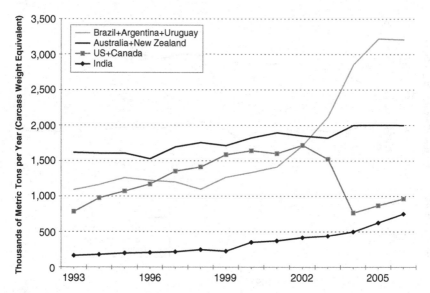

FIGURE 12.2   Major Exporters of Beef and Veal
Source: Livestock and Poultry: World Market and Trade Circular (Foreign
Agricultural Service, USDA) Comment: EU-15 through 1999; EU-25 afterwards

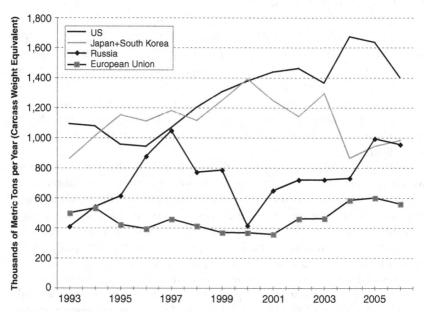

FIGURE 12.3   Major Importers of Beef and Veal
Source: Livestock and Poultry: World Market and Trade Circular (Foreign
Agricultural Service, USDA) Comment: EU-15 through 1999; EU-25 afterwards

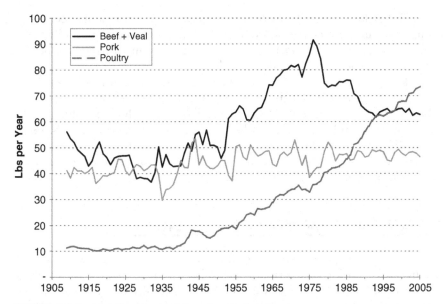

FIGURE 12.4 U.S. Per Capita Meat Consumption
Source: Economic Research Service, USDA

U.S. citizen consumes only 60 pounds of beef per year. The decline in beef consumption is more than made up for by the increase in poultry consumption from 35 to 70 pounds per capita per year.

Bovine Spongiform Encephalopathy (BSE), or mad cow disease, is a chronic, degenerative nervous system disorder. First encountered in Great Britain in the mid-1980s, it is thought to have arisen from the practice of feeding cattle ground animal remains, specifically of sheep. The disease appears to be transmitted both maternally and by consumption of abnormal proteins contained primarily in the neural system, including the brain and spinal cord. The incubation period for BSE ranges from two to eight years.

On its own, BSE is a nasty, debilitating disease for animals, but scientists tied it to CJD (Creutzfeld-Jacob disease) in humans in 1996. The United States and Canada banned mammalian protein from ruminant feed in 1997 as a precautionary measure. But BSE emerged in North America via a Canadian cow in May of 2003. Since then there have been roughly 10 instances of BSE in Canada and the United States, some of which have arisen in animals born after the feed ban. This has led to bans on importation of U.S. and Canadian beef in many countries, most importantly in East Asia. Subsequently, some markets have reopened, allowing certain low-risk parts from animals less than 30 months old to be exported.[12]

BSE has had no readily discernible impact on U.S. per capita beef consumption figures. Referring back to Figure 12.4, the decline in per capita beef consumption occurred prior to 1995. The U.S. consumer certainly appears to have a high degree of confidence in domestic beef.

Clearly foreigners have not felt the same way. As seen in Figure 12.2, U.S. and Canadian beef exports from 2002 to 2004 fell by 55 percent. The subsequent recovery of U.S. and Canadian exports has been sluggish at best. Australia and New Zealand beef has replaced much of the U.S. beef that had been exported to Asia, while U.S. beef has been absorbed at home. Meanwhile, South American beef has gone on a tear, supplanting traditional sources of beef and developing new markets.

FUTURES PRICES AND MARKET MOVING EVENTS

The most volatile period for cattle futures has been the past five years (see Figure 12.5). During that period, BSE has been a major market mover. The discovery of BSE in Canada in May 2003 sent prices skyrocketing as already tight supplies were compounded by a U.S. ban on Canadian imports. Then, in December 2003, the discovery of BSE in the United States sent prices plunging as consumer confidence in beef slipped and U.S. exports were banned abroad. Note that BSE has not had any obvious long-term negative impact on cattle prices. Future prices have actually risen since 2003. Of course, the impact of BSE may have been obscured by other forces.

The long-term prospects for cattle are predominantly positive. Increased wealth and demand for meat products worldwide will continue to support

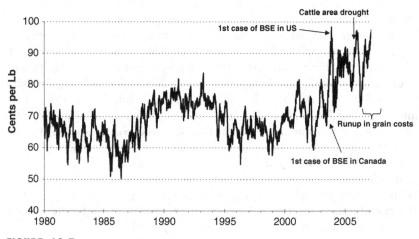

FIGURE 12.5 Cattle Futures Price

demand for beef. Furthermore, a rise in grain prices, as biofuels and ethanol play a more significant role in energy supply, will drive up feed costs and, therefore, the price of cattle.

The impact of higher grains costs merits further elaboration. When the price of grain rises permanently, this must pass through to feeder cattle and live (fed) cattle prices in the long run. Feeder cattle prices rise to reflect grain consumption by pregnant and lactating cows as well as any grain supplementation of the calves. Fed cattle prices rise to accommodate both the increase in the price of feeder cattle and the grain fed directly to the feedlot animals. In the short run or when the price of grain rises only temporarily, we often see a fall in the price of feeder cattle. This is because retail prices are relatively sticky, more or less fixed in the short run, so the cost increase in the price of grain must be shared between the players somewhere along the chain of production. Ranchers receive less for their animals, feedlot operators see their margins fall if not turn negative, and packers see their margins fall as well. Accompanying these shifts in prices, ranchers are inclined to keep feeder cattle on pasture longer, passing along heavier, more mature animals. Meanwhile, feedlot operators pass along lighter, less mature, lower-grade animals. In fact, feeder cattle can even trade at a discount to fed cattle in these situations. It is not too surprising, then, that even temporary surges in grain prices can halt expansions or cause outright contractions of the breeding population. Thus, culled beef and dairy cows enter the market and fewer heifers are retained.

There are some risks to that rosy view of high prices for beef in the future, however. First, a resurgence of BSE in the United States could affect consumer confidence in domestic beef. More cases of BSE in Canada, on the other hand, would likely drive up the price of beef in the United States as supplies become scarcer. Second, continued growth of the cattle industry in Argentina, Brazil, and Uruguay may put some downward pressure on beef prices, particularly if hoof-and-mouth disease can be eradicated. Third, relative demand for beef could fall as a result of the perception of beef as less healthy than other possible meat choices. This appears to be one reason for the decline in per capita U.S. beef consumption from the mid-1970s to the mid-1990s. Admittedly, per capita U.S. beef consumption has since stabilized.

CONTRACT SPECIFICATIONS

There are actually two cattle contracts: live cattle and feeder cattle. We describe live cattle, by far the more liquid contract, here. Live cattle trades on the Chicago Mercantile Exchange (CME) from 9:05 AM to 1:00 PM CST. The trading unit is 40,000 pounds of 55 percent Choice, 45 percent Select,

Yield Grade 3 live steer as defined by the USDA. Unlike lean hogs, which may be cash settled, the live cattle contract may be settled only by delivery of live cattle to approved public livestock yards and slaughter plants. The contract trades in cents per pound, with a tick size of 0.025. One tick is worth $10. Daily price limits are $0.03 per pound above or below the previous day's settlement. The main live cattle contract trading months are February, April, June, August, October, and December (G, J, M, Q, V, and Z). The electronic, Globex, market is growing quickly, and volumes will likely exceed those in the pit before long.

Many of the most important public sources of information come from the USDA. These include the daily slaughter reports, monthly Cattle on Feed reports, weekly and monthly export reports, and so forth. To get up to speed on the cattle industry, the USDA's website is a good source of information as is the *Daily Livestock Report* put out by Steve Meyer and Len Steiner for the CME. For high-quality data and market insight, Informa based in Louisville, Kentucky is an excellent source for paying customers.

Understanding Industrial Metals

Copper

Notable for its shiny reddish color, hardness and malleability, copper has been used in jewelry and weapons for as long as 10,000 years. By 3000 B.C., humans had learned that mixing copper with tin or arsenic yielded a significantly harder material, an alloy that had a low enough melting point to be cast in open hearth pit fires. This was bronze, and with its discovery came the Bronze Age and the continued blossoming of Western civilization. Today, copper's importance is little diminished. The metal's electrical conductivity, corrosion resistance, ductility, malleability, and rigidity render copper an essential part of electrical wiring, plumbing, brass valves and fittings, air conditioning, electric motors, and integrated circuits. That is, as long as its price does not rise too high.

PROCESSING AND PRODUCTION

In contrast to its ubiquitous industrial use, copper is a relatively rare element. It is roughly the twenty-fifth most common element in the Earth's crust, accounting for only 0.006 percent on a mass basis.[1] Fortuitously, some copper comes in high-concentration deposits rather than being uniformly spread through the Earth. The next few paragraphs describe how copper in these deposits is transformed into the high levels of purity required for industrial processes.

Copper processing begins with mining. U.S. mines at the turn of the twentieth century contained 3 to 3.5 percent copper. Today, U.S. mines recover copper economically at concentrations of less than 0.5 percent. The copper ore dug from the mines is crushed and ground before being loaded into an aerated water bath. In the presence of specialized reagents, copper attaches to rising air bubbles and can be skimmed from the top of the bath. The result is copper concentrate at 20 to 40 percent pure.

Traditionally, the next three major steps in production are pyrometallurgical; they use heat to purify copper. First, the powdered copper concentrate is roasted and smelted to yield a 60 to 80 percent pure liquid known as matte. Second, matte is heated in the presence of air to produce blister copper, which is 97 to 99 percent pure. In these two processes, copper sulfides are first oxidized and then reduced to form copper metal while silicon, iron, sulfur, oxygen, and other impurities are liberated from the ore. Third, most remaining sulfur and oxygen are removed from the blister copper in a furnace, and the resultant metal is cast as anode copper, greater than 99 percent pure. In the final, electrorefining stage, the anode copper is placed in a tank bearing sulfuric acid electrolyte and subjected to an electric current. The current deposits copper at the cathode, at purity greater than 99.9 percent. Copper cathode is the refined (grade A) copper that trades on metal exchanges.

Pyrometallurgical approaches to processing copper, such as the first three steps in the previous example, have been used throughout history and are particularly effective for copper sulfides. For copper oxides, a relatively new hydrometallurgical process has been commercialized during the past 30 years. This is known as solvent extraction-electrowinning (SX-EW).[a]

SX-EW begins with leaching copper ore or mine waste in a weak acidic solution. The leachate is then mixed with an organic solvent, the extractant, which attaches to the copper, enabling the copper to be extracted. The copper is then separated from its organic extractant in a stronger acidic solution. Finally, electrowinning subjects the copper in the stronger acidic solution to an electric current, depositing the copper as copper cathode.

Recycling also plays an important role in copper production, accounting for 10 to 15 percent of total refined copper production worldwide. Secondary copper is the name for refined copper produced through recycling. There are two major types of recycling. The first takes new copper with a shelf life of a few months, commonly returns from manufacturing, and converts it to secondary copper. This procedure involves mostly a simple remelt with no cleanup required. The second takes old, used copper and fire-refines it to produce copper anode, which is then electrolytically refined. Old copper accounts for about 80 percent of available scrap in the United States.[2]

One-third of world mined copper originates in Chile, with another 5 to 10 percent coming from the United States, Peru, Australia, Indonesia, and China; the remainder is divided among another half-dozen countries (see Figure 13.1). South America, Australia, and Indonesia are the

---

[a] SX-EW has been applied to copper sulfides as well but on a more limited basis.

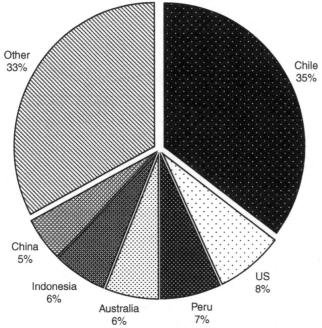

Total: 15.3 million metric tons

FIGURE 13.1 Mined Copper Production by Country, Average of 2005–2006
Source: United States Geological Survey

major exporters of concentrate, with much of their copper being refined elsewhere.

World refined copper production has grown at nearly 4 percent per annum since 1995 (see Figure 13.2). This growth has not been evenly distributed. Figure 13.3 documents the shares of the major producers of refined copper during the past decade. Most importantly, Chile and China are the dominant refiners, and China's production has almost exactly offset the decline in the United States on a percentage basis. More generally, refining in Asia has risen while refining in the West has fallen. For example, India has increased its share of world production from virtually 0 percent to nearly 4 percent, not enough to merit a position in the top-five producers club but substantial growth and worthy of notice nonetheless.

Smelters not associated with a mine—custom smelters—obtain their copper through the market. The mines may either retain ownership of the metal or sell it outright to the smelter. In the former case, smelters receive

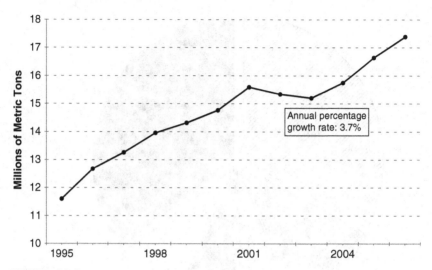

FIGURE 13.2 World Refined Copper Production
Source: World Bureau of Metal Statistics

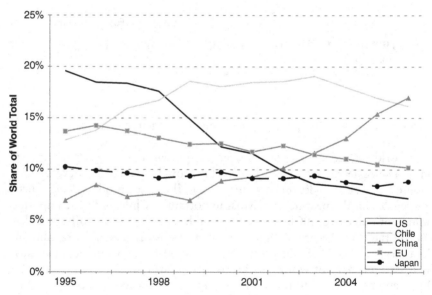

FIGURE 13.3 Top Five Refined Copper Producers
Source: World Bureau of Metal Statistics

concentrate treatment ($/ton) and refining charges (cents/pound) from the mines in exchange for converting concentrates to refined metal. The charges vary with the availability of concentrates. If concentrates are abundant, charges are high and smelters may get price participation (escalation) if the price of copper increases. If concentrates are scarce, price participation disappears and charges are low, as was the case for many East Asian smelters in 2007. Some traders track spot treatment and refining charges.

Production of copper varies from year to year for various reasons. Technology and investment push output up while wars, strikes, mine and natural disasters, and normal declining yields from old mines pull output down. Declining yields are a major part of the story in the United States, and the giant Grasberg mine in Indonesia was shut down for several months in 2005 as a result of a landslide. Much of the short-term volatility in prices resulting from physical supply–demand imbalances (e.g., ignoring purely financial sources of volatility) probably derives from supply shocks. Demand tends to grow more steadily. This is difficult to demonstrate in practice, however, as consumption is never really observed but rather estimated as the residual from production, net trade, and the change in inventories. Measured or *apparent* consumption, therefore, shows substantial measurement error.

CONSUMPTION

Fabricators purchase refined copper and process it via extrusion, drawing, rolling, forging, melting, electrolysis, and atomization into products such as wire, rod, tube, sheet, plate, strip, castings, and powder. Some of these products are pure copper, and others are alloys such as brass and bronze.

In the United States, these intermediate products are used in building construction (50 percent), electrical and electronic products (20 percent), industrial machinery and equipment (10 percent), transportation equipment (10 percent), and consumer and general products (10 percent).[3] Across these categories, 75 to 80 percent of use is in electrical applications, and applications of copper alloys such as brass account for most of the remainder. The predominance of electrical applications holds across Germany and Japan, and presumably elsewhere as well.[4]

Consumption of copper worldwide has increased at an annual rate of 3.3 percent since 1995 (Figure 13.4). The major story in world consumption is much the same as the major story for world production—China. Figure 13.5 reveals that China is now the number-two user of refined copper following the European Union. More impressively, China has gone from 7 percent of

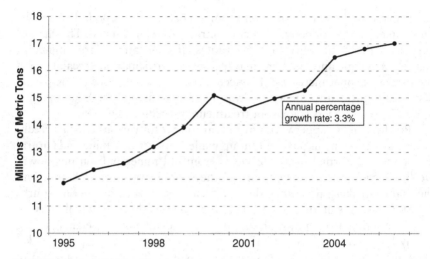

FIGURE 13.4 World Refined Copper Consumption
Source: World Bureau of Metal Statistics

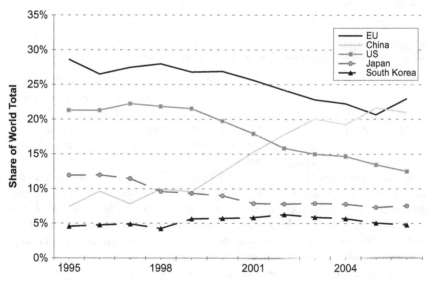

FIGURE 13.5 Top Five Refined Copper Consumers
Source: World Bureau of Metal Statistics

world consumption in 1995 to 21 percent in 2006 and accounts for more than 50 percent of all incremental copper use over that period.

If, as hypothesized above, changes in production are less forecastable than changes in consumption, one could try to use consumption of copper to forecast price movements.[b] This still leaves the problem, however, that apparent consumption is quite noisy. As a proxy for consumption, one could use world GDP growth. Admittedly, parts of GDP growth are little related to copper usage, and this had led some traders to use industrial production. Industrial production is particularly attractive, because it comes out on a monthly basis rather than quarterly as does GDP. Of further benefit, in many countries, industrial production comes out by sector, thus enabling the trader to pick and choose the components relevant for copper. Be careful if you go down this route, however, as the potential for data mining is a big problem. We can all find data series that are highly correlated with returns on a historical basis. The question is: What will be correlated with returns on an ongoing basis? This need not be the series that was most correlated historically.

STOCKS

The primary balance measures the difference between production and consumption. Many analysts believe it to be an important indicator of price movements. A positive primary balance means that production exceeds consumption and prices are likely to fall. Yet a positive primary balance when stocks are low may be quite a different animal from a positive primary balance when stocks are high. Furthermore, recall that consumption is a residual, embedding substantial measurement error. The primary balance itself, then, is likely to contain quite a substantial error component.

One could use stocks themselves. After all, stocks rise when the primary balance is positive and fall when it is negative. It would then be possible to look at trends in stocks or, better yet, trends in stocks relative to usage. The key reason for incorporating usage is the normalization. A change in stocks of 500,000 metric tons meant more in 1995 when consumption was 30 percent lower than it does today.

In an ideal world, we would measure stocks all along the production chain from upstream components such as reserves, concentrates, and blister all the way to refined and then on to downstream components such as wire,

---

[b] As previously discussed, demand growth tends to be smooth and incremental. Supply changes such as strikes and disasters tend to be punctuated.

strips, and brass. Furthermore, we would collect information from stocks held by producers, consumers, merchants, and speculators. In practice this is impossible. Exchange stocks are available daily from the exchanges, but little else is readily available. Some countries do report stocks held domestically, and a few organizations, including the International Copper Study Group, collect and report them. Yet this data is available only with a considerable lag and is not readily verifiable. Thus, which specification constitutes a useful indicator of stocks becomes an issue of empirical testing and judgment.

To gain a sense for the importance of these issues, 2006 was a year in which the Chinese government is believed to have liquidated 375 thousand tons from its refined copper stockpile, 2 percent of annual world consumption.[5] This is an estimate; Chinese government sales are not publicly reported. If true, this release would be enough to switch the World Bureau of Metal Statistics estimate of the refined copper primary balance for that year from surplus to nearly perfect balance, an issue the WBMS acknowledges and has discussed.

Traders look at other measures of stocks as well. For instance, stocks that are on warrant (metal in a London Metal Exchange (LME) warehouse for which a warrant has been issued) can be canceled if the owner has found a seller.[c] One measure of future metal scarcity is the percentage of warrants canceled or trends in percent of warrants canceled. Of course, these numbers are typically very short term and can easily be manipulated; the line between warranted stocks in an LME warehouse that show up in the LME stocks numbers and stocks in an LME warehouse that do not show up in the LME stocks numbers is very, very fine. The owner can move his stocks on and off warrant for a small cost without any physical movement of the metal. This has reputedly led some players to try to game the system by strategically making stocks warranted or canceled. The benefits to this are unlikely to be tremendous, however, and market participants can always choose to play these games outside of LME warehouses as well.

One additional warning should be given with respect to the use of exchange stocks. Exchange stocks have risen in quantity as exchange warehouses have opened up for business and as exchanges themselves have opened up for business. This can lead to misleading interpretations. Suppose a new LME warehouse opened up in Atlanta in 2004, and 100k tons of material were moved in. Should this be treated as an increase in LME stocks? It depends. If the stocks would have gone to an LME warehouse in New Orleans, certainly yes. If the stocks would have gone into a non-LME warehouse in Mobile, probably not. The reason for *probably not* rather than

---

[c] For more on the London Metal Exchange (LME), see the Appendix.

certainly not is that as the market grows, stocks will have to grow and new warehouses will have to open up. Some of these will be LME warehouses. When implementing trading models, these considerations need to be thought through carefully. The extreme case is the opening of the Shanghai Futures Exchange (SHFE). Stock movements in the SHFE are clearly informative. However, it would be a mistake to compare changes in exchange stocks including the SHFE today with changes in exchange stocks before the SHFE was open.

FUTURES PRICES AND MARKET-MOVING EVENTS

As shown in Figure 13.6, two periods stand out in copper: the boom from 1987 to 1998 and the spike since 2004. The first boom corresponds, perhaps coincidentally, with the tenure of Yasuo Hamanaka, "Mr. Copper," as head copper trader at Sumitomo. This is an amazing story, one that is well covered elsewhere. In brief, Mr. Hamanaka has been convicted of unauthorized trading, and Sumitomo has attributed losses of $2.6 billion to trades Mr. Hamanaka placed on the LME over a period of 10 years. It is unclear what proportion of this loss arose from natural hedging operations, and it is even less clear how this trading could have been hidden from Sumitomo for such a long time. It does not appear that Mr. Hamanaka was trying to corner

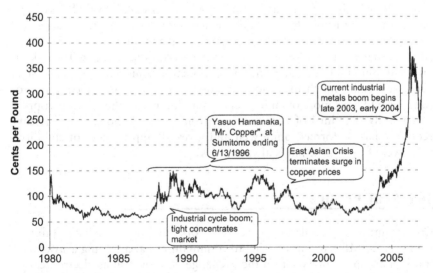

FIGURE 13.6 COMEX High-Grade Copper Price

the market, but it seems likely that his unauthorized long position had some upward impact on the copper price over that period, especially given the notable decline shortly after his reign ended and the subsequent downward trend of copper over the next five-plus years.

The period since 2004 corresponds with booming growth in China, the rise of the commodity index funds, and the rise of the hedge funds. It is unclear precisely what has driven the price boom in copper over this period; probably all three have contributed. We can say with confidence that world demand for copper has grown much faster than world supply ever since the East Asian crisis. We can also say that investments in long-only commodity index funds have grown phenomenally during this period, as discussed in Chapter 21. In addition, there are rumors of large metal positions being taken by individual funds. This can be partially confirmed using the LME Banding reports, which reveal anonymously, with a two-day lag, the presence of LME members and customers with large warrant and futures positions.

The future for copper is cautiously optimistic. Copper will likely stay strong as long as the world industrial cycle stays strong and the current cycle is being driven by growth foremost in China and secondarily in other emerging markets in Asia. The main risk is, therefore, a major economic downturn, especially one extending to China. Another risk is that the high price of copper relative to substitutes will lead to substantial demand destruction. This can already be seen in the substitution of PVC for copper pipes for plumbing and the replacement of copper by aluminum in power cables. It will also be seen as copper applications make do with less copper, perhaps by using thinner and smaller components. In the absence of technological changes, betting on copper relative to aluminum seems wise. Aluminum is far more abundant in the earth's crust than copper. The risk of upside to aluminum is that aluminum production is highly energy intensive per unit weight, much more so than copper. If energy prices continue to rise, this will have more of an impact on aluminum. Another risk for copper is that fully one-third of copper comes from Chile. Although the Chilean economy has performed quite well and gives all appearances of stability, that level of concentration is always a risk.

CONTRACT DETAILS

Copper futures are available on the New York Mercantile Exchange (abbreviated as COMEX when referring to commodities), and trading is available through an open outcry pit on the exchange floor as well as electronically. This side-by-side trading has increased liquidity since the electronic trading was launched in September 2006, and electronic trading volume is increasing significantly. Each COMEX copper contract has a size of 25,000 pounds, with a tick size of $0.05 and a tick value of $12.50. This means for each $.05 move in the futures contract the value changes by $12.50.

The equivalent LME contract for COMEX copper is Grade A Copper and is quoted in $/metric ton. Contract specifications are for 25 tons of copper at better than 99 percent purity. Like the other LME metals, for physical delivery each lot must be of an LME-approved brand and form residing in an LME-approved warehouse. The minimum quoted tick size is $0.25 on LME Select, but in the ring it is $0.50. The ring tick size is equivalent to the tick value of the COMEX copper contract—$12.50. The copper rings for the first session are from 12:00 PM to 12:05 PM and 12:30 PM to 12:35 PM. The second session rings for copper are from 3:10 PM to 3:15 PM and 3:50 PM to 3:55 PM. The kerbs are from 1:15 PM to 2:45 PM and 4:15 PM to 5:00 PM, at which time the ending day evaluation price is determined. All times are quoted in London Standard Time. For more information or clarification of terms, see the Appendix, which discusses the LME, or visit the LME's website. Kerbs are discussed in the LME appendix.

For those interested in long-term data series, be aware that the exchanges have changed copper grades over time. At the COMEX, high-grade copper has traded since January 1989. The earlier contract had been standard grade, which was terminated in December 1989. At the LME, Grade A copper has been traded since April 1986, although prices were quoted in pounds sterling rather than U.S. dollars until July 1993. Standard-grade copper, quoted in pounds sterling, traded from September 1981 to December 1988. High-grade copper traded from September 1981 to March 1986. The primary differences relate to degrees of purity and acceptable tolerances for specific impurities.

Copper also trades on the Shanghai Futures Exchange (SHFE).

CHAPTER 14

Aluminum

Aluminum is the third most common element in the earth's crust after oxygen and silicon, accounting for 8 percent of the ground we walk on. We don't think twice about aluminum as we remove our sandwiches from aluminum foil, drink soda from an aluminum can, and toss the foil and the can into the recycling bin. Yet 150 years ago, aluminum was more valuable than gold and platinum.[1] Of course, this was before the modern electrolytic method of producing aluminum was discovered in 1886. But even this example understates the value of certain forms of aluminum. Rubies and sapphires are no more than aluminum oxide with a sprinkling of impurities. Surprisingly, this same aluminum oxide is the feedstock for aluminum metal. The major difference is that the gems are crystals and the feedstock is powdered.

PROCESSING AND PRODUCTION

Primary aluminum processing proceeds in three steps: bauxite mining and milling, conversion of bauxite to alumina via the Bayer process, and conversion of alumina to aluminum via the Hall-Heroult process.

Elemental aluminum oxidizes too readily to exist in nature. Instead, aluminum must be recovered from aluminum hydroxide and aluminum oxide hydroxide (commonly known as bauxite) deposits. Bauxite deposits are found primarily in tropical regions, with 80 percent of world production coming from Australia, Brazil, Guinea, China, Jamaica, and India (see Figure 14.1). After mining, bauxite typically requires little additional processing other than removal of clay, crushing, and milling.

The Bayer process for refining bauxite to produce alumina was discovered in 1888 and commercialized in 1893. The first stage of the process involves dissolving bauxite in sodium hydroxide at high temperature and pressure, discarding settled insoluble residues (*red mud*), and precipitating

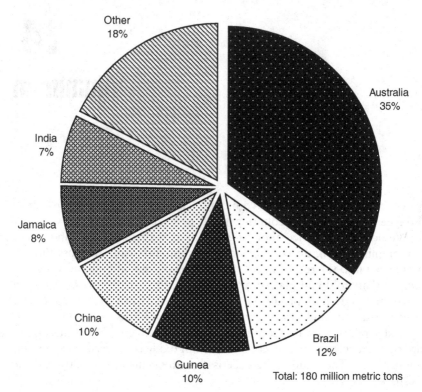

FIGURE 14.1 Bauxite Production by Country (2006)
Source: World Bureau of Metal Statistics

aluminum trihydroxide from solution. In the second stage, the precipitate is calcinated in a kiln to drive off water, releasing the fine white powder known as alumina. Roughly speaking, 2.0 to 2.5 tons of bauxite are required for each ton of alumina produced.

The Hall-Heroult process for converting alumina to aluminum predates the process for converting bauxite to alumina by two years. The essential problem for creating aluminum was to find a solvent that would permit electrolysis of alumina at what was considered a reasonably low temperature: 950°C. This solvent, discovered independently by Hall and Heroult, is sodium aluminum fluoride or cryolite. Modern plants dissolve alumina in complexes of graphite lined steel *pots* filled with cryolite. Low-voltage, high-amperage current, passed through the electrolyte, deposits molten aluminum metal at the bottom of the pot, which can then be siphoned off. Aluminum production remains an energy-intensive process, with even modern

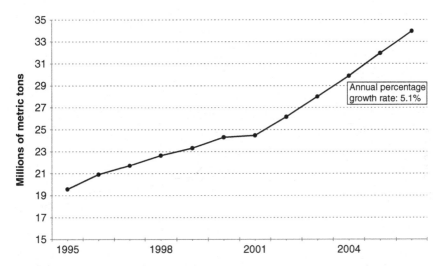

FIGURE 14.2   World Primary Aluminum Production
Source: World Bureau of Metal Statistics

plants requiring 13 to 16 kilowatt-hours (kWh) of direct electrical energy per kilogram of output.[2] Two tons of alumina are required for each ton of aluminum produced and therefore four to five tons of bauxite produce one ton of aluminum at a purity level of 99.7 percent. Aluminum produced from bauxite via alumina is commonly known as primary aluminum.

World primary aluminum production has grown at 5 percent per year since 1995 (Figure 14.2). As with all the metals, the major story is the growth of Chinese primary production. Chinese production has risen from 1,600 kilotons per year in 1995 to 9,300 kilotons per year in 2006, as its share of world production increased from 8 percent to 28 percent.[3] The major supply story over the next 10 years will likely be the continuing shift of production from West to East as new plants come online in China, India, Russia, and the Middle East. Cheap, captive power supply is driving capacity expansion in Russia and the Middle East, while economic growth is driving the expansion in China and India. Notable exceptions to this trend, Iceland and Canada, will likely see capacity increases due to available geothermal and hydroelectric energy sources.

While Chinese primary production skyrocketed during the past 10 years, U.S. production fell by one-third. Much of the U.S. story relates to energy prices: more than half of the U.S. decline came during the winter of 2000–2001, when natural gas prices spiked to $10/btu for the first time and from which production has never recovered. Natural gas provides winter

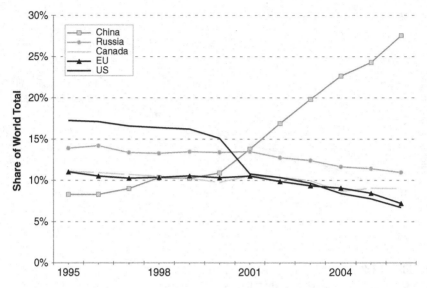

FIGURE 14.3 Top Five Primary Aluminum Producers
Source: World Bureau of Metal Statistics

home heat to most of the United States and is also the source of incremental supply during periods of peak electricity demand. (For more information on natural gas, see Chapter 7, "Natural Gas.") Primary aluminum production has been roughly flat in the other major producing countries, causing their share of world production to fall in the face of China's dramatic growth (see Figure 14.3). Overall, primary aluminum production is more dispersed than bauxite mining.

Secondary production, or recycling, remains an attractive source of production for aluminum. Recycling aluminum incurs only 5 percent of the energy costs required to convert alumina to aluminum.[4] Currently, recycling accounts for roughly 40 percent of global production, significantly higher than the proportions for other metals.[5] Recyclable material is commonly subdivided into two categories: new scrap and old scrap. New scrap encompasses surplus from manufacture and fabrication of aluminum product, including alloys, prior to sale to the consumer. As such, new scrap tends to be of known quality and requires little preprocessing prior to electrical reformation. Old scrap consists of consumer discards of unknown quality and is more likely to undergo preprocessing. The major aluminum recyclers are, unsurprisingly, the United States, Europe, and Japan. In the United States, recycling accounts for a full 60 percent of aluminum production, and in Japan recycling accounts for nearly all aluminum production.[6]

CONSUMPTION

Primary and secondary aluminum are frequently but not necessarily alloyed with other metals and then converted into semifabricated products (semis) such as sheet, foil, rod, and plate via rolling, casting, extrusion, forging, and powdering. These semis are then used in a variety of applications. As of 1998, end use of aluminum worldwide consisted of: 26 percent transportation (vehicles), 20 percent packaging (foil and cans), 20 percent construction (commercial and residential), 9 percent electric (transmission), and 25 percent other uses (machinery, consumer durables, etc).[7] More recent data, as of 2004, is publicly available for the United States and Canada: 37 percent transportation, 22 percent packaging, 16 percent construction, 7 percent electric, and 18 percent other uses.[a] Regarding the set of end uses, GDP, industrial production, and their components would seem to be promising indicators of demand for aluminum.

World primary aluminum consumption has grown at slightly less than 5 percent since 1995 (Figure 14.4). The consumption picture is dominated by China. From 9 percent of world consumption in 1995 to 25 percent of world

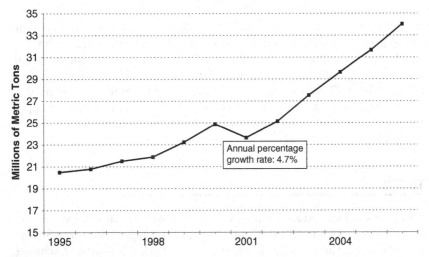

FIGURE 14.4 World Primary Aluminum Consumption
Source: World Bureau of Metal Statistics

---

[a] Base data comes from the Aluminum Association. We have allocated end-use exports, which have no sectoral designation, in proportion to domestic use, which has a sectoral designation.

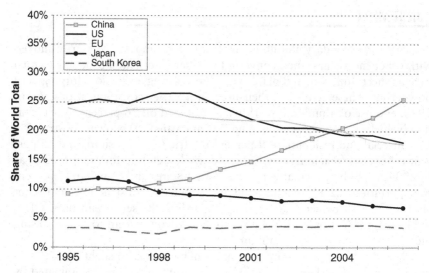

FIGURE 14.5 Top Five Primary Aluminum Consumers
Source: World Bureau of Metal Statistics

consumption in 2005, incremental aluminum use in China accounts for fully 50 percent of incremental use worldwide. As a consequence, Japan, the United States, and Europe have all seen their shares of world consumption fall, even though absolute levels of consumption have increased mildly (see Figure 14.5). If China can continue to maintain high rates of growth, this process has a long way to go. In 2006, primary aluminum consumption per capita was more than three times higher in the United States at 41 pounds than in China at 13 pounds.[b]

STOCKS

Aluminum stocks are available from a variety of sources. Most important are the exchange stocks from the London Metal Exchange (LME), the Shanghai Futures Exchange (SHFE), and the New York Mercantile Exchange (COMEX), which are available on a daily or weekly basis. The International Aluminum Institute (IAI) reports two additional types of stocks: unwrought aluminum and total aluminum. Unwrought aluminum consists of

---

[b] U.S. population of 298 million and Chinese population of 1.313 billion from the *World Factbook 2007*, published by the CIA. Primary aluminum consumption from the World Bureau of Metal Statistics.

metallurgically unworked primary metal stocks. Total aluminum adds un-processed scrap, metal in process, and finished semi-fabricated mill products. Both may be useful to the trader. The IAI stocks dwarf all other stocks and are available only on a monthly basis. To be specific, absolute variation in exchange stocks tends to be quite small compared with variation in IAI unwrought or total stocks. If you do examine the IAI stocks, be aware that the reporting rules changed in 1999; therefore, any series constructed over a longer history needs to meld the old and new reporting rules. One final source of stocks is Japanese port stocks available from Mitsubishi and Marubeni. These are also reasonably well regarded and available on a monthly basis.

FUTURES PRICES AND MARKET MOVING EVENTS

As the COMEX aluminum market is not particularly liquid and has a rel-atively short history, we examine the LME three-month contract to under-stand the movement of prices over time. This has the disadvantage of missing information contained in the rolls, but for our purposes that is not crucial.[c]

The black line in Figure 14.6 traces the path of three-month aluminum prices over time. The two principal spikes in aluminum occur at the be-ginning and the end of the series. The run-up in metals over the past few years coincides with surging demand in emerging economies, particularly in China, the astonishing (for many reasons) growth of long-only commodity index funds, and the rise of the hedge funds. Each of these developments has probably played a role in aluminum's boom, most likely in the order listed, but the precise contributions of each are debatable.

The earlier spike occurred in the summer of 1988. This peak arrived as a consequence of a typical industrial cycle, with a period of abundant supply in the early 1980s heralding underinvestment, which then led to a period of tight supply in the late 1980s. The unraveling of the 1988 price spike, which led to the prices lows from 1991 to 1993, is particularly interesting and merits further comment.

The gray line in Figure 14.6 plots the evolution of aluminum stocks, portraying the sum of IAI unwrought producer stocks and LME stocks and ignoring the SHFE and COMEX, which are smaller. The contemporane-ous correlation between prices and stocks is -0.43. The 1991–1993 price

---

[c] It is certainly possible to take the three-month figure at the end of every month and follow that through until the end of the next month, rolling the contract when it has effectively become the two-month. This would make the series more consistent with the other futures contacts in this book at the cost of a little more complexity. However, raw LME historical evaluations (end-of-day prices for all tradable prompt dates) data are not available from the exchange prior to 1997.

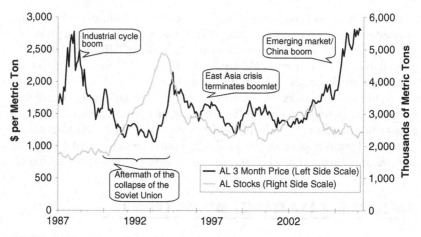

FIGURE 14.6 Aluminum Stocks versus LME Three-Month Prices
Sources: LME; SHFE; COMEX; International Aluminium Institute

lows reflect the collapse of the Soviet Union. As the USSR's defense industry scaled back and internal trade patterns and business relationships disintegrated, Soviet Union producers sent surplus primary aluminum to the West, where it showed up in mounting LME warehouse stocks. By 1991, primary aluminum prices were already headed well south and eventually fell below $1,100/metric ton in the fall of 1993. This led to the erection of trade barriers against Russian aluminum in the European Union. In January 1994, the major aluminum-producing countries met to encourage aluminum producers to cut production, with Russia pledging to reduce 1994 production by 500,000 tons. Indeed, Russian production subsequently fell. Some argue that this was a Pyrrhic victory; production would have declined even without the pledge as the Russian aluminum industry struggled with logistics, access to alumina, and access to Western currency in the chaotic post-revolutionary environment.[8,9] Regardless, prices had recovered to the $1,500/metric ton range by mid-1994.

These wide swings in prices may leave the impression that aluminum is volatile. That would be incorrect. Aluminum prices have relatively low volatility compared with copper and zinc, let alone nickel.[d] This can be seen in Figure 14.7 where we have taken a consistent time period, January 1989

---

[d] We do not discuss nickel because of its low liquidity relative to the other industrial metals.

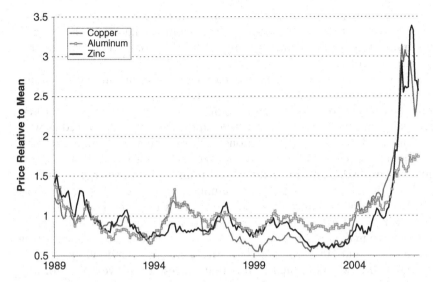

FIGURE 14.7 Relative Price Movements—Industrial Metals

to March 2007, and plotted the price of each metal relative to its mean over that period.[e] For copper and zinc, the standard deviations of the relative price movements are about 0.50, whereas that for aluminum is about 0.25. That is, copper and zinc are twice as volatile. The higher volatility of copper and zinc is not driven just by the recent price spike. If we omit the period since January 2004, the standard deviations for copper and zinc remain one-third higher than aluminum, with the standard deviations for copper and zinc falling to 0.20 and aluminum falling to 0.15.

Simple eyeball-ometrics suggests the existence of an industrial metals cycle. Statistically, over the full sample, the correlations between the three metals' prices average 0.9. Even ignoring the period since January 2004, they still average 0.6. Putting together aluminum's low volatility and the existence of an industrial metals cycle, one could interpret aluminum as a low *beta* metal, with the beta referring to the metals cycle and not the stock market.

The low volatility of aluminum may well be a consequence of its geological abundance (low relative scarcity) in conjunction with the presence of mothballed capacity. If this is the case, as seems reasonable, aluminum will

---

[e] The length of the time series is limited by the availability of a three-month LME zinc price.

remain less volatile than the other metals, benefiting less from the boom in emerging markets but suffering less if the boom should crash. Investing in aluminum may thus provide exposure to the industrial (metal) cycle with a defensive posture.

Thus, as long as investment in capacity remains prudent and the industrial cycle stays strong, aluminum is likely to stay strong. Neither of these is guaranteed, however. While the strength of the current commodity markets makes it tempting to forget, growth in supply can certainly exceed growth in demand. Rapidly growing nations such as China may build excessive aluminum capacity, looking to export the excess abroad, until they grow into the available capacity. Similarly, nations with low energy costs such as the Gulf States are ramping up aluminum production to supply export markets. A heavy reliance on export markets, a potential issue in both of these scenarios, leaves aluminum exposed to downward price pressure from a slowdown in the rest of the world. The crisis in the U.S. sub-prime housing market as of mid-2007 may well be a precursor of such a downturn.

There are two additional factors that suggest a positive future for aluminum. First, the energy intensity of aluminum means it should benefit more than the other metals from any future increases in energy prices. The recent spike in energy prices saw the closure of marginal (i.e., high-cost) capacity particularly in Europe. As futures markets for energy products are reasonably liquid a couple of years out, their forecasts can give a good sense for a major component of future aluminum marginal costs.[f] Second, the larger surge in copper and zinc prices will lead to their substitution by aluminum. Working in the other direction, the rise in aluminum prices may engender switching to plastics. Of course, this will depend on the price of plastics, which are themselves products of the increasingly pricey petroleum complex.

CONTRACT DETAILS

Primary aluminum trades on the LME and is quoted in $/metric ton.[g] Contract specifications are for 25 tons of aluminum at 99.7 percent purity. For physical delivery, each lot of metal must be of an LME-approved brand and form residing in an LME-approved warehouse. The minimum quoted tick size is $0.25 on LME Select, but in the ring it is $0.50. The aluminum rings for the first session are from 11:55 AM to 12:00 PM and 12:55 PM to

---

[f] Here, we are invoking the expectations hypothesis.
[g] There are also aluminum alloy contracts that are significantly less liquid.

1:00 PM. The second session rings for aluminum are from 3:15 PM to 3:20 PM and 3:55 PM to 4:00 PM. The kerbs are from 1:15 PM to 2:45 PM and 4:15 PM to 5:00 PM, at which time the ending day evaluation price is determined. All times are quoted in London Standard Time. For more information or clarification of terms, see the Appendix, which discusses the LME.

There have been a few substantial grade changes in aluminum. The current Primary Aluminum High Grade contract has been trading since June 1987. An alternative High Grade contract traded from 1987 to 1990, and a Standard Aluminum contract traded from 1978 to 1988. All of these contracts have traded in U.S. dollars, whereas earlier contracts traded in British pounds. The historical data are a bit noisy but do not provide strong evidence of a significant change in prices as a consequence of the grade changes.

Aluminum also trades on the Shanghai Futures Exchange (SHFE) and the COMEX.

CHAPTER 15

Zinc

Zinc is a bit of a mystery. When was the last time you saw a piece of zinc? Unlike copper and aluminum, zinc is hardly ever used on its own. It is used to galvanize steel (preventing rust), to make alloys such as brass and bronze, and in various other chemical applications. One of zinc's most familiar applications, zinc oxide, hardly even seems like a metal. After all, why should a metal be put in a microwavable burrito or used as sunscreen to prevent sunburn? Yet zinc does have these applications. Zinc's unjust lack of recognition has a long history. Despite having been used for more than 5,000 years as an important constituent of brass and, frequently, of bronze, zinc was not recognized as a metal in Europe until the sixteenth century.

PROCESSING AND PRODUCTION

Zinc accounts for roughly 0.007 percent of the Earth's crust on a mass basis, making it only slightly more common than copper.[1] Economically, zinc sulfide is the most important mineral form of the metal with mined ores having concentrations from 1 to 15 percent zinc sulfide. These levels of concentration are far from what is required for cost-effective smelting, so zinc undergoes beneficiation to increase the concentration of zinc in the ore.

Beneficiation has two stages. First, the zinc is milled, or crushed, to increase surface exposure. Second, the zinc is separated from other minerals and low value rock (gangue) by froth flotation. Froth flotation refers to the process by which milled ore submerged in water becomes attached to rising air bubbles and forms a froth on the surface of the water, which can then be skimmed off. The particular minerals which rise with the air bubbles are selected by the application of specialized reagents. Careful application of these chemicals enables the processor to sort out and concentrate desirable minerals in sequence. Typical zinc concentrates exiting froth flotation are on the order of 50 to 60 percent zinc.

It should be noted that lead and zinc are frequently associated in industry and trade publications. This is because zinc sulfide (sphalerite) and lead sulfide (galena) are commonly found together. A typical froth flotation process would first concentrate lead by application of reagents to collect lead (collectors) and depress zinc (depressants). Once the lead has been skimmed, the processor would then float the zinc. Of course, other valuable minerals present in the ore could be concentrated along the way as well.

As shown in Figure 15.1, China accounts for one-quarter of the world production of zinc concentrate, with Australia and Peru together accounting for another quarter. The United States, Canada, Europe, Mexico, and India combine for a little more than the third quarter, with the remainder split among several countries.

Smelting, the next step of zinc production, involves roasting zinc concentrate at 950°C to replace the sulfide with oxygen, yielding impure powdered

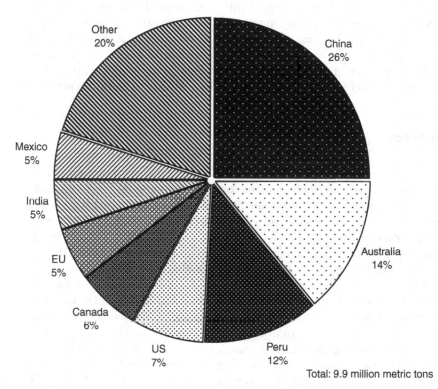

Total: 9.9 million metric tons

FIGURE 15.1 Zinc Concentrate Production by Country (2006)
Source: World Bureau of Metal Statistics

zinc oxide (calcine). The powder can then be leached with weak sulfuric acid to remove the impurities. Some impurities, such as lead, silver, and iron, do not dissolve; others, such as cobalt and nickel, do. These latter impurities can be precipitated out of solution by *cementation,* whereby the addition of powdered zinc at known temperatures forces other metals to fall out of solution.

Finally, an electrical current is run through the zinc sulfate solution, causing zinc to become deposited on an aluminum cathode. The resultant zinc metal, at 99.99 percent or higher purity, can then be melted and cast into ingots or worked as desired. For the trader, the most important grades of zinc, with associated minimum purities, are (LME) Special High Grade at 99.995 percent, High Grade at 99.9 percent and Prime Western at 98 percent. Slab zinc refers generically to commercially cast zinc of assorted shapes and sizes.[a]

Worldwide, 30 percent of zinc production derives from secondary sources.[2] This also holds true for the United States. Of U.S. secondary production, 70 percent of zinc comes from new scrap (pre-end consumer use) and 30 percent comes from old scrap (post end-consumer use). Interestingly, only 10 percent of old scrap supplies are recovered each year. The low recovery rate arises because chemical uses of zinc are largely dissipative while galvanized zinc products have long product lives.

Worldwide, slab zinc production has grown at a nearly 4 percent rate since 1995 (Figure 15.2). As seen in Figure 15.3, China accounts for 30 percent of current slab zinc production, with Europe and Canada together combining for another quarter. Japan and Korea, with their large steel-producing and steel-using industries are next. The United States, remarkably, processes very little zinc and is a major exporter of zinc concentrate as well as a major importer of slab zinc. Growth in China accounts for 60 percent of the increase in global output since 1995 in both zinc concentrate and slab zinc. Production in Canada, the United States, and Europe has fallen from 42 percent to 28 percent of the world total.

CONSUMPTION

Zinc is the fifth most commonly used metal after iron, copper, aluminum, and lead. It is highly sought after for its low weight and corrosion resistance.

---

[a] There also exists a purely pyrometallurgical process for creating zinc metal. Although this process was important historically, it now accounts for less than 20 percent of zinc production. (Ronald Woods. *Electrochemistry Encyclopedia* Web site, November 2004.)

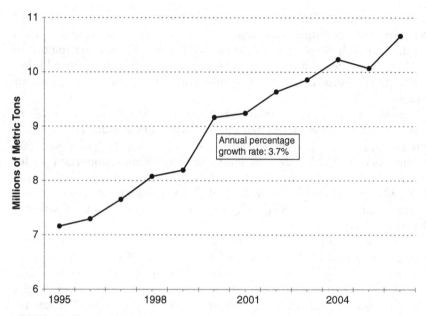

FIGURE 15.2   World Slab Zinc Production
Source: World Bureau of Metal Statistics

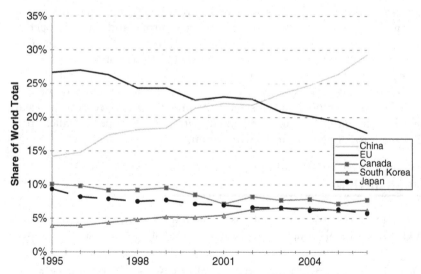

FIGURE 15.3   Top Five Slab Zinc Producers
Source: World Bureau of Metal Statistics

Competition, to a large extent, comes from aluminum, magnesium, and plastics.

Nearly half of all zinc is employed for galvanizing steel, whether for sheets, structures, fences, storage tanks, fasteners, or even wire. Construction, power generation, agriculture and transportation, especially automobiles, are the major users of galvanized steel. Another 20 percent of zinc is blended with copper to form brass. Major applications of brass include tubes, valves, fittings, electrical connections, heat exchangers, and ammunition. The automotive, construction, and electrical sectors are particularly important users of brass. The remaining third of zinc use is divided across die cast alloys, chemical applications, and semi-manufactures.[3] Worldwide, 45 percent of zinc is consumed in construction, 25 percent is consumed in transport, and 10 percent is consumed in industrial machinery and in consumer products.[4]

Growth of zinc consumption during the past decade falls just short of 4 percent annually (Figure 15.4). The growth of China, illustrated in Figure 15.5, is once again astounding, as China accounts for nearly 30 percent of consumption, up from 12 percent a decade ago. Meanwhile U.S., European, and Japanese consumption has dropped from 52 percent to 34 percent. Since 1995, Chinese end-use growth accounts for more than 60 percent of worldwide growth.

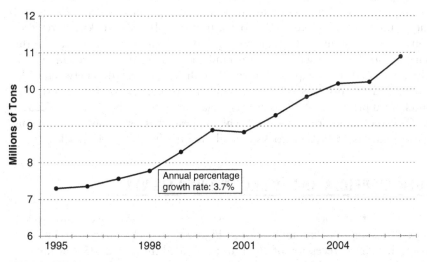

FIGURE 15.4 World Slab Zinc Consumption
Source: World Bureau of Metal Statistics

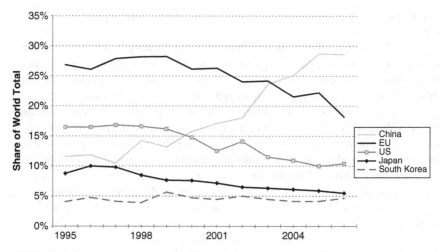

FIGURE 15.5 Top Five Slab Zinc Consumers
Source: World Bureau of Metal Statistics

STOCKS

Zinc trades on the London Metals Exchange (LME). Clearly, LME stocks are important to follow. In addition, the International Zinc and Lead Study Group (ILSZG) also tracks zinc stocks, reporting consumer, producer, and merchant stocks. Unlike LME stocks, however, ILZSG stocks are revised, sometimes substantially. Furthermore, they rely on the thoroughness of the survey and the good will of the respondents and are thus not readily verifiable. If we consider the period since 1996, the raw correlation between LME stocks and zinc prices is −0.57, whereas the raw correlation between ILZSG stocks and prices is −0.29 and the correlation between the sum of LME and ILZSG stocks and prices is −0.63. This suggests that, on a contemporaneous basis, unadjusted ILZSG stocks contribute little beyond LME stocks.

FUTURES PRICES AND MARKET-MOVING EVENTS

The story of zinc prices during the past 20 years involves two major spikes on either side of a long internal lull (Figure 15.6). The lull reached its low point during the recession of 2001 and extended through 2003. During this period, the phrase *zinc is in the sink* became a common refrain. Far better to have been zinc than lead, however, as *lead is dead* sounds quite a bit worse.

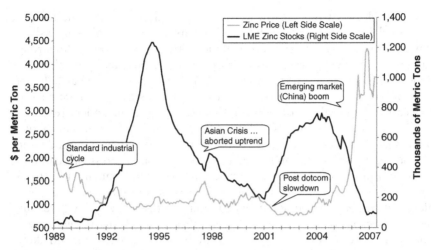

FIGURE 15.6 Zinc Exchange Warehouse Stocks versus LME 3-Month Prices
Source: LME

The first spike arose from strong demand relative to supply, compounded by strikes, hurricanes, and technical problems. This led to significant increases in the price of zinc beginning in 1987 and extending to 1989, where our graph picks up. During 1989, new mines and refineries as well as restarts brought about an increase in refined metal supply that enabled prices to begin their slide back down. In 1990, prices initially recovered on strong demand, but zinc prices fell back during the second half of the year, when mining and refining reached all-time highs and the North American economy slowed.[5]

The more recent zinc spike has been part of a larger boom in the metals complex. Demand from emerging economies, particularly China, has led to a shortage of refined zinc, as can be seen in the evolution of stocks or of the primary balance. An analogous but smaller surge in the price of zinc occurred during the first half of 1997. This surge was equally attributed to strong growth in emerging markets, in this case East Asia. It was short lived, however, as the East Asian crisis began in July, triggering a slowdown in economic activity and a corresponding decline in zinc prices.

The juxtaposition of the 1997 boomlet and the current boom is suggestive. In both cases, emerging market growth caused a surge in prices. In the first case, a collapse occasioned the return to the $1,000-per-ton price range. Clearly, a slowdown of growth in China represents one of the major risks to today's elevated metals prices.

The risk of a Chinese slowdown exposes a deeper truth: zinc follows the world industrial cycle. While China may present an obvious risk, a slowdown in any of the major areas of the world poses a problem for strong zinc prices. Of course, developments specific to the zinc industry are also very important. Most significantly, if investment in new capacity remains driven by financial discipline, zinc prices will likely remain strong; if investment in new capacity runs ahead of demand, zinc prices will come under pressure.

In the medium term, zinc will have to be recovered from less attractive sources as the better mine deposits become tapped out. This natural decline will be at least somewhat mitigated by technological progress, which helps to expand the set of economical mines. Another factor that should help to contain zinc prices is recycling: unlike the products of the petroleum complex, zinc can be recycled. Relative to aluminum, though, zinc is less readily recycled because of the dispersive nature of its uses (chemicals, galvanization). Since zinc is also less commonly available in the ground, this will likely mean an increase in the price of zinc compared with that of aluminum. If the price of zinc rises too high, however, substitution will occur. Aluminum, magnesium, and plastics are all possible substitutes for zinc. Admittedly, all these materials are currently experiencing strong prices.

Clearly, quite a few fundamental factors are at work in zinc. Luckily the economic intuition behind many of these fundamentals is relatively clear. As such, they have the potential to provide a strong foundation for an attractive trading strategy. The difficulty comes in figuring out how to weight them and how the weights should change over time.

CONTRACT DETAILS

Special high-grade zinc trades on the LME and is quoted in $/metric ton. Contract specifications are for 25 tons of zinc at 99.995 percent purity. Like the other LME metals, for physical delivery each lot must be of an LME-approved brand and form residing in an LME-approved warehouse. The minimum quoted tick size is $0.25 on LME Select, but in the ring it is $0.50. The zinc rings for the first session are from 12:10 PM to 12:15 PM and 12:50 PM to 12:55 PM. The second session rings for zinc are from 3:05 PM to 3:10 PM and 3:45 PM to 3:50 PM. The kerbs are from 1:15 PM to 2:45 PM and 4:15 PM to 5:00 PM, at which time the ending day evaluation price is determined. All times are quoted in London Standard Time. For more information or clarification of terms, see the Appendix, which discusses the LME, or visit the LME's website.

There have been three major grade changes. From 1964 until 1988, European Producer Prices were the principal basis for world zinc pricing, with the LME playing second fiddle. European Producer Prices were based on good ordinary brand (gob) at 98 percent. From 1968 to1986, the LME offered a competing contract known as Standard Zinc. Both these prices were quoted in pounds sterling. In December 1984, the LME introduced High Grade at 99.99 percent which lasted until March 1990. Yet it was the introduction of Special High Grade zinc in September 1988 (quoted in dollars), that spelled the demise of European Producer Prices. By the end of 1988, LME pricing had become the standard reference. The next substantial change came on November 1, 2000, when the LME moved to 99.995 percent pure. The historical data are a bit noisy, but they do not provide strong evidence of a significant change in prices as a consequence of the grade changes.

Understanding the Softs

CHAPTER 16

Coffee

Coffee is the world's premiere caffeine delivery device; 1.6 billion cups are drunk everyday.[1] It provides about 54 percent of the world's total caffeine, followed by tea and soft drinks.[2] In the United States, 52 percent of the population drinks coffee—down from 1975, when it was consumed by 65 percent of the population.[3] In recent decades, coffee has encountered increased competition from soft drinks.

The coffee plant is a woody evergreen shrub or tree that is grown in subtropical and tropical climates. Coffee beans are the seeds of this plant. There are two major types of coffee: Arabica and Robusta. Arabica coffee is generally considered superior to Robusta, which is often described as having a harsh taste.[a] In the United States, Robusta is typically used in blends with Arabica and in instant coffee. About two-thirds of world production is Arabica, and one-third Robusta.[4] The best Arabica coffee is grown in volcanic soil, at altitudes of 2,000 to 6,000 feet, depending on the proximity to the equator. Robusta grows at lower elevations and closer to the equator. From planting, it takes three to five years before the coffee plant begins bearing cherries. This long lead time can create periods of supply–demand imbalance, as farmers plant coffee when prices are high but then do not produce a crop for several years, by which time circumstances may differ.

HISTORY

Coffee originated in East Africa, probably in the region that is today Ethiopia, during the ninth century. Nobody knows its exact origin, but its legendary discoverer is Kaldi the goatherd. One day Kaldi came upon his goats and found them behaving in a most energetic fashion. They were

---

[a] For a more detailed discussion see "Ready for Robustas?" by Shanna Germain, *Roast Magazine*, March/April 2006.

eating the leaves and berries of a particular shrub. The next day the goats hurried back to the same spot. Pretty soon Kaldi decided to get in on the act, and it wasn't long before both he and the goats were having a grand time dancing around.

From Ethiopia, coffee moved across the Red Sea to Yemen in around 1000 A.D. and then spread throughout the Muslim world. It was the Muslim Arabs who began the coffee trade—hence the name Arabica coffee.[b] It entered Europe around 1600, and in 1683 retreating Turks left bags of coffee outside Vienna, hastening its move into northern Europe. The Dutch planted coffee in Java (an island of what is now Indonesia) in 1700, and the vernacular appellation *java* has stuck.

In the early 1700s coffee made its way to the new world. In 1723 the French planted coffee in their possession of Martinique, where it flourished. A few years later coffee seeds were smuggled to Brazil, initiating the coffee industry in what is today the world's largest coffee producer.

PROCESSING

Coffee beans are the seeds of the coffee plant. They are located inside the fruit of the plant, called a cherry, and require many stages of processing before they can be brewed into a cup of coffee. First the coffee cherries are picked from the plant. They can be picked by hand or stripped by machine. Machine picking is obviously less labor intensive, but it has the disadvantage of picking all coffee cherries whether ripe or not. Next, the coffee must be processed. The purpose of processing is to separate the coffee bean from the cherry and to dry it. Once this is done it is known as green coffee. There are two processing methods: the dry (unwashed) method and the wet (washed) method. The dry method basically involves laying the coffee cherries in the sun and letting them dry out. The fruit is later separated from the bean by a hulling machine. The wet method differs from the dry method in that it uses lots of water, as one would expect, but the more important difference is that in the wet method the fruit is separated by machine from the seed before drying. This pre-dry separation produces higher-quality—and therefore higher-priced—green coffee. Importantly, only washed Arabicas are deliverable to the New York Board of Trade coffee contract. Most Brazilian coffee and almost all Robusta coffees are processed with the dry (unwashed) method. Almost all Arabica coffee (Brazilian being the main

---

[b] Robusta coffee was discovered in West Africa during the second half of the nineteenth century.

exception) is processed by the wet method. Once processed, the green coffee is ready to be exported to the consuming country.

The next step in the coffee preparation process is roasting. Roasting brings out the flavor in coffee by heating it to temperatures of around 400°F. Before roasting coffee has little flavor (though all the caffeine), but after roasting it has the taste so many know and love. Roasting generally takes place in the importing country, in part because once roasted the beans begin to lose their freshness.

COFFEE PRODUCTION

For the 2006/2007 marketing year the U.S. Department of Agriculture (USDA) estimates that the world will produce 128.6 million (60 kilogram) bags.[5] Figure 16.1 shows world production since 1973. Coffee production has increased fairly steadily at an annual rate of growth of about 2.1 percent. Producing countries export most of what they grow but not all, as the export line shows. Coffee is produced in approximately 70 countries,[6] but the world's largest coffee producer by far is Brazil. For the 2006–2007

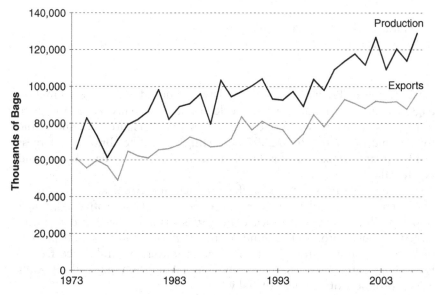

FIGURE 16.1 Coffee Production and Exports
Source: USDA

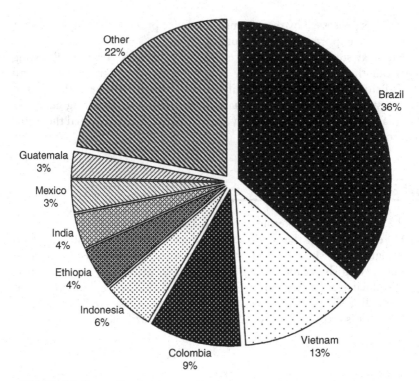

FIGURE 16.2   Coffee Production by Country
Source: USDA

marketing year, Brazil is estimated to have produced more than 46 million bags, which is over one-third of world production. This makes the price of coffee sensitive to weather conditions in Brazil. Figure 16.2 shows the top producers for the 2006/2007 marketing year. After Brazil the largest producers are Vietnam, Colombia, Indonesia, Ethiopia, India, Mexico, and Guatemala.

About two-thirds of world coffee production is Arabica. The countries of Western Africa and Vietnam produce mostly Robusta coffee. Although Brazil produces mostly Arabica coffee, it is actually the world's second largest Robusta producer, behind Vietnam. A bit more than 20 percent of Brazil's crop is typically Robusta. The producers of Arabica coffee are located in Central America, Africa, and South America. Brazil is the world's largest producer of Arabica coffee by far.

Figure 16.3 shows how the production of these countries has varied over time. Notice how Brazil's production has varied. In the mid-1970s, very severe frosts cut production tremendously. In the mid-1990s, frost and

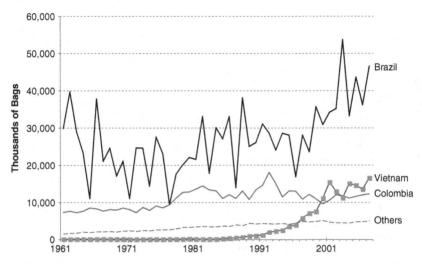

FIGURE 16.3 Top Coffee Producers Over Time
Source: USDA

drought again cut production. In both periods, the world price of coffee increased. Recently, the second largest producer of coffee has been Vietnam, surpassing Colombia, which has historically been the second-biggest producer. This represents quite a change to the coffee supply dynamic, given that as of the mid-1980s Vietnam was only a trivial producer of coffee. The value of Colombia's production is still greater, however, as it produces premium Arabica beans whereas Vietnam's production is primarily Robusta. As can be seen in Figures 16.1 and 16.3, in the first few years of the twenty-first century coffee production has been at historically high levels. This has led to a drop in price that has been particularly painful for coffee growers in the developing countries.

COFFEE CONSUMPTION

Figure 16.4 presents coffee consumption for the major coffee importers[c] as reported by the International Coffee Organization (ICO). From 1975 through 2005, coffee consumption grew by only about 0.7 percent a year.

---

[c] The countries are: Austria, Belgium/Luxembourg, Cyprus, the Czech Republic, Finland, France, Germany, Greece, Hungary, Ireland, Italy, Japan, Malta, the Netherlands, Norway, Poland, Portugal, Spain, Sweden, Switzerland, the United Kingdom, and the United States.

FIGURE 16.4   Coffee Consumption of Major Importers
Source: International Coffee Organization

During the same period, coffee production grew by about 1.50 percent. Thus, coffee consumption among the major importing countries has not been growing rapidly; in fact, it has been growing more slowly than production. Coffee-producing nations have responded to this by, among other things, seeking new markets (such as in Asia), by seeking to differentiate themselves based on the quality of their coffee (such as Colombia has successfully done), and by increasing domestic consumption. Given that coffee is produced in many different countries and that many of these countries are poor, there is likely to be continued upward pressure on supplies. If so, it will be difficult for coffee to show a strong upward trend in the future.

FUTURES, FUTURES PRICE HISTORY, AND MARKET-MOVING EVENTS

Coffee trades on two major exchanges. The New York Board of Trade[d] (NYBOT) lists a contract for washed Arabica deliverable from a predetermined set of countries. Even though Brazil is the largest producer of Arabica

---

[d] Previously, this contract traded on the Coffee, Sugar, & Cocoa exchange (CSCE). The CSCE merged with the NYCE in 2004 to form the NYBOT.

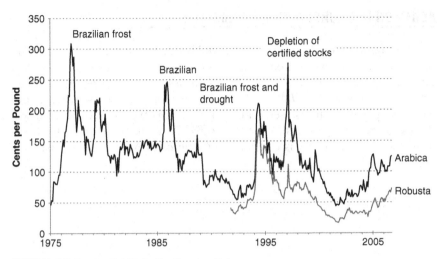

FIGURE 16.5   NYBOT Coffee Futures Price

coffee, Brazilian growths are not deliverable against the NYBOT contract. Robusta coffee trades on the Euronext-Liffe exchange. Like the NYBOT contract, this contract also specifies a set of countries whose growths are deliverable. Interestingly, Brazilian Robustas are deliverable against the Euronext contract.

Figure 16.5 displays the price history of the front New York Board of Trade contract and the front Euronext contract. Arabica trades at a premium to Robusta, and the two prices tend to move together. There is no long-term discernible trend in the price of coffee. Its history, however, is punctuated by a number of price spikes, most of which are due to weather in Brazil. The severe frost in Brazil in the mid-1970s drove the price of coffee ultimately to over $3 a pound, a price that has not been seen since. During the first few years of the twenty-first century, very low coffee prices prevailed. Among other reasons, these resulted from favorable weather in Brazil and increased Robusta supplies from Vietnam. A data release that can affect the market is NYBOT warehouse stocks. This is released every afternoon after the close and measures the level of coffee inventories in NYBOT-approved warehouses. The steady increase in coffee supply and the only moderate increase in demand make it unlikely that there will be a secular demand/supply imbalance that will put upward pressure on the price of coffee. More likely, the price of coffee will remain trendless or mildly increasing and will continue to have weather-related price spikes.

ADDITIONAL SOURCES OF INFORMATION

The International Coffee Organization and the National Coffee Association of U.S.A. are two organizations that collect and report statistics related to the international coffee trade. The USDA publishes a quarterly report entitled *Tropical Products: World Markets and Trade*, which presents estimates of world supply and collects useful information from other sources. Currently, the December and June issues feature coffee. A recent book on coffee that provides a breezy history is *Uncommon Grounds* by Mark Pendergrast.

Sugar

Sugar is made by plants to store energy that they don't need immediately, similar to the way animals store fat. All plants produce sugar using photosynthesis, but only sugarcane and sugar beets store enough for commercial production. Once processed, the end product produced from both crops is nearly identical. Sugarcane stores the sugar in its stalk, whereas sugar beets store the sugar in its white root. Sugarcane is a perennial grass that looks like bamboo and is grown in tropical and semitropical climates. Sugar beets are an annual crop grown in the more temperate climates of the Northern Hemisphere. Sugar is a pure carbohydrate that supplies energy to the body. It plays an important role in the world's food supply. Most people think of sugar as only a sweetener, but it can also be used for many other cooking and baking functions—for example, as a bulking agent or a preservative.

Sugar has a market structure that is completely different from that of the other commodities discussed in this book. The world market for sugar as well as the corresponding futures contract does not bear any relationship to the true global supply and demand conditions. This is because nearly every sugar-producing country in the world intervenes in its production, consumption, and trade of sugar. Only approximately 20 percent of global sugar production is traded on the open market.[1] The rest is consumed or stored in the country in which it is produced. This makes it extremely hard to derive a true assessment of the fundamentals that drive the world sugar price. The sugar on the open market is heavily subsidized, and often the price received is lower than the cost of production.

PRODUCTION

During the past 25 years, approximately 70 percent of world sugar production has come from sugarcane and 30 percent from sugar beets.[2] More recently, those percentages have shifted to account for more sugar from sugarcane and less from sugar beets. This is because the cost of producing sugar from sugarcane is cheaper than from sugar beets. In addition, expansion in world production has come from countries in tropical regions that produce sugarcane, such as Brazil, China, and India, as shown in Figure 17.1. The world's largest sugar producers are Brazil, the European Union, China, and India. They account for more than 50 percent of world production.[3] Of the four, the European Union is the only country to produce most of its sugar from sugar beets. Other smaller but important sugar producers include Thailand, Australia, Pakistan, Mexico, and the United States.

Sugarcane and sugar beets go through different processes in order to arrive at the end product, refined sugar. Sugarcane is first processed at a sugar mill where the cane is shredded, mixed with water, and crushed. This creates the cane juice, which contains sucrose along with remaining fibrous solids. These solids are called bagasse; they constitute a biomass that can be used for power generating. The bagasse makes sugar mills that process sugarcane very energy efficient as they actually burn the bagasse to create power to run the mill. The remaining cane juice is mixed with lime and goes through an evaporator to create syrup. The syrup is cooled and the raw sugar is separated from the remaining liquid, or molasses. The raw sugar is yellowish brown in color and can be bleached to make crystal sugar or refined to create white refined sugar. When raw sugar goes through a sugar refiner, it is purified even further to white refined sugar. This is the sugar

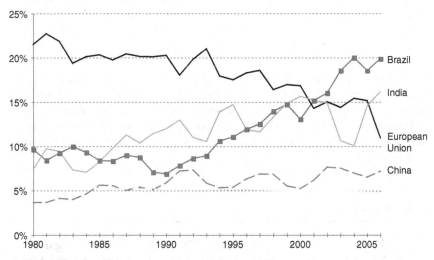

FIGURE 17.1   Percent Share of World Sugar Production
Source: United States Department of Agriculture

commonly found in Europe and the United States. White refined sugar is usually dried and packaged as granulated sugar.

Sugar beets go through a similar process to create refined sugar. The major difference is that sugar beet processing is normally accomplished in one continuous method that does not involve the raw sugar stage. The products leftover from sugar processing, including sugar pulp and molasses, can be used as an ingredient in livestock feed. Some of the residual products still may contain a fair amount of sugar and are recycled back into the process in order to extract the maximum amount of sugar.

Sugar beets and sugarcane can also be processed into sugar-based ethanol for transportation fuel. Of the two, sugarcane is the most cost-effective input for making ethanol. Brazil is the largest producer of ethanol using sugarcane. This is the result of the National Alcohol Program in Brazil initiated in 1975 after the 1973 oil embargo. Sugar mills in Brazil are sugar only, ethanol only, or joint production. Most Brazilian sugar mills are joint production and able to alternate between the production of raw sugar or of fuel ethanol. This gives them the ability to respond to shifts in the fundamentals of either market very quickly. Demand for ethanol both domestically and abroad from countries such as the United States and Japan has the potential to divert more Brazilian sugarcane to ethanol production and away from raw sugar production.

CONSUMPTION

Sugar is found in many foods, listed using terms such as sucrose, glucose, fructose, and lactose. When sugar is added to food it improves the taste and texture. Important uses of sugar are as a sweetener, as a preservative, and to add color to baked goods. Figure 17.2 shows the world's five largest consumers of sugar for human consumption. This chart follows a period of almost 50 years, and there are dramatic shifts in some countries' percentage of world consumption. Growth in consumption by countries such as India, China, and Brazil has occurred as both their population and their wealth continue to increase. Both the European Union and the United States were the major sugar consuming countries during most of the twentieth century. U.S. sugar consumption stabilized in the early 1990s after years of decline. Much of this decline occurred when sugar consumers switched to a different sweetener, high fructose corn syrup (HFCS). HFCS is derived from the wet milling of corn. Its production increased rapidly during the 1980s as the two major beverage manufacturers, Pepsi-Cola and Coca-Cola, both switched from sugar to HFCS. One reason for this switch is the U.S. government keeps the price of its sugar above the world sugar price in order to protect

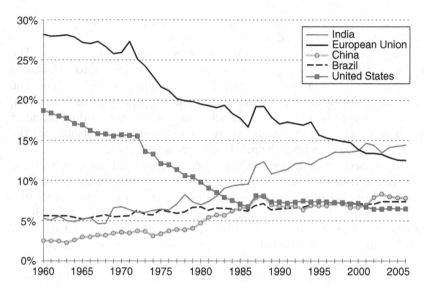

FIGURE 17.2 Percent Share of World Sugar for Human Consumption
Source: United States Department of Agriculture

U.S. sugar farmers. Both Pepsi and Coke were able to get the same flavor in their products using lower-cost HFCS. Demand for HFCS comes from sources that use that sweetener as an ingredient in many products, including baked goods, soda and other beverages, cereal, and various confectionary goods. Other sweeteners, that are not sugar based, have also begun to take market share away from white refined sugar. Health concerns about the consumption of sugar, such as obesity and diabetes, have contributed to the growth in these alternative products.

The expansion into biofuels has increased demand for raw sugar from sugarcane to make fuel ethanol. As discussed previously, Brazil is the largest producer of ethanol from sugarcane. Brazil has been a model for the rest of the world in weaning itself of energy imports. It helps that Brazil has a large amount of available land and the right climate for growing sugarcane to make ethanol. Ethanol demand comes not only from Brazil's governmental program, which requires certain levels of ethanol consumption. It comes also from similar governmental programs in the United States, Europe, and Asia, making Brazil the largest exporter of ethanol in the world. This creates an interesting market dynamic given that Brazil is also the largest sugar exporter in the world. Shifts in Brazil's or other countries' policies regarding increased ethanol consumption can tighten the availability of sugar on world export markets.

Ethanol is a biofuel made from the fermentation of sugars and is used as an alternative to gasoline. It can be blended with gasoline or used as 100 percent ethanol or pure ethanol. In Brazil, flexible fuel vehicles are manufactured to use a blended gasoline called gasoline type C or hydrated ethanol fuel. The flexible fuel vehicles in Brazil allow the consumer to fill up on whichever fuel is cheaper at a given time. Gasoline type C is gasoline blended with ethanol. The percentage of ethanol used has been between 20 percent-25 percent. Brazil's Ministry of Agriculture changes the percentage of ethanol blended each year depending on the outlook for the sugarcane crop. Hydrated ethanol is a mixture of ethanol (93 percent) and water (7 percent). In the United States, because the vehicles are not set up to burn hydrated ethanol they use anhydrous ethanol, or ethanol without water. In other countries, ethanol is made from corn, wheat, or even sorghum. These feedstocks are not as economical as raw sugar. The low-cost production of ethanol using sugarcane will allow Brazil to have a foothold in the global ethanol industry for many decades to come.

GOVERNMENT SUBSIDIES

Government sugar subsidies have a significant impact on the fundamentals of the world sugar market. Nearly every country in the world that produces sugar has some form of subsidy, either directly or indirectly. This makes sugar the most subsidized commodity in the world. Direct subsidies can be in the form of domestic market controls such as production quotas and guaranteed prices, export controls such as export subsidies, or import controls such as import tariffs or quotas. Indirect subsidies occur in the form of income support and debt financing or additional long-term support programs such as government ethanol programs.

The result of these sugar subsidies is overproduction of sugar and a sugar surplus in the world market. This occurs because subsidized producers overproduce and then dump their excess sugar on the world market for whatever price they can get. The price received is often a fraction of the cost of production. This *dumping* of sugar on the market is why the world market for sugar is often referred to as the world dump market and the price received is called the dump price. Compared to actual supply and demand, the dump market for sugar is fairly small. Approximately 20 percent of world sugar production is openly traded on the world dump market.[4] Some countries do not allow or minimize access to the dump market for both consumers and producers. This distorts the market even further in that consumers may be required to pay the domestic price, which is higher than the dump market price. In addition, countries can limit their sugar production by not allowing producers to sell excess sugar on the dump market. This will make them produce only what the government will pay for, because additional production would not be of any value.

A good example of how government subsidies affect the world sugar market is Brazil's ethanol program. The heavily subsidized Brazilian ethanol program has resulted in a rapid increase in its sugar production compared with other sugar producers as shown in Figure 17.1. This increase in production has resulted in Brazil's having excess supply of raw sugar for its domestic market. Brazil then turns to the world dump market for raw sugar, flooding the export market. From 1990 to 2006, Brazil's exports of raw sugar increased an average of 30 percent each year.[5] This expansion has depressed the price on the world dump market. Brazil now dominates the world dump market, and the increased competition in the export market has caused all sugar exporters to suffer.

FUTURES

There are two active sugar futures in the world, one for the delivery of raw cane sugar and one for the delivery of white refined crystal sugar. The raw sugar future is traded on the New York Board of Trade (NYBOT). It is the world sugar #11 future and has been trading since 1914. The NYBOT sugar future calls for delivery of raw cane sugar from a list of 28 countries of origin with delivery made to that country's customary port of export. Brazil plays an important role in the NYBOT sugar #11 future. Since 1994, Brazilian sugars have accounted for 80 percent of the tonnage delivered against the NYBOT sugar future.[5] One sugar #11 future contract is equal to 112,000 pounds of raw cane sugar and is priced in cents per pound. The minimum fluctuation, or tick size, for the contract is .01 cents per pound with a tick value of $11.20. That means for each hundredth of a cent move in the sugar #11 future the value of the contract changes by $11.20. This future trades both side-by-side on an electronic platform and in the NYBOT pit. Over time it will move to an all-electronic market, since the Intercontinental Exchange (ICE) purchased the NYBOT in 2006 and ICE uses an electronic platform for its trading.

The London International Financial Futures Exchange (LIFFE) trades the white sugar future. The LIFFE white sugar future is for delivery of white beet or cane crystal sugar (any refined sugar) with delivery at ports specified by the LIFFE exchange. One LIFFE white sugar future is equal to 50 metric tons of refined sugar and trades in dollars per ton. The minimum tick size for this contract is $0.10 with a tick value of $5.00. This future trades electronically.

In terms of liquidity the NYBOT sugar #11 future is the premier sugar future. It has approximately 10 times the open interest and significantly more daily volume than the LIFFE white sugar future. In this chapter when reference is made to sugar futures, it is made with the NYBOT sugar #11 future in mind.

PRICE HISTORY AND MARKET REPORTS

The price history of sugar shows two very different fundamental periods. Figure 17.3 shows the NYBOT sugar #11 future price since 1970. Here you can see the two different periods. The first period, in the early history, shows tremendous price volatility, whereas the second period shows the price holding below 20.00 cents per pound and ranging around 10.00 cents per pound. The high sugar prices in 1974–1975 and in 1980 were the catalyst for this structural shift in the sugar markets. Prior to the mid-1980s the United States, Japan, Canada, and the European Union dominated the sugar import market. The price increases during 1974–1975 and 1980 did little to

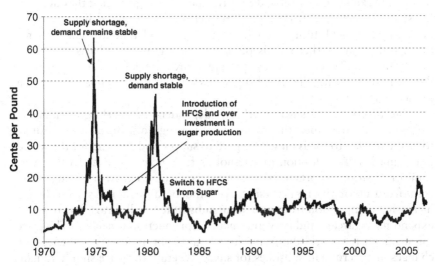

FIGURE 17.3 NYBOT World Sugar Future Price

curb demand for sugar from these countries. The major consumers of sugar in these countries were companies that used sugar to make a final product. Because these companies did not want to lose market share, they cut into their profit margin and continued to buy sugar at increasing prices, making prices rise even further. These high prices led to the development of the HFCS industry in the United States and Japan. Sugar consumption in both countries began to be replaced by HFCS. The beverage industry, one of the largest consumers of sugar, switched to HFCS in the 1980s. Because of this switch to HFCS, the United States and other developed countries became less reliant on the sugar import market as their demand for sugar declined.

The stability of the sugar market since the 1980s is due not only to the greater availability of sweetener substitutes but also to Brazil's increased role in the world export market. In addition the countries that utilize the sugar import market have changed over time. At this time the sugar import market is made up of many developing countries that will lower their consumption when prices increase. This has allowed prices to remain stable. This is different from the 1970s when the major importers were developed countries that were price inelastic because sugar was a small part of their disposable incomes.

The USDA publishes *Sugar: World Markets and Trade* biannually in May and November. This report is one of the most comprehensive available to the public and includes supply-and-demand estimates for the major sugar producing and consuming countries. One of the things to focus on in this report is Brazil's production and export expectations given that they account for such a large part of the dump market and the sugar delivered to the NYBOT sugar #11 future. It is hard to find good fundamental data for the world sugar market that is published on a consistent basis without a significant lag. There are a few private sources that publish supply-and-demand estimates for the world sugar market, but these estimates are often revised many times.

The future of the sugar market is dependent on world governments' curtailing subsidies and other sugar support programs. Brazil will continue to be the market to focus on with regard to supply and demand for the world dump market. As adoption of ethanol as fuel increases, Brazil will divert some of its sugar exports to ethanol exports. Demand growth for sugar will come from alternative markets such as ethanol because refined sugar is facing increasing competition from non-sugar substitutes. Still, Brazil has room to expand its sugarcane industry and increase production if needed. The price for sugar on the world dump market should continue to be influenced by changes in government subsidies for sugar. Overall, the price should remain steady, but production shortfalls due to weather events could lead to price spikes.

ADDITIONAL SOURCES OF INFORMATION

Other sources of fundamental information for the sugar markets can be hard to come by. Some Brazilian agencies, such as São Paulo Sugar Cane Agroindustry Union (UNICA) and the Agricultural Ministry of Brazil, publish production and stock estimates for the sugarcane industry. In addition, the International Sugar Organization (ISO) publishes studies and statistics relevant to the sugar industry.

CHAPTER 18

Cocoa

Cocoa is the fundamental ingredient in all things chocolate: milk chocolate, dark chocolate, and cocoa powder, among other things. It is the seed[a] of the cacao tree (*theobroma cacao*, literally *food of the Gods*), a tropical understory tree that grows only in wet environments near the equator. The seed pods grow directly from the trunk and branches. It originates from South America, but today it is mostly grown in Africa. Cocoa has a rich and storied history. It has been the exclusive delicacy of royalty, it has served as currency, and it has become what it is today—an everyday treat for people worldwide and an important cash crop for many developing countries.

HISTORY

The cacao tree is native to the equatorial region of the Western Hemisphere. Its documentary record dates back to the classic period of the Maya civilization of Mesoamerica (600–900 A.D.), though as a wild food source, it was almost certainly in use before then. With the rise of Aztec society chocolate became a drink reserved for the royalty. One of the names used by the Aztecs was chocolatl, which eventually became the word chocolate. The first westerner to see chocolate was Christopher Columbus, who encountered it as a form of currency used in the new world. Soon after that came Hernando Cortès and the Spanish conquest, and chocolate finally made its way to Europe in 1544. In the early 1800s Coenraad Van Houten developed an alkalizing process that made chocolate less acidic. This eventually led to the first chocolate bars in 1847. Previously, chocolate had always been taken

---

[a] *Cocoa* is also commonly used, in English, to refer to cocoa powder specifically. However, the NYBOT uses the term *cocoa* to refer to the seed of the cacao tree that will be processed into chocolate products.

as a drink. A major breakthrough in chocolate came in 1879 when Swiss chocolate manufacturer Daniel Peter thought to mix powdered milk in with chocolate, thus creating milk chocolate. In recent years scientific research has identified the possible health benefits of flavanols—antioxidants that are found in cacao beans—and manufacturers are developing methods of processing chocolate that preserve these flavanols.[1]

PROCESSING

The cacao tree is unusual in that it produces both flowers and seeds at the same time; thus, where rainfall is adequate, it can produce more than one crop during the year. The world's main crop, however, is produced from October to March. Cacao pods are harvested and opened by hand. The seeds are suspended in a pulp and they, pulp and all, are dumped into boxes to ferment. The pulp eventually dissolves away and the seeds are laid out to dry. Once dry, processing by machines begins. First the beans are separated from the shell, roasted, and ground. This produces what is called chocolate liquor (though it contains no alcohol). From this point there are two paths that can be taken. The chocolate liquor can be pressed, separating the oil (cocoa butter) from the cocoa cake. The cake becomes cocoa powder, and the butter can be used in other chocolate products. The other path is to process the chocolate liquor into chocolate; the liquor undergoes additional processing, and additional ingredients, such as milk, sugar, and cocoa butter, are added.

COCOA PRODUCTION AND CONSUMPTION

Figure 18.1 displays production and consumption of cocoa beans.[b] Consumption is not measured directly but is inferred from grindings—that is, how much cocoa bean enters processing. Both production and consumption have risen steadily during the past 25 years. Production is more volatile than consumption but much more steady than production in, say, coffee. Both production and consumption have grown by about 3 percent a year, on average, from 1980 through 2005.[2]

The five largest cocoa producers are shown in Table 18.1. The largest by a wide margin is Cote d'Ivoire (Ivory Coast) which produces just under

---

[b] The marketing year for cocoa runs from October to September.

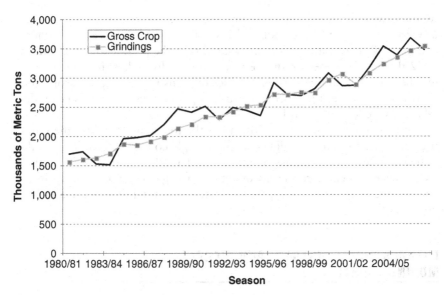

FIGURE 18.1 Cocoa Production and Grindings
Source: International Cocoa Organization

40 percent of all cocoa. Of the top five producers, four are in Africa. Of all cocoa estimated to be produced in the 2005–2006 crop year, African countries are expected to produce about 70 percent. The other continent represented in the top five is Asia with Indonesia. Notice that the native range of cocoa is not represented in the top five (though Brazil is number six). The importance of Cote d'Ivoire to the supply of cocoa makes events there important for the price of cocoa. A bad crop, perhaps due to dry

TABLE 18.1 Top 5 Cocoa Producing Countries
2006/07 (Preliminary)

Country	Tons (Thousands)
Cote d'Ivore	1300
Ghana	720
Indonesia	440
Nigeria	175
Cameroon	160

Source: International Cocoa Organization

weather, would certainly push the price of cocoa up worldwide. Also, Cote d'Ivoire has had periods of political instability. In 1999 there was a coup, and in 2000 there was violence associated with the presidential election. In 2002 there was a rebellion that left the country divided, as it is today. The number-one and number-two export destinations for cocoa are Europe and North America. Because cocoa is a luxury good, consumption is generally related to a country's wealth.

In recent years, perhaps following in the footsteps of coffee, there has been increased interest in higher-quality, single-country cocoa. This could potentially lead to a double or multi-tiered market in the future. Other recent developments are the introduction of organic cocoa and, again as with coffee, fair trade cocoa, which guarantees a minimum price to the grower.

FUTURES, PRICE HISTORY, AND MARKET-MOVING EVENTS

Cocoa trades on two major exchanges: the New York Board of Trade (NY-BOT), which was recently purchased by Intercontinental Exchange (ICE), and the Euronext-Liffe. The main difference between the contracts is that the NYBOT contract is denominated in U.S. dollars and the Euronext contract is denominated in British pounds sterling. Accounting for the currency difference, the Euronext contract typically trades at a premium because of warehouse location and the quality of the cocoa deliverable at par. It also has a moderately higher open interest. The Euronext contract is traded electronically, whereas the NYBOT contract trades electronically side-by-side with open outcry (but eventually it will all be electronic). For both exchanges, the contract size is 10 metric tons, the tick size is 1, and the value of a tick is $10 or 10 pounds. Both exchanges list contracts for March, May, July, September, and December (HKNUZ).

Cocoa does not have as many regularly released statistics that move the market as some other commodities. One such report is the quarterly grindings report released by the Chocolate Manufacturers Association, available on the NYBOT's website. The NYBOT also releases data on daily warehouse stocks.

Figure 18.2 displays the price history of the front NYBOT cocoa contract. Aside from spikes, the price of cocoa has increased only very slowly. The price of cocoa today is about the same as it was 30 years ago. The primary price spike occurred in 1977. In this year the crop from Ghana, then the world's largest producer, was small as a result of disease and neglect during previous years when prices were lower. More recently, in 2002

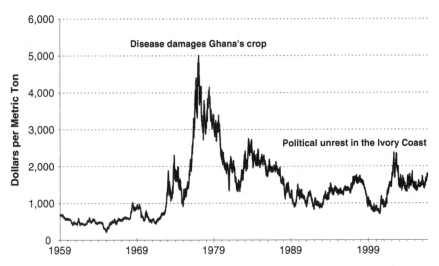

FIGURE 18.2 NYBOT Cocoa Futures Price

and 2003, the price of cocoa spiked because of the political unrest in Cote d'Ivoire.

Looking forward, as with all commodities, there will be price spikes. In cocoa they will likely be related to weather and possibly also to political unrest. Increasing world wealth and newly found health benefits bode well for demand, which should grow steadily, as it has. Supply should increase as producing countries increase acreage devoted to cocoa, but it will be limited by the fact that cocoa can be grown only in equatorial regions. Thus, the long-term outlook for price is flat to modestly increasing.

ADDITIONAL SOURCES OF INFORMATION

The best source of information on cocoa and the cocoa trade is the International Cocoa Organization (www.icco.org). That organization is the source of the main statistics on production and trade and provides useful information on cocoa in general.

CHAPTER 19

Cotton

Cotton is the soft fiber seed casing of the cotton plant that is grown world-wide in tropical and subtropical regions. The fiber is spun into thread and used to make a textile or cloth. Cotton has been in use for more than 5,000 years, with the Romans and the Persians being among the first empires to use cotton goods as a currency in world trade. Cotton spread north to Europe and eventually to the Americas, where it became the first cash crop of the colonies.

The Industrial Revolution in Europe brought about the creation of the cotton mill, which sped up the process of spinning and weaving the cotton fiber into cloth. However, the separation of the cotton fiber, or lint, from the seed was still being done by hand. This changed in 1793, when Eli Whitney patented a machine called the cotton gin. The cotton gin separated the lint from the seed, allowing each worker to produce more lint at a faster pace than ever before. Both the cotton mill and cotton gin further launched the economic power of cotton. Its economic importance in many countries around the world resulted in cotton being known as *white gold*.

Cotton is the world's most important textile. It is used in hundreds of textile products, including clothing, bed sheets, and bath towels. All parts, not just the cotton fiber, of the cotton plant are valuable. The cottonseed part of the cotton plant is an oilseed like soybeans. Cottonseed is crushed to produce its three products: cottonseed oil, cottonseed meal, and hulls. Both the cottonseed oil and cottonseed meal have uses similar to those of soybean oil and soybean meal. The cottonseed oil is used primarily for human consumption in the form of cooking oil, salad dressings, and other food products. Cottonseed meal is a protein source used for livestock feed. See Chapter 10, "Soybeans," for additional information regarding oilseeds.

PRODUCTION

Today's cotton plant was created using a combination of genetic modification and specific breeding of a variety of wild cotton species. These modifications have enabled the cotton plant to be resistant to some insects, to require less fertilizer, and to make the cotton fiber better for textile processing. There are five major types of cotton being grown around the world—American Pima, Asiatic, Egyptian, Sea Island, and Upland. The majority of the cotton grown in the United States and worldwide is Upland cotton. Each type of cotton is differentiated by its staple length and the fineness of the fiber. The staple length is the average length of the cotton fiber. American Pima, Egyptian, and Sea Island have long staple lengths, which allow them to be woven into stronger and lighter fabrics. Asiatic cotton is primarily grown in Asia and is a coarse fiber with a short staple length. Upland cotton has a staple length and fineness that falls between the two. Cotton plants require a sunny growing period with at least 160 frost-free days and an ample supply of water. Wild cotton is a perennial plant, but cultivated cotton must be planted annually.

World production of cotton is dominated by China, the United States, India, and Pakistan. These four producers account for approximately 70 percent of world production.[1] Each country may have a different crop marketing year depending on its planting and harvest schedule. The cotton marketing year for the United States extends from August through July. This means the 2006–2007 cotton marketing year is August 1, 2006 through July 31, 2007. The chart in Figure 19.1 shows the four largest producers and their percentage of world cotton production since 1990. This chart is interesting in that it shows that each country's share of world production has been relatively flat during the past 15 years. Only India has managed to increase its share of world production, and it is competing with the United States to be the second-largest producer. In the United States the loss of cotton mills to Asia along with demand for acreage from other agricultural products such as corn and soybeans has resulted in fewer cotton acres and lower production. The movement of the textile industry away from the United States to China and other Asian countries has fueled the expansion of cotton production in China. Other smaller cotton producers such as Brazil and Uzbekistan have emerged as swing cotton producers. A large amount of their excess production goes to the export market. This results in more competition and supply in the cotton export market, benefiting importers with lower prices.

CONSUMPTION AND TRADE

Once cotton is harvested it is brought to a cotton gin, where the cotton fiber is separated from the cotton seed. The cottonseed is sent to a processing facility

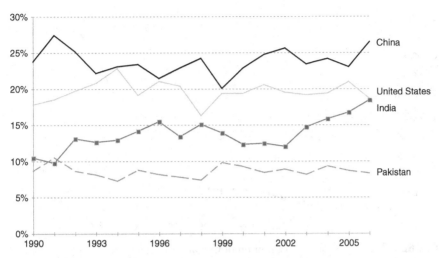

FIGURE 19.1 Percent Share of World Cotton Production
Source: Foreign Agricultural Service, USDA

where cottonseed oil and meal are made. After the cotton goes through the cotton gin, the raw fiber produced is called lint. The lint is compressed to form cotton bales. Cotton bales have an industry standard of being 55 inches tall, 28 inches wide, and 21 inches thick, with each bale weighing approximately 500 pounds. Cotton is priced in cents per pound, but it is bought and sold in bales.

These raw bales are then brought to textile mills, where they are processed into yarn or cloth. This yarn or cloth is then used to make the many consumer products that we use everyday. One bale of cotton can produce approximately 215 pairs of denim jeans or 1,256 pilowcases.[2] These are just a few of the items created using cotton fiber. Other products include diapers, socks, shirts, towels, and even U.S. currency bills. Approximately 80 percent of all cotton fiber–based products are articles of clothing.[3]

The largest consumers of cotton for textile mills are China, the United States, India, and Pakistan. These countries then re-export the finished apparel and household goods back to the United States. Figure 19.2 shows how domestic consumption of cotton in these four countries has changed since 1980. Why is there such a rapid rise in Chinese and Southeast Asian cotton consumption? One reason is the expansion of the textile industry in this region. Cotton production there is high, creating a potentially lower input cost to the textile mills. The Multifiber Agreement (MFA) encouraged the expansion of the textile industry in Asia. The MFA was a quota-based trade agreement for textiles and clothing that began in 1974 and was replaced in

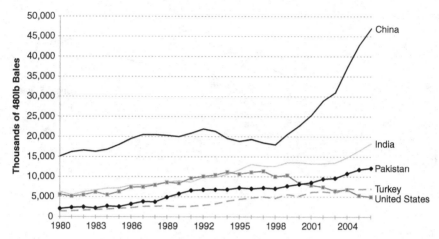

FIGURE 19.2 Domestic Consumption of Cotton
Source: Foreign Agricultural Service, USDA

1995 by the Agreement on Textiles and Clothing (ATC). The MFA's goal was to protect the domestic textile and clothing markets in the European Union and United States by limiting the amount of imports from developing countries. Yet the MFA started with imposing quotas on Japan and Hong Kong; naturally, production shifted to countries with no quotas at that time, such as South Korea and Taiwan. Eventually these new producers were also hit with quotas, but resources continued to flow to countries without restrictions, creating an industry in some countries that might not otherwise have existed. This allowed the textile and clothing industries to build up within many developing countries and specifically around Southeast Asia, where a large amount of cotton was produced.

The ATC was established in 1995 as a way to schedule elimination of the MFA quotas, which occurred on December 31, 2004. The removal of quotas has changed the geography of textile and clothing production but has not affected cotton consumption. The economics of comparative advantage favor textile and clothing production in lower-income countries. Without the MFA, production can move to the lowest-cost country. This will result in the continued decline of textile and clothing production in the United States and the European Union. Instead, these two countries export cotton to developing countries, which produce the textiles, apparel, and household goods. These goods are then re-exported to the United States and the European Union, among many other consumers.

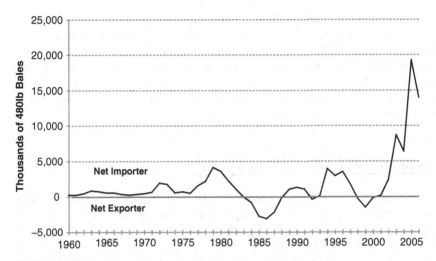

FIGURE 19.3 Chinese Cotton Trade Flow (Imports–Exports)
Source: Foreign Agricultural Service, USDA

World cotton trade has two major players—the United States and China. The United States is the single largest exporter of cotton, as its textile and clothing production has been declining but its cotton production has been increasing. China is the largest importer of cotton as its textile production has had tremendous growth. Figure 19.3 shows China's trade flow of cotton bales. For a long time China fluctuated between being a net importer and a net exporter. China's emergence as the world's largest net importer of cotton coincides with the liberalization of the global textile trade. In 2005 with the end of the MFA agreement, China began importing more cotton than ever before.

FUTURES

In terms of both volume and open interest, the cotton futures on the New York Board of Trade (NYBOT) are the most liquid in the world. This future trades side-by-side electronically and in the NYBOT pit, but over time it will move to an all-electronic market. This is because the Intercontinental Exchange (ICE) purchased the NYBOT in 2006 and ICE uses an electronic platform for its trading. The NYBOT cotton futures are priced in cents per pound with a contract size of 50,000 lbs (approximately 100 bales). The minimum fluctuation, or tick size, for the contract is .01 cents per pound when the price is under 95 cents per pound. When the price is over 95 cents per pound the tick size changes to .05 cents per pound. The value of one tick (.01 cents per pound) is $5.00. This means that for every hundredth of a cent move in the price of the cotton future, the value of the contract changes by $5.00. The NYBOT cotton futures are deliverable to five locations in the southern United States and must be quality Strict Low Middling Upland cotton (SLM). SLM cotton is the average Upland cotton in terms of color and other cotton qualities. Cotton futures also trade on the Zhengzhou Commodity Exchange (ZCE) in China.

PRICE HISTORY AND MARKET REPORTS

Figure 19.4 shows the price history for the prompt month NYBOT cotton future since 1980. There does not appear to be an apparent long-term trend in price over this time frame. The chart clearly shows a price spike above $1.00 that occurred in 1995. This price spike was the result of extremely strong demand for U.S. cotton in the export market during the 1994–1995 crop marketing year. This extra demand was primarily from China, which was a large net importer that year (as can be seen in Figure 19.3). Farmers in the United States reacted to this price increase by planting more cotton acreage for the next year. That, combined with lower export demand during the next few years, resulted in prices declining once the 1995–1996 marketing year harvest arrived. Export demand did not recover to 1994–1995 levels until 2001–2002, but it has continued to grow each year as textile

FIGURE 19.4 NYBOT Cotton Futures Price

production and demand for cotton has shifted to regions outside of the United States. Prices declined sharply in the 1985–1986 marketing year as the United States had extremely low exports that year due to competition from China in the cotton trade market. Price changes in the U.S. cotton market seem to be largely driven by export demand. The fluctuation on the demand side stems from the results of China's cotton harvest. During 1984–1985 China produced 35 percent more cotton than in the year before.[4] Because this extra cotton was not all needed domestically, China turned to the export market and competed with the United States for export share. This resulted in low exports for the United States, because China did not need any additional cotton that year and there was more competition in the trade market. If China has low production compared with domestic demand, it will import cotton from the United States, increasing prices for the NYBOT cotton future. This is why it is important to monitor cotton production in China to gauge demand for U.S. cotton. On the supply side in the United States, the total number of acres harvested for cotton has not changed dramatically, averaging approximately 13 million acres harvested during the past 10 years, with little change from one year to the next.[5]

Data on U.S., Chinese, and world supply and demand statistics are reported monthly by the U.S. Department of Agriculture (USDA) in the *World Agricultural Supply and Demand Estimates* (WASDE). The WASDE has a section that breaks down the United States cotton supply and use and includes important data such as acreage planted, yield, and the USDA's estimate for exports. Another section of the WASDE focuses on world cotton supply and use, with emphasis on countries that are major exporters and importers. The U.S. Export Sales report from the Foreign Agricultural Service (FAS) division of the USDA is released weekly and includes data regarding the previous week's exports for cotton and other agricultural commodities. With the Export Sales report you can keep track of each week's net sales, exports to China, and the accumulated sales for the current marketing year. Since the export market for United States cotton constitutes a large part of usage, the pace of these exports over the year will play an important role in future price action.

Cotton's future remains mired between the competition for acreage among agricultural products and demand for textile products. As population and global wealth increase, demand for clothing, household goods, and other textile products will increase. This demand increase will come at a time of lower available acreage for cotton, as it faces competition globally from food crops such as corn, soybeans and other oilseeds, and wheat. Still, cotton production will be dependent on the weather, and price spikes will occur. Overall cotton prices should remain steady to higher going forward in order to *buy* acreage each year as needed for production.

ADDITIONAL SOURCES OF INFORMATION

Additional information regarding the cotton market can be found at the USDA division Economic Research Service briefing room page dedicated to cotton. Another great source for information on the United States cotton market is the National Cotton Council of America (www.cotton.org). Its website has economic data on and analysis of cotton supply, demand, and prices.

Seven

How to Invest

CHAPTER 20

Some Building Blocks of a Commodity Futures Trading System

In this section we explore how one might start bringing together important information to construct a trading system. The key steps in constructing a trading system are (1) determining what the important information is, (2) constructing and testing a system or model to use the information, and (3) developing appropriate risk control. The purpose of this section is not to present a full-blown system, but instead to show how one might go about constructing such a system.

The main reason one would construct a trading system, of course, is to make money. But there are other reasons to develop methods for forecasting the direction a price is likely to go. An equity analyst who analyzes a commodity-producing company may find it useful to have a forecast, or at least a sense, of the direction in which the price of the underlying commodity is likely to go. Both producers and consumers of a commodity will have an obvious interest in future price movements. Fund managers and investors who are considering investing in passive commodity indexes may wish to look at some indicators to get a sense as to whether commodity future investments will offer a positive or negative return. So, even though this section presents the development of a simple trading system, its methods and tools have broader applications.

It is important to emphasize that it may not be possible to construct a trading system. Though it may be possible to predict returns, there is no reason why it must be. And even if it is possible, competition among investors may render a system that has been profitable in the past unprofitable in the present. In addition, trading futures entails significant risk, and individual investors will generally not be successful.

The presentation here deals with directional forecasting. For example, will a crude oil future go up or down? Another popular approach to commodity future trading among professionals is spread trading. For example, one could take a view on the price differential between two different commodities or between two futures contracts on the same commodity that expire at different times.[a] People are often led to believe that spreads are less risky than outright positions because they have a built-in hedge against directional price movements. However, this is not necessarily true in practice. The reason is that to achieve a reasonable level of profitability in spreads often requires that very large positions be taken. This larger position size will often cancel out any inherent safety in a spread trade.

The first part of what follows considers some factors that are potentially useful in forecasting commodity futures returns. The first, the shape of the curve, is very important to understand and should always be given serious consideration. Following this is a discussion of trend following, which, next to passive index investing, is probably the most common commodity trading strategy. After that come anchor variables. Subsequent to the discussion of potential factors, a sample trading system is constructed, followed by a discussion of risk control.

THE FUTURES CURVE

Future Curve Basics

What should be the relation between future prices and spot prices? Between different futures contracts for the same commodity? These questions are important because commodity investors will generally invest in futures as opposed to the physical commodity. Also, as time passes, a future contract may *creep* along the curve in a way that substantially affects investment returns.[b] In this section, we will explore the determinants of the shape of the futures curve and how that shape may affect investment returns.

A very simple explanation is that futures prices reflect what investors expect the price of a commodity to be in the future. This is a reasonable conjecture, but it immediately runs into difficulty in commodities where arbitrage can be applied. In what follows, the expectations model is subsumed by Keynes's theory of normal backwardation.

A basic tenet of financial theory is that if there exists an enforceable arbitrage between two financial instruments, the arbitrage relation—and nothing else—will determine the relative price of the two instruments. To

---

[a] These are called calendar spreads.
[b] This is also referred to as the *roll yield*.

illustrate this principle, consider a futures contract on a ticket to a Philadelphia Eagles game one month from today. Suppose that the cost of the ticket today is $50. Also suppose that the interest rate is 5 percent. It doesn't cost anything to store the ticket (it's small and thin), and tickets can be sold short. What should the price of the future be? First consider the problem from a buyer's perspective. She can buy the ticket today, or she can buy the future. When a future contract is bought, no money changes hands today, it is an agreement on a price today for a transaction at a later date. Either way, she'll have the ticket one month from today. If she buys the ticket today, she forgoes the interest she would have earned had she left the money in the bank. This interest is

$$.05 \times (1/12) \times \$50 = .21$$

Therefore, she will be indifferent between buying the ticket today for $50 or buying a future contract at a price of $50.21. In both cases the total cost to her (including forgone interest) one month from today is $50.21.

Now consider the problem from a seller's perspective. If he sells the ticket today, he gets the $50. He can invest this money at 5 percent, and over the next month he will earn .21, putting his total at the end of the month at $50.21. He would be indifferent between selling the ticket today or selling a future contract for a price of $50.21. In both cases his financial position (including earned interest) one month from today will be $50.21.

So will the price be $50.21? All we've said at this point is that both the buyer and seller are indifferent to this price, which is a fairly weak statement. After all, the buyer would be very happy to see a futures price of $45. And who's to say the futures price wouldn't be $55? The buyer wouldn't like it, but so what? Here is where arbitrage comes in. Suppose the price of the future was $55. One could sell the future while simultaneously borrowing $50 and buying the ticket. At the end of one month, the seller would receive $55, deliver the ticket, and repay the loan. This would make his financial outcome:

$$\$55.00 - \$50.00 \times (1 + .05/12) = \$4.79$$

He would have earned a profit of $4.79.

Now suppose the futures price was $45. One could buy the future while simultaneously selling short the ticket for $50 and investing the proceeds. (Note that here is where we use the assumption that short sales are permissible.) At the end of one month he would receive the ticket, pay $45 (the future price), and have the $50 plus interest. This would make his financial outcome:

$$\$50 \times (1 + .05/12) - 45 = \$5.20$$

In words, he would have earned a profit of $5.20.

In fact, we can show that any future price other than $50.21 will leave an arbitrage opportunity. Since the profit motive is very powerful, someone will always be willing to exploit that opportunity, and the future price will be driven to $50.21.

It is interesting to ask what the price of the future would be today if we expected the price of the ticket to change? For example, suppose we thought the price of the ticket would probably go up tomorrow. The answer is that nothing would change; the price of the future would still be $50.21. Every step of the foregoing argument would still hold even if the price of the ticket were expected to change. This is what makes arbitrage so powerful.

Periodic Supply and Excess Stocks   Arbitrage relations tend to hold very well in financial markets, where the instruments are not consumed and short selling is easy. In commodity markets the arbitrage theory is an ideal that never holds exactly and is often off by a lot. If the structure of the market is such that an arbitrage between the spot commodity and the future can be enforced, then an arbitrage pricing relation should work well. If the structure of a market makes arbitrage difficult, then one must look to other explanations to understand the spot–future relation and the shape of the futures curve.

This arbitrage theory works best in commodity markets where new supply is only periodic and supply exists in excess of immediate consumption needs. Consider the corn market, for example. The United States is a major supplier of the world corn market. In the United States corn is planted in the spring and harvested in the fall. Once this crop is harvested there is no more supply until the following fall. On November 11, 2006, the front contract was the December 2006 contract and the second contract was the March 2007 contract. The settlement price of the December contract on this day was 342.50 (in units of cents per bushel). If the theory of arbitrage held, what would be the price of the March contract?

Price of December 2007	342.50
Rate of interest	5.37%
Storage cost	.15 cents/day
Days between December and March first notice dates	90

On November 11, the December contract was close to its first notice day, so we will assume that this is a good proxy for the spot price.[c] The cost

---

[c] There are actually many different spot corn prices in the United States, depending on location, and the delivery of corn in satisfaction of the contract can be to more than one location.

of carry to March is:

$$(.15 + 342.50 \times .0537/360) \times 90 = 18.1 \text{ cents}$$

So we might guess that the price of the March 2007 contract would be:

$$342.50 + 18.10 = 360.60$$

It turns out that the actual price of the March contract on this day was 358.50, fairly close. Another way to think about it is that the March contract was priced at 88.4 percent of full carry.

$$(358.50 - 342.50)/18.10 = .884$$

Figure 20.1 displays this measure of full carry beginning in 1993. When July is the front contract and December the second,[d] the percentage of full carry is set to 50 percent, roughly the average for the other periods. The reason for this is that corn is harvested in the fall, so the supply of corn is not fixed between July and December. What can we see from the graph in Figure 20.1? Notice that the percent full carry measure fluctuates, but it is almost always below 100 percent. Why is this? One reason is that it is very difficult or even impossible to go short the actual physical corn. In the preceding example, an arbitrageur would like to buy the March contract and sell short the physical corn. An additional complication is that even if the arbitrageur could short the corn, he would not receive the storage costs (though he would have to pay them if he went long the physical corn).

A second reason is the mysterious concept of convenience yield (Kaldor 1939). Convenience yield refers to the notion that there can be value to having a commodity on hand for immediate use, which a forward buyer does not receive. For example, a farmer who raises hogs must keep a minimum amount of corn feed on hand or else the pigs will starve to death. They can only be fed corn, not corn futures. The theory of convenience yield is not well developed, and often an expositor will simply refer to the residual in a model as the convenience yield with little attempt to explain the economic processes at work. In general, in that there is a convenience yield, it is generally assumed to be bigger when supplies are low. As can be seen in Figure 20.1, in the spring and summer of 1996 the percentage full carry measure became very negative (the price of nearby corn was much higher

---

[d] The September corn contract is not generally considered an active contract and is therefore skipped.

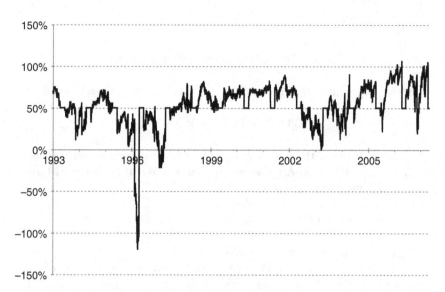

FIGURE 20.1   Percent Full Carry in Corn Market

than corn for more distant delivery). Why was this? 1995 was a year of drought in the corn-growing regions,[e] and fewer than normal acres were planted. Stocks grew tight, and corn users bid up the price of existing stocks.

Continual Supply and No Excess Stocks   Crude oil is a market that is very different from corn in that it tends not to be stored above ground in abundance (leaving it in the ground is much cheaper), and what has been produced tends to be consumed relatively quickly, leaving little in the way of excess stocks. At any point in time crude oil inventories in the United States may be about 20 or 25 days worth of consumption, whereas immediately after the corn harvest there is enough corn inventory to supply the United States for the entire upcoming year, leaving plenty to export to other countries. If would-be arbitrageurs cannot easily get hold of inventory and cannot cheaply store it if they could, then an arbitrage pricing relation is not likely to determine the shape of the futures curve.

Two other theories often invoked to help understand the shape of the futures curve are Keynes's theory of normal backwardation (Keynes 1930),

----

[e] The yield of the crop harvested in 1994 (the 1994–1995 marketing year) was 139 bushels per acre, while the yield of the crop harvested in 1995 (the 1995–1996 marketing year) was 114 bushels per acre.

and Hotelling's theory of exhaustible resources (Hotelling 1931). Keynes's notion of normal backwardation is that producers of a commodity will want to lock in the price at which they can sell their product by going short futures contracts. However, in order to entice speculators to buy futures contracts, the producers must offer to sell at prices that are lower than the current prices, or, if prices are expected to change, lower than future expected prices. Speculators are effectively getting paid to provide insurance and make the difference between the current (or expected) price and the price that was paid for the future contract. This argument also works in reverse if it is the buyers of a commodity who wish to lock in the price. In this case futures prices would exceed spot prices. This situation is called contango. So, according to this line of reasoning, if the marginal hedger is a producer, then the market should be in a state of normal backwardation, and if the marginal hedger is a consumer, then the market should be in a state of contango.

The theory of Hotelling is not strictly about the shape of the futures curve but more generally about how the price of a nonrenewable resource should evolve over time. Suppose the production of a finite resource, perhaps oil or a base metal, was controlled by producers and the interest rate was r. The producer has the choice to produce now or wait and produce later. If he produces now, he will be able to earn a return of r on the selling price. What the producer should do depends on what he thinks the price of the resource will be in the future. If he thinks the price of the resource will rise at a rate less than r, he should sell everything he can right now so that he can invest the proceeds and earn r. If he thinks the resource will increase at a rate greater than r, he should withhold supplies from the market and earn a return higher than r. Because all producers act in the same way, the price of the resource must increase at the rate r. If it increases less than r, producers will sell all they can today, driving down the price. If it increases by more than r, sellers will withhold supplies, driving up the price today. Transferring this logic to the futures curve, the futures prices should increase across expirations at a rate r.

Do any of these theories fit the data? Figure 20.2 displays the percentage spread between the first and second monthly contracts:

$$(\text{contract } 1 - \text{contract } 2)/\text{contract } 1$$

The spread has fluctuated, but it has averaged 0.5 percent and has been positive 57.1 percent of the time. Clearly the simple explanation offered by the theory of Hotelling does not explain this pattern. Normal backwardation also cannot be the only explanation, inasmuch as the distant contract is priced higher than the nearby contract more than 40 percent of the time.

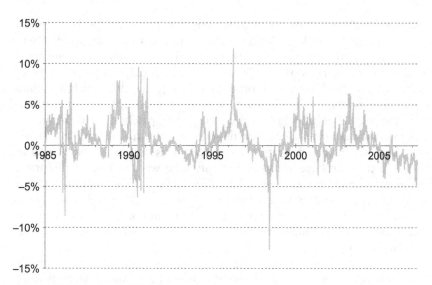

FIGURE 20.2   Crude Oil Percentage Spread

It is also interesting to note that since the beginning of 2005 the crude oil curve has mainly been in a state of contango (the distant future trading at a higher price than the nearby future). From January 2005 through April 2007, the average one-month spread has been −1.6 percent. If the spot price of crude and the shape of the curve had not changed, an investor who was long the oil futures contracts and rolled the position monthly would have lost approximately 18 percent annually!

With corn, we saw that nearby futures prices can be higher than distant futures prices when supplies are tight. This is consistent with the notion of convenience yield. In the case of crude oil, the correlation between the percentage spread and the year-on-year change in inventories is −71 percent. When oil inventories are high compared with the previous year, nearby prices are lower and vice versa.[f] Thus, as with corn, available stocks would seem to be at least one of the important determinants for the shape of the futures curve.

Another explanation related to normal backwardation is hedging pressure. In the normal backwardation story, it is the producers who wish to

---

[f] This is for the period January 1991 through November 2006. Oil prices (for the spread) are month end. The oil inventory data is the last release prior to month end. Oil inventories are for the United States and are from the U.S. Department of Energy. The change in inventories is crude oil inventories—the five-week weekly average centered on one year ago, divided by the five week average.

lock in their selling price, which pushes the price of distant futures down relative to nearby prices. Of course, there is no reason why it could not go in the other direction with users of the commodity wanting to lock in their purchase price. Perhaps hog farmers wish to lock in the price at which they can provide corn feed to their hogs, or homeowners in the northeastern United States wish to lock in what they will be paying for heating oil during the winter. If hedging by buyers dominates, we might expect the curve to be in a state of contango. The substantial increase in oil prices in the first few years of the twenty-first century, and the supply disruptions caused by hurricane Katrina, may have convinced buyers to hedge their oil purchases and convinced oil producers that hedging was less necessary. This could potentially explain the shift to contango that the oil futures price curve exhibited in 2005 and 2006.

A final issue that will be considered here is seasonality. For some commodities, the amount of available stocks or the amount demanded naturally changes across the year. Gasoline is in higher demand in the summer, when people drive more, whereas heating oil is in higher demand in the winter. These supply-and-demand fluctuations can cause price patterns over the course of the year, which are reflected in futures prices. Consider natural gas. Figure 20.3 displays the prices of the front 14 natural gas contracts on November 27, 2006: January 2007 through February 2008. There is an

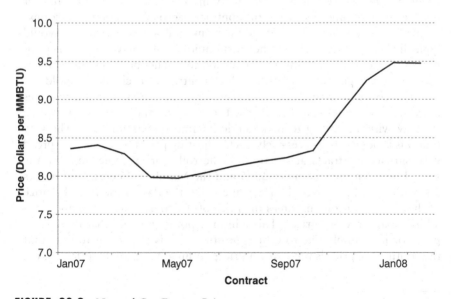

FIGURE 20.3 Natural Gas Futures Prices

obvious seasonal pattern present: Prices are high in the winter, during the heating season, and lowest in the spring and summer. When accounting for the effect the shape of the curve has on returns, it is important to know what the seasonal price pattern is so it can be adjusted for.

The Futures Curve and Investment Returns

This section focuses on the effect the shape of the futures curve can have on investments in commodity futures. The previous section showed that several explanations can be called on to help understand the shape of the futures curve. One way to use this information from an investment perspective would be to hypothesize that one theory is correct for one or more commodity markets and invest based on that theory. For example, one could start from the position that Keynes's theory of normal backwardation is the best explanation and accordingly go long a diversified basket of commodities, hoping to earn a positive return from the future price converging upward to the spot price. If Keynes's theory of normal backwardation were the best explanation for the shape of the futures curve, then it could justify the passive, long-only approach that commodity indexes provide.

In this section we will start more simply. We will look at a few commodities and try to understand how the typical shape of the futures curve affected the return of a buy-and-hold investment. Given that future contracts expire, a buy-and-hold investment will actually involve rolling a position further out the curve as time passes and the contract approaches expiration. For example, if an investor wishes to hold the front natural gas contract (as would typically be the case, since it is the most liquid), he will have to roll the position every month. A corn investor may have to roll her position four or more times a year, depending on exactly which contracts she chooses to hold.

It is convenient to create a continuous *price* series that incorporates the rolls. This series can then be used to compute the profits of a trading strategy without having to make periodic adjustments for rolls. The way that this is done is by successively back-adjusting prices based on the spread between two contracts at the time of the roll. For example, suppose the spread between the December 2005 and the March 2006 corn contracts is 14 (with the March over the December). On the day of the roll, the price of the March contract becomes the price of the continuous series and 14 is added to all previous prices. This will incorporate the fact that there is no profit or loss simply due to rolling positions.[g] It is important to note that the continuous price is not really a price; nothing was actually priced at the

---

[g] One could incorporate transaction costs.

continuous price at a point in history, it is simply a construct to allow for the easier computation of investment returns. A long investor can measure his return in points by simply comparing the current price with the continuous price at his time of purchase.

As was shown previously, corn is generally a carry market. That is, most of the time the price of a distant contract is higher than the spot price, reflecting the cost of carrying the physical corn. This implies that if the spot remains unchanged, a long position in corn will lose money. The futures price will converge downward to the spot price as time passes. It is said to have negative creep or a negative roll yield. Figure 20.4 displays the continuous corn price and the actual nearby future corn price from January 1993 through the beginning of April 2007. The actual corn price begins at 215.75 and ends at 366. The continuous corn price also ends at 366, by construction, but begins at 519. Thus, while the price of corn went up over time, the return from being long corn futures was significantly negative. This is because the long investor must pay the carry charge.

This illustrates a more general rule-of-thumb: Commodities that are grown (i.e. crops) will have futures curves that tend to be in a state of contango. Professionals in the grain markets, for example, simply use the term *normal market* to refer to the state in which the future price increased as the expiration date did. These types of commodities tend to fit the periodic-supply-excess-stock model discussed previously. As such,

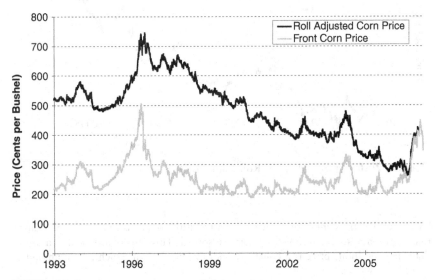

FIGURE 20.4   Front Corn versus Roll-Adjusted Corn

buy-and-hold positions will tend to have a negative return built in and the spot price will have to rise that much more to overcome this.

Now consider NYMEX crude oil. As discussed previously, this market has been backwardated about 57 percent of the time. That is, nearby future prices have generally been above distant future prices. How has this affected investment returns in this market? Figure 20.5 displays the actual price of the front future contract and the continuous price of the front future contract.[h] The continuous contract appreciates more than the actual price, showing that a strategy of buying the front contract and rolling it every month beat the return of the spot price. This is because, on average, when an investor rolled he would be buying a cheaper contract than the one that was expiring. Note, however, that since the end of 2000 the strategy of buying the front contract and rolling has returned less than the actual price. This is because for most of the period since 2000 the market has been in a state of contango. If periods of contango were to occur more frequently in the oil market that would have important implications for commodity

FIGURE 20.5   Front Oil versus Roll-Adjusted Oil

---

[h] The fact that the continuous price is negative at the outset is immaterial as it just reflects the repeated addition of a negative spread. This also reinforces the notion that the continuous price is a construct and not the price at which the commodity ever traded hands.

index investing, because oil is an important component of most commodity indexes. An experiment with the S&P GSCI Index in Chapter 21, "The Rise of the Indexes," highlights this further.

The main point of this section is that investors do not directly buy commodities, they buy commodity futures. These futures positions must be rolled as they expire. Because of this, the shape of the curve can have a significant effect on returns. In general, returns in markets that are backwardated will be increased and returns in markets that are in a state of contango will be decreased.

TREND FOLLOWING

Trend following is a simple strategy based on the simple conjecture that if the price of something has been going up, it will continue to go up, and if the price of something has been going down, it will continue to go down. Trend following does not have a strong basis in theory, but the perception is that it has worked well enough historically to be viable. This strategy has generally been practiced by the class of managers known as commodity trading advisors (CTAs).[i] In this section we explore the results of a simple trend-following strategy applied across a wide range of commodity futures.

One simple trend-following strategy is a moving average strategy. The rule is: Whenever the price is above its n-day moving average, the strategy is long, and whenever the price is below its n-day moving average, the strategy is short. It is convenient to work with the continuous price so that the profit for a trade is simply the price at which a trade was closed minus the price at which the trade was opened (multiplied by negative one for a short position). All intervening rolls would have already been accounted for in the continuous adjustment process.[j] This strategy will do well when the price is trending. It will do poorly when the market is choppy.

To explore the potential of this strategy a simple 100-day moving average strategy is run on a wide selection of commodities. Reasonable slippage and commission are assumed for each commodity, based on its own individual characteristics. The starting date for each contract is either January 1, 1984 or the first available date for the commodity. The ending date is early

---

[i] *Commodity* in this use is misleading. CTAs are identified by whether they trade mainly futures, not by whether they trade physical commodities such as corn.
[j] Though the transaction cost involved in rolling would not have been.

April 2007. The returns are computed in terms of continuous price points and are displayed normalized by standard deviation to allow for comparison across contracts.[k]

Table 20.1 displays the results, which are very weak. The average monthly Sharpe ratio across all contracts is almost exactly zero. The best performers are zinc and nickel with monthly Sharpes of 0.12, and the worst performer is silver with a monthly Sharpe of –0.18. Most commodities produce a Sharpe ratio fairly close to zero. No class of commodities stands out as being positive, and often within related commodities some are positive and some are negative.

It is true that all we have done here is to pick a simple strategy and show how poorly that one does. It has not been shown that all trend-following strategies do not work. There are many tools that trend followers can use, and some may form the basis for a successful investment strategy. It is also possible that trend following works on some commodities and not others. Diversified trend followers do weight asset classes differently, for instance. For example, they invest much more in fixed-income and currencies than in equities. One must be very careful in making such an intellectual leap, however, as it could easily be fallacious and simply lead to data mining. In this example, 10 of the 23 commodities yield positive profits. Without a clear reason, it would be nonsensical to simply throw away the negative commodities and put a portfolio together of the positive commodities. A final caveat is that results are often sensitive to the time period. For example, in zinc almost all of the returns are in 2006 during the big run-up in industrial metal prices.[l] Investors' patience is generally less than saint-like, and one good year every 20 is a weak foundation on which to base one's prosperity.

It is worth noting that the trend following discussed here and the curve effects discussed previously are potentially related. As was shown, if a market is generally backwardated, the continuous price will typically have an upward trend as the future price continually converges up to the spot price. Since the continuous price tends to be in an upward trend, a trend-following system will usually be long. Profits generated by trend following may just be due to a tendency to be long in a backwardated market.

---

[k] This can be thought of as the Sharpe ratio. An actual trend following investment strategy would involve posting capital, which would earn interest. This interest would then simply be subtracted when computing the Sharpe ratio.

[l] The results for zinc and the other LME contracts are based on a constant maturity three-month forward price. Thus, strictly, they are only indicative of the results of a trading strategy.

TABLE 20.1 Trend Following

Commodity	Monthly Sharpe Ratio	Number of Months
NYMEX Crude	0.05	280
NYMEX Unleaded	−0.01	263
NYMEX Heating Oil	−0.03	280
Natural Gas	0.01	205
Canola	−0.05	206
Wheat (CBOT)	−0.07	280
Corn	0.06	280
Soybeans	−0.02	280
Soymeal	−0.02	280
Bean Oil	0.03	280
Palm Oil (Kuala)	0.12	134
Cotton	0.08	280
Cocoa	−0.14	280
Coffee	−0.05	280
Sugar (New York)	0.04	280
Lean Hogs	0.00	280
Live Cattle	−0.05	280
Copper (COMEX)	0.04	280
Gold	−0.10	280
Silver	−0.18	280
Aluminum (LME)	−0.01	280
Zinc (LME)	0.13	280
Nickel	0.13	280
Average	−0.002	

Notes: Start date is 1/1/84 or the earliest the contract is available and runs through early April 2007. The Sharpe ratio is the average monthly return in continuous price terms divided by the average monthly standard deviation. Reasonable slippage and commission has been assumed for each contract. The LME contracts (aluminum, zinc, and nickel) are three-month forwards, not futures. For these, the results are not realized returns but merely indicative of the pattern of the price series. Gasoline ends in November 2006 because of the switch to RBOB.

Even though trend following looks weak as a standalone strategy it may be helpful in the context of a richer strategy. Controlling for other variables, a trend following variable may be helpful. This will be explored further subsequently. To sum up, trend following: It has both its adherents and its detractors, but many find it a useful tool and there is a whole industry built up around it. One must be very careful to approach trend-following strategies very rigorously and always be on guard for data mining.

ANCHORS

We will define an anchor as a number, constructed or otherwise, to which the price of something else is logically attracted to. It is a weaker concept than arbitrage. It is meant to capture the notion that there can be strong economic reasons why the price of something should be anchored to something else. To illustrate, consider the price of a stock and the per-share discounted value of all future cash flows accruing to equity holders. Assuming that a reasonable discount rate is chosen, the price of a share should tend to gravitate to the value of the discounted cash flows. They may never exactly match, but they will not differ by an order of magnitude. The share price may differ from the discounted cash flow for a long time, but not indefinitely. Another example is purchasing power parity (PPP) in currencies. The notion is that there is an exchange rate that equalizes the cost of goods in two different countries. The nominal exchange rate may differ from the PPP exchange rate for long periods of time, perhaps years, but it should converge back to it over time. The PPP exchange rate should serve as an anchor for the nominal exchange rate.

Anchor variables are very comforting to have in a model because they provide a reality check that other variables do not. For example, suppose one was running a simple moving average trend following system. Suppose that the price of aluminum was $2,800 a metric ton, which was above its moving average, thus yielding a buy signal. If the price went to $28,000, the signal would still be a buy and, indeed, if it went to $280,000 it would still be a buy. In a simple trend-following system, there is no sense of fundamental value. The same issue arises in curve variables since parallel shifts in the curve do not affect how any particular future is creeping down the curve. Of course, there is no guarantee anchors will exist for commodities of interest or that conjectured anchors will work in an investment model.

Where might we look for anchor variables in the commodity markets? One place might be the cost of inputs. It takes known quantities of corn and soymeal to bring a hog to maturity. It is reasonable to postulate that the price of hogs should have some relation to the cost of this corn and soymeal. Similarly, the price of outputs may provide a reasonable anchor. Another place to look is substitutes. If consumers of commodity A can also use commodity B for the same purposes, and vice versa, then A and B are said to be substitutes. For example, consider natural gas and fuel oil. Both are fossil fuels. Natural gas is pumped from the ground in the form in which it is used, and fuel oil is a heavy residual left after the lighter products have

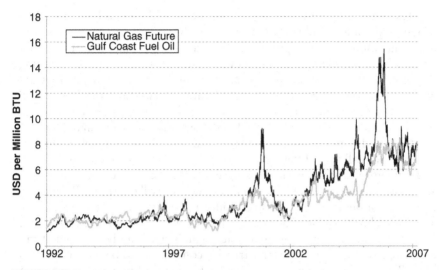

FIGURE 20.6   Natural Gas versus Fuel Oil

been taken out during the crude oil refining process. Many industrial users can choose to use either natural gas or fuel oil.[m] If natural gas becomes expensive, those who can will switch to fuel oil. So it is reasonable to hypothesize that if natural gas moves far away from the price of fuel oil (stated in BTU equivalents), there will be a tendency for it to move back. Figure 20.6 displays the price of natural gas and fuel oil on a BTU equivalent basis. The relation is clearly not perfect, but the prices do generally move together. Of particular interest to those constructing investment models is that when natural gas prices have spiked up relative to fuel oil they have subsequently come back down.

BUILDING A SIMPLE TRADING SYSTEM

In this section we combine some of the previously discussed topics to construct a simple trading system. This is meant to be illustrative of one approach to putting together a trading system, and it is in no way meant to suggest that this is the only way, or the best way, or even that the system constructed here will work in the future.

---

[m]See the EIA website. www.eia.doe.gov/emeu/consumptionbriefs/mecs/fueloil/mecs_fueloil_use.html#fuelswitch

There are many different approaches one could take to build a trading system that combine more than one variable. One very good approach is to use a regression. Simply regress the commodity's returns on the variables that you think might have forecasting power. If the fit is reasonable, the resulting model might provide the basis for an investment strategy. Regressions are often good choices when there is lots of data available and the data is well behaved. (Keep in mind, of course, that there is no guarantee that anything will work and that what has worked in the past may not work in the future.)

Commodity prices are very volatile and often have relatively short histories, so we will try a different approach. We will build a very simple index and implement a strategy that is long when the index is above a threshold and short when the index is below a threshold. We will use the CME lean hog contract[n] for our commodity and consider a trend variable, a curve variable, and an anchor variable. The trend variable will be the average of the 60-, 80-, 100-, and 120-day moving average signals. Each individual signal can either be a +1 or a −1. A positive trend is conjectured to be bullish for lean hogs. The curve variable is the deseasonalized spread between a collection of USDA cash prices and the price of the lean hog contract. A spot price that is higher than the future price is considered bullish (i.e., when the curve is backwardated). The anchor variable is the de-meaned gross feeding margin, the difference between the price of the hog and the price of the corn and soybean feed input prices. It is conjectured that it is bearish for hogs when the price of hogs is high relative to the price of feed and vice versa.

In order to construct an index the variables must be made quantitatively comparable to one another. The spread between spot and futures prices is divided by its standard deviation. The gross feeding margin is de-meaned and also divided by its standard deviation. These two variables are capped at +3 and −3 to prevent either from having extreme influence. The trend variable by construction is between −1 and 1, so no adjustment is needed. Thus the index takes the form:

$$\text{Index} = \text{trend} + \text{creep}/\sigma(\text{creep}) + \text{GFM}/\sigma(\text{GFM})$$

A trading rule also must be constructed: When do you buy? When do you sell? We will implement a simple rule that is long hogs when the index is greater than or equal to 0.25, flat when the index is between 0.25 and −0.25, and short when the index is less than −0.25. Returns are computed in terms of percent on the lean hog contract's face value,[o] and a transaction

---

[n] At the end of 1996 this was switched from a live hog contract to the current lean hog contract. Presumably, the hogs did not have a say in the switch.
[o] More precisely, daily log returns are computed based on the price of the lean hog future's face value. No interest is added to the return.

TABLE 20.2   Lean Hog Trading System Performance

Average	1.3%
Standard Deviation	6.6%
Median	1.0%
Sharpe	19.9%
Best Month	27.4%
Worst Month	−30.1%
Max Drawdown	−41.1%
Number of Months	204

cost of 12 basis points is charged for every trade (not including rolls). The results are displayed in Table 20.2 and the cumulative returns are displayed in Figure 20.7. With an average monthly return of about 1.3 percent and a monthly Sharpe ratio of 0.20 the results are promising and this strategy merits further exploration.

The major trap that trading strategy researchers fall into is *data mining* (or *curve fitting*). This occurs when a researcher searches over model forms and explanatory variables until a trading strategy is found that looks good (usually, really good) even though there is no true relation between the model and the return series. There are no statistical tests that can provide

FIGURE 20.7   Cumulative Profits

one with certainty as to whether one is data mining or not. The best test is generally to test a trading strategy over a time period or set of data other than what was used to construct the model. However, even here there are concerns; people do not live in vacuums, and they often construct models that they have a sense have worked historically. The best protection against data mining is intellectual honesty. One should not consider explanatory factors for which one cannot give a solid explanation as to why they should affect returns.

RISK CONTROL

In the late summer of 2005, as a result of hurricane Katrina, several well-known hedge funds suffered large losses in the natural gas market.[1] One year later, the hedge fund MotherRock closed as a result of losses in natural gas.[2] One month later, the hedge fund Amaranth went out of business because of losses in natural gas.[3] In April 2007 Bank of Montreal announced that it had lost up to $400 million trading, you guessed it, natural gas.[4] Clearly, trading commodities entails risks.

With investing, risk cannot be avoided. The purpose of risk control is to have tools that allow one to assess with some degree of confidence (1) how much will be lost if something really bad happens and (2) how likely it is that something really bad will happen. There is never certainty. All the most sophisticated risk-control models reduce to educated guesses.

Risk control is a wide-ranging and important subject. However, space considerations necessitate that only a brief consideration be given here. In particular, we will look at maximum drawdowns and value-at-risk. The reader is encouraged to seek out additional sources on the subject.[5]

A maximum drawdown is the maximum peak-to-trough decline suffered by an investment strategy. The maximum drawdown is a common consideration for evaluating investment strategies or investment managers. It is meant to give a sense of what is the worst that can happen. For example, the lean hog trading system developed previously had a 41 percentage point (in terms of the price of hogs) drawdown in 1999. The overall equity curve looks very attractive, but an investor who began this strategy on the day the drawdown began would have lost 41 percent of his initial investment (assuming he could have lasted that long). And this is just based on a historical simulation. Historical simulations have a way of overstating what a strategy will actually produce; thus, on a going-forward basis, a bigger drawdown could reasonably be expected.

A second problem with the maximum drawdown is that it is not very useful for strategies with short track records. There is no reason to believe that the drawdown that a strategy experiences in its first year or two is in any way representative of what will happen over a longer time horizon. Related to this, evaluation by maximum drawdown puts strategies with a longer track record at a disadvantage. A maximum can only grow over time, since by its definition it is the biggest of something that has ever happened. Thus strategies with long track records are more likely to have bigger maximum drawdowns than strategies with shorter track records.

The second risk analysis tool discussed here is value-at-risk. Value-at-risk can be defined in different ways, but it generally refers to the loss that will be equaled or exceeded a given fraction of the time. Every value-at-risk measure has two numbers: a probability level and the loss (stated in dollars or as percentage of an account's equity) that will be equaled or exceeded at that level of probability. Suppose you chose your probability level as 5 percent and the strategy you are considering lost 8 percent or more 5 percent of the time. Then the value-at-risk is 8 percent.

After determining what is to be measured, the key task is to then measure it. The most typical way to do this is to look at the historical distribution of returns for the instrument or portfolio in which one is interested. It is then assumed that the future will resemble the past in that the same distribution of returns will be realized in the future. It is important to keep in mind that you are making this assumption. Though the past is often a good guide to the future, just because something happened in the past does not mean it will happen again in the future.

Figure 20.8 displays the distribution of monthly returns for the front soybean contract from August 1959 through October 2006. This histogram has the typical bell shape—most returns are clustered in the middle of the distributions, and the distribution narrows as one moves away from the center. This means that multiple standard deviation events—outcomes far from the mean—are also low probability events.[p] In this case, the average monthly return is about 0.13 percent, but there are also many months where the return is much greater and much less than this. Suppose one picks a probability level of 1 percent. What is the value-at-risk? This can be determined by taking the first percentile of the return series. For monthly soybean returns, the first percentile is –18.1 percent. So one percent of the time an outright position in soybeans would have lost 18.1 percent or more. For a portfolio containing more than one instrument, the same procedure is followed, with the exception that the historical distribution of the portfolio's returns is used.

---

[p] It is important to keep in mind that if the underlying distribution is not bell-shaped then high standard deviation events may or may not be less likely than low standard deviation events.

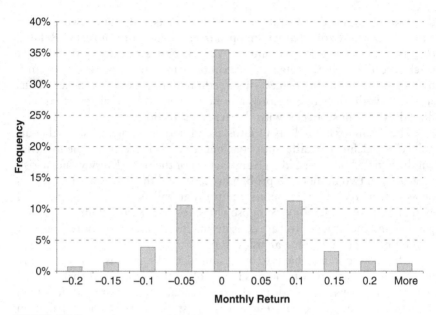

FIGURE 20.8 Soybean Monthly Return Distribution

Note that value-at-risk, as defined here, is independent of the investment strategy. It is purely a function of the positions in a portfolio. Good strategies and bad strategies will both have the same value-at-risk. This is the way it is most typically done, especially when the risk monitoring is done by an outside party.

Finally it is worth noting that though basing value-at-risk on the historical distribution of returns is the most common approach, it is not the only approach. Remember, the point of the exercise is to determine how big a loss is likely to occur at a given level of probability. The past may be a good guide for the future, but if you have information that helps predict your risk profile, you should use it. The most common additional information you might have is a volatility forecast. The volatility of markets can change over time, or it can be seasonal. If current volatility is higher than normal, the true value-at-risk is higher than an approach based on the historical distribution of returns would indicate. The standard approach to volatility forecasting has been the ARCH and GARCH models, but these models often work poorly. In recent years, however, great progress has been made in volatility forecasting, and a better approach is that of forecasting realized volatility, as laid out in Anderson et al. (2003).

The Rise of the Indexes

For most of this book we have been taking a do-it-yourself approach to investing. In this chapter we take a well-deserved break and let someone else do the work as we look at passive investments. Some investors may want commodity exposure in their portfolios but are not interested in opening a futures account or tracking petroleum inventories. During the past several years, many investors have been choosing commodity indexes, so that will be our main topic. However, there are a few additional ways investors can obtain exposure, so we will tackle exchange-traded funds, commodity trading advisors, and mutual funds as well.

THE RISE OF THE INDEXES

During the years 2002–2006, a dramatic increase occurred in the level of institutional interest in the commodity sector. This shift was likely a result of investors looking at the historical returns of long-only commodity indexes and finding that they compared favorably to gross equity market returns in both average return and typical levels of risk, but with low levels of correlation to equities. The trusty tool of mean variance optimization meant that this was too good to pass up, and this analysis is fine as far as it goes. However, it misses the source of the returns and does not take likely future returns into account. In this section we discuss the indexes, their composition, their potential role in a portfolio, and their prospects for continued attractive excess returns.

The increased interest in these indexes is shown in Figure 21.1, which is our estimate of the assets in all long-only commodity indexes gathered from a variety of industry sources. This is an especially difficult area to measure, since much of the investment is over the counter and thus not subject to public disclosure, so these estimates should be considered only rough guidelines. We can see that in the four years ending in 2006, long-only

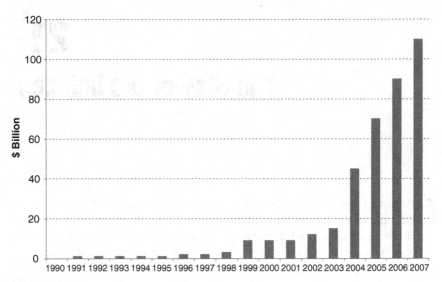

FIGURE 21.1 Commodity Index Assets

commodity assets have grown from about $15 billion to about $90 billion. By way of comparison, 2007 worldwide daily crude oil consumption is worth about $4 to $6 billion, with the daily notional value traded of exchange listed petroleum futures contracts at about $40 to $60 billion. The reason for the flow to long-only commodity indexes is likely similar to the logic laid out in Chapter 2: good long-run returns with low correlation with stocks and bonds. The S&P GSCI has been the most popular choice; as a consequence we will examine its construction and returns in some detail in this chapter.

HISTORY OF THE INDEXES

As discussed in Chapter 3, "Commodities for the Long Run," the ancient predecessor of the current craze for commodity indexes is The Economist Commodity Price Index, which has been published since 1864. In the 1930s the CRB index was launched at the request of the U.S. Commerce Department to provide insight into the U.S. business cycle, even though commodity prices were already widely disseminated. The *Wall Street Journal,* for example, dedicated an entire page (no small thing in what was then a 20-page newspaper) to prices of commodities futures and daily reportage from distant ports about the state of the cotton market in New Orleans, the grain markets in Chicago, and the metals markets in London. In the 1930s there were also three (now defunct) commodity price indexes reported daily in the newspaper: the Dow Jones commodity futures index, the Moody's spot commodity index, and the Reuters UK commodity index. An index of *sensitive material prices* (which were mainly the same commodities we have discussed in earlier chapters) was later included in the Bureau of Economic Analysis's index of leading economic indicators when it began to be published in 1961 (Conference Board, 2001). It seems likely that the intuition behind examining commodity prices was that when the economy heats up, demand for raw materials increases and the price of those materials increases as well, thus immediately reflecting the state of the business cycle. Over the subsequent years the empirical relationship between commodity prices and the business cycle failed to hold and in 1996 commodity prices were removed from the index of leading economic indicators.

In 1991 Goldman Sachs launched the Goldman Sachs Commodity Index (GSCI), which was designed from inception to be an investable index—one that reflects returns investors could have achieved. The index was sold to Standard and Poor's in 2007 and is now known as the S&P GSCI. The key characteristics of the S&P GSCI are that it is an index of the performance of liquid futures contracts, with careful consideration of rolling from one contract to another and a quantitative criteria for deleting illiquid contracts and adding ones that are newly liquid. In addition, the weight on each future will shift over time, depending on the importance of the commodity, a function of both volume produced and the price of the future traded. We explore this in greater depth when we discuss the S&P GSCI returns in detail.

INDEXES COMPARED

Looking again at Figure 21.1, we can see that at first the S&P GSCI had solid but not spectacular growth in assets until the turn of the millennium, when the combination of popular concern with commodity prices along with a sobering bear market in equities made investors cast about for something new. Soon assets were flowing to the S&P GSCI, and long-only indexes began to proliferate. Like so many bankers trying to get the same fashionable briefcase, by 2007 it seemed that every investment bank had its own commodity index—which makes one wonder why Goldman Sachs sold its index. Summary information about the various indexes is presented in Table 21.1.

The indexes differ mainly in their allocation to the individual commodities, though rules on when contracts are rolled can differ as well. The S&P

TABLE 21.1   An Overview of Many Passive Commodity Indexes

	Reuters/ Jeffries/ CRB Index	S&P GSCI Index	Dow Jones AIG Commodity Index	Rogers International Commodity Index	Deutsche Bank Liquid Commodity Index	Lehman Brothers Commodity Index
Descriptive Information						
First month of data	1/1940	12/1969	1/1991	7/1998	11/1988	12/2000
When index was constructed	1/1940	1/1991	7/1998	7/1998	2/2003	7/2006
Returns collateralized?	No	Yes	Yes	Yes	Yes	Yes
Bloomberg Code	CRY Index	SPGSCITR Index	DJAIGTR Index	RICIGLTR Index	DBLCMAVL Index	LBCITR Index
ETF Ticker		GSG, GSP	DJP		DBC	
Estimate of Assets Tracking Index		$60 Billion	$35 Billion	$7 Billion	$1 Billion	
Returns						
Annual return 1/70–12/06	3.0%	11.5%	7.8%	15.7%	13.2%	7.2%
Annualized std. dev.	12.0%	18.8%	12.3%	16.7%	19.7%	19.6%
Number of years	37	37	16	8	18	6
Annual return, in sample		15.8%	4.1%		12.7%	
Annual return, out of sample		6.0%	11.2%		15.1%	

Correlation of Monthly Returns	CRB	S&P GSCI	DJ/AIG	Rogers	Deutsche Bank	Lehman Bros.
CRB	1	0.72	0.81	0.81	0.57	0.78
S&P GSCI	0.72	1	0.88	0.93	0.92	0.96
DJ/AIG	0.81	0.88	1	0.91	0.84	0.95
Rogers	0.81	0.93	0.91	1	0.96	0.90
Deutsche Bank	0.57	0.92	0.84	0.96	1	0.89
Lehman Brothers	0.78	0.96	0.95	0.90	0.89	1
Weight by Sector						
Energies	39%	79%	33%	44%	55%	59%
Grains	13%	7%	21%	20%	23%	11%
Base Metals	13%	6%	18%	14%	13%	17%
Precious Metals	7%	2%	8%	7%	10%	8%
Tropical	21%	3%	9%	10%	0%	3%
Livestock	7%	4%	10%	3%	0%	3%
Other Industrial	0%	0%	0%	2%	0%	0%
Number of Commodities	19	24	19	36	6	20

GSCI has a well-defined methodology for including and weighting contracts based on the total value (a function of both price and volume) of physical production of the commodity. The DJ–AIG and Lehman Brothers indexes base their weights on the average volume of the futures contracts included in the index, but still have somewhat different weights. The other indexes take a more discretionary approach. This leads to the two extremes of the Rogers Commodity Index with its plethora of illiquid and non–dollar-denominated commodities and Deutsche Bank, which has chosen what it considers the six most liquid commodities.

Although returns vary substantially across indexes and are extremely period dependent, the correlation of the monthly returns is quite high. Where appropriate we break out returns that are generated with the benefit of hindsight called in-sample returns, and returns realized subsequent to the codification of the index rules known as out-of-sample returns. As shown in the table, the indexes out-of-sample returns are often substantially different from in-sample returns, but they are not consistently superior or inferior. There is no obvious way to predict which index will do the best in the future.

A ROUGH DECOMPOSITION OF S&P GSCI RETURNS

Since the S&P GSCI index is the market leader, we will examine its construction and return in some detail.

While older indexes simply set static weights on each commodity, the S&P GSCI was designed instead to build in a weighting mechanism. This weighting scheme is responsible for some peculiarities of the S&P GSCI return. The first step is to yearly cull the world of potential commodity futures down to those that are (1) denominated in U.S. dollars, (2) traded on a developed country futures exchange, and (3) have a significant volume traded. Once the set of contracts is chosen, the weight is set as a function of both the total production (worldwide or regional, as appropriate) of the commodity and the price of the commodity future. The weights on each sector have changed dramatically over time, as is shown in Figure 21.2. Perhaps most surprising is the 60 percent weight on livestock in the early 1970s—a very different index from the current 70 percent weight on energy.

There are three types of S&P GSCI indexes reported: spot, excess return, and total return. The *spot* index is derived from the returns of the front futures contract with no adjustment made for rolls from one expiry to another. With no roll adjustment, these returns are not realizable. A change in this index tells you, roughly, what has happened to the level of the front contract's price over the period studied. Note that in much of the futures market the *spot* market can refer casually to either the front futures

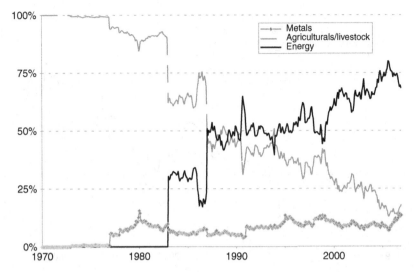

FIGURE 21.2   S&P GSCI™ Monthly Weight by Sector

market or the cash market. For clarity, in this chapter we refer to the *cash* market when talking about physical commodity prices and use *spot* only to refer to the S&P GSCI series by that name. *Excess* returns are what we have heretofore been calling noncollateralized futures returns. The rule in the S&P GSCI is to roll from the first to the second contract in equal amounts over the fifth to ninth business day of the month. *Total* returns are what we have been referring to as collateralized returns, where the margin is assumed to be invested in the three-month U.S. Treasury Bill. Standard and Poor's disseminates all three types of returns for the S&P GSCI, for various sub-indexes, and for each individual commodity included.

The rules for constructing the S&P GSCI were codified in 1991, and the history prior to 1991 was back-filled—that is, the developers of the index went back and applied their rules to that 1970–1990 period.

Including the price of the commodity in its weighting scheme has lead to the dramatic emphasis on petroleum products (67 percent as of 2007) in the S&P GSCI since the inclusion of the crude oil contract in 1987. It has also led to a surprising composition of returns in the simulation period, when Goldman was testing its rules. Sugar is a dramatic example. It was added to the index in 1973. The weight went from 10 percent to 30 percent in 12 months as the price of sugar briefly increased fivefold and decreased back down again to 10 percent 15 months later as the price subsided. The weight on sugar drifted further lower until crude was added to the index in 1987 and the weight settled near the 2 percent, which has characterized the

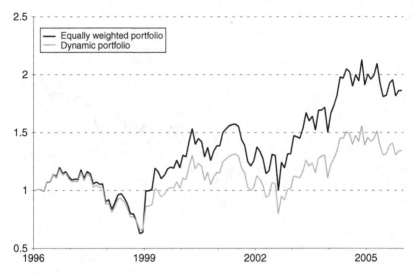

FIGURE 21.3   Comparing Livestock Portfolios

more recent period. Investors relying on performance from the 1970–1987 period should think about the historical structure of the index. Specifically, one distinguishing characteristic of the S&P GSCI today is that it is mostly energy. Given that energy is so important to the economy, many investors feel this is a good choice as a focus. Substantially fewer investors would be interested in an index today that was 30 percent sugar.

There is a performance-related issue to consider with the S&P GSCI approach as well. Suppose commodity prices are fluctuating around a long-term mean; in that case, this strategy will amount to buying as the price gets expensive relative to its long run average (and by assumption, its expected) price and selling as it gets cheap. In other words, the index will constantly be buying high and selling low. This is demonstrated in Figure 21.3, which compares two livestock portfolios, one equally weighted between the lean hogs and live cattle, and a second that starts out evenly weighted but follows S&P GSCI–like weighting rules to reset the portfolio monthly. Though both these futures move broadly higher over the period, we still do much better with the equally weighted portfolio (about 6.5 percent per year) than with the dynamic portfolio (3 percent per year). If an investor believes that in fact some commodities will appreciate relative to others, then a dynamically weighted index with reference to the price of the commodity is a better choice than a static index.

Table 21.2 shows that from the inception of the simulation period, 1970, the S&P GSCI Total Return series has had similar, though somewhat inferior, returns to the equally weighted index we constructed in Chapter 2. Compared with traditional assets, the S&P GSCI has had roughly comparable returns to stocks and superior returns to bonds with low correlation with either asset. Since the launch of the index in 1991, returns have been inferior to stock returns, though still with low correlation.

It is natural to ask how much of the returns that come with holding a collateralized commodity index is due to changes in commodity prices and how much is due to creeping along the futures curve. Standard and Poor's does not produce these returns, perhaps because of the difficulty in calculating cash commodity returns. The main issue is choosing the exact cash series to use. Despite this issue, we took the month-end S&P GSCI weights and applied them to the cash series for each contract to try to decompose the returns. This is not a perfect analysis, but we think the exercise is still worth the effort. Table 21.3 shows the results.

Column A shows the sum of the change in cash prices weighted according to the S&P GSCI weighting scheme. Column B shows the S&P GSCI *excess returns*. or the noncollateralized returns for holding the futures. Column C shows the S&P GSCI Total Returns, or what we have been calling the collateralized returns. In the last two columns we get some rough estimates as to the decomposition of the returns an investor would have obtained. Over the full period, investors would have received about 11.5 percent per year by being in the S&P GSCI. Of that, slightly more than half the return was due to the assumed margin interest, and most of the balance was due to changes in the price of the commodities.

Our approximation of creep, or the difference between the futures and cash returns, was slightly negative over both the whole period and the period since crude oil was added to the index. In other words, our calculations show that the money investors have given up because of contango has more than offset the money they have made in backwardated contracts. This is consistent with holders of futures paying at least some of the carrying costs. Negative *creep* returns might be slightly surprising to investors raised on charts of crude oil backwardation, so we perform two additional analyses—the S&P GSCI since the crude contract was added in 1987 and the crude considered on its own.

Considering crude alone gives the expected result that the creep along the curve and the movement in the cash have contributed roughly equal amounts to the return, since the crude oil curve has been backwardated on average over this period. The last two years of our history tell a different story. In this period the crude oil curve has been mainly in contango.

TABLE 21.2 An Analysis of S&P GSCI Returns

	Full Period: Jan. 1970–Dec. 2006				Out of Sample Period: Jan. 1991–Dec. 2006			
	S&P GSCI Total Returns	Collateralized Equally Weighted Portfolio	S&P 500 Total Returns	U.S. 10-Year Bond Total Returns	S&P GSCI Total Returns	Collateralized Equally Weighted Portfolio	S&P 500 Total Returns	U.S. 10-Year Bond Total Returns
Annual Returns (Geometric)	11.51%	13.16%	11.23%	8.25%	5.36%	8.34%	11.78%	7.33%
Analysis of Monthly Returns								
Avg. Monthly Return	1.06%	1.12%	0.99%	0.69%	0.58%	0.71%	1.01%	0.61%
Std. Dev. Monthly Return	5.43%	4.20%	4.39%	2.19%	5.44%	2.86%	3.94%	1.72%
Avg. Std. Dev.	0.19	0.27	0.22	0.31	0.11	0.25	0.26	0.35
Best Month	25.8%	25.1%	16.8%	11.4%	16.9%	8.1%	11.4%	5.4%
Worst Month	-15.6%	-12.8%	-21.5%	-7.4%	-14.4%	-6.1%	-14.5%	-5.7%
Correlations								
S&P GSCI Total Returns	1	0.75	-0.04	-0.07	1	0.73	-0.01	0.06
Equally Weighted Portfolio	0.75	1	0.02	-0.16	0.73	1	0.17	-0.05
S&P 500 Total Returns	-0.04	0.02	1	0.20	-0.01	0.17	1	-0.01
U.S. 10-Year Bond Total Returns	-0.07	-0.16	0.20	1	0.06	-0.05	-0.01	1

TABLE 21.3 Decomposing S&P GSCI Returns

Decomposing S&P GSCI Total Returns

	Cash [A]	S&P GSCI Excess Returns [B]	S&P GSCI Total Returns [C]	Approximate Interest [C]–[B]	Approximate Creep [B]–[A]
Full Period (1/1970–12/2006)	5.87%	4.88%	11.51%	6.63%	–0.99%
Since addition of crude to S&P GSCI (1/1987–12/2006)	6.94%	4.86%	9.82%	4.96%	–2.07%

Decomposing Crude Oil Excess Returns

	Crude Cash	GSCI WTI Crude Only Excess Returns	Approximate Creep
Since crude added to GSCI (1/1987–12/2006)	6.31%	11.21%	4.90%
Recent period when crude has been in contango (1/05–12/06)	13.12%	–8.62%	–21.74%

Source: Column A is our calculation, see data appendix for sources. Columns B and C are based on Goldman Sachs data.
Note: Annualized Geometric Returns.

One of the most important changes coincident with the increased assets in long-only commodity indexes is that the crude oil curve has been spending more time in contango at the front, not backwardated as it had been historically. Therefore, an interesting exercise is to take the average shape of the petroleum curve which was obtained recently and apply it to the historical performance of the S&P GSCI. Figure 21.4 plots three curves. The highest curve is the S&P GSCI excess returns series, which comprises the noncollateralized futures returns weighted according to the S&P GSCI weighting scheme. The line in the middle, "S&P GSCI—Petroleum Cash," replaces the futures returns with cash returns for the petroleum contracts—that is, instead of futures returns we use cash returns for crude oil (Brent and WTI), heating oil, and unleaded gasoline. The chart suggests that movement along the curve in the petroleum complex was a key source of S&P GSCI returns over the period examined.

The most interesting line in Figure 21.4 is the one labeled "S&P GSCI—Adjusted Petroleum Cash." This represents the same cash petroleum returns as in "S&P GSCI—Petroleum Cash" and subtracts the average difference[a] between the price of the first and second contracts in the 12 months

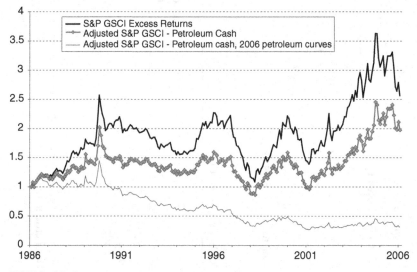

FIGURE 21.4   S&P GSCI Excess Return Index

---

[a] This adjustment comes out to −1.8%, −0.7% and −1.8% for WTI crude, unleaded gasoline and heating oil respectively. We use the same adjustment for WTI and Brent crude.

ending March 2007. Again, our goal is to answer the question: How would the S&P GSCI have done if the petroleum curves had looked as they have in the more recent periods? Remember that this spread price is not quite the exact thing we would like to measure; we are using the difference between the second and first futures contract as a proxy for the difference between the first futures contract (which is what the S&P GSCI is invested in) and the cash. Also remember that we are assuming that the shape of the curve will be unchanged over the period. Our third line shows that if the contango headwind of the 2005–2007 period had been in place in the past, the S&P GSCI would have had negative returns. Equivalently, we could say that the contango in the petroleum market curves in 2007 was large enough, if persistent, to erase the average capital gain in petroleum over the 1987–2007 period as well as all profits made in non-petroleum futures over that period.

NEWER COMMODITY INDEXES

As commodity investments became more popular and the crude oil curve shifted from backwardation to contango at the front end, sponsors began to list commodity-related products that we might call semi-actively managed—that is, products that take the shape of the forward curve into account. Deutsche Bank launched one such index in 2006, the *optimum yield* version of its liquid commodity index. This index will place its trade in the futures contract with the most attractive roll yield. The idea is compelling and, unsurprisingly, the simulated returns have been quite strong, but it is too early to review the out-of-sample returns of these approaches.

COMMODITY TRADING ADVISORS

Investors might be interested in an actively managed commodity program as opposed to an index, and it would be natural to assume that a commodity trading advisor (CTA) would fill the bill. A *commodity trading advisor* suggests a manager who invests in commodities, but in fact it simply means anyone who is registered as providing futures trading advice for profit with the National Futures Association (a self-regulatory body under the supervision of the Commodity Futures Trading Commission). So even though CTAs have *commodity* in their title, all it means is that they trade futures contracts without specifying the type of futures traded. Although we have been talking only about commodity futures in this book, in fact financial futures such as those based on stocks, bonds, and currencies trade much more than the commodity-based futures.

There is a sense in the alternative asset industry that CTAs in fact trade mainly financial futures and moreover that they do so with *trend-following* systems, price-driven trading strategies similar in principle to those spelled out in the Chapter 20, "Some Building Blocks of a Commodity Futures Trading System." If we take data from one of the leading trackers of CTAs, The Barclay Group, as of 2007 only 20 programs are in its agricultural index while 114 and 133 are in its currency and financials indexes, respectively. Further to the issue of underlying trading strategy, according to The Barclay Group, as of the third quarter 2006, fully 59 percent of the programs Barclay tracks are systematic and only 18 percent are discretionary, with the rest being hybrids. The discretionary number includes systematic traders who include fundamental data in addition to price in their trading decisions.

We can see from Table 21.4 that CTA returns, as measured by the Barclays' CTA Index, are not correlated to the S&P GSCI. However, it could be the case that because CTAs are actively going from long to short, in other words they could be earning positive returns in periods when the S&P GSCI is down, thus reducing the correlation. To account for this possibility we break out periods of positive and negative commodity returns and find only low levels of correlation, regardless of whether commodities are appreciating or depreciating. So commodity exposure is not a good reason to invest in most CTAs as a group.

TABLE 21.4   The Returns of Commodity Trading Advisors

Returns	CTAs	S&P GSCI Total Return
Annualized Geometric Return	12.35%	8.10%
Annualized Standard Deviation of Monthly Return	16.18%	17.73%
Return/Standard Deviation	0.76	0.46

Correlation of Monthly Returns	All Months	Months When S&P GSCI Is...	
		Positive	Negative
	0.04	0.17	0.03

Note: CTAs = Barclays CTA Index. Monthly data from 1/1980 to 12/2006

EQUITY MARKET COMMODITY EXPOSURE

There are a number of ways an investor can add commodity exposure by way of the equities markets, opening up these markets to anyone with a brokerage account. Commodity-related equities (invested in directly or through a mutual fund) will add both commodity exposure and idiosyncratic company exposure. Commodity equities will also be subject to the fluctuations of the broader stock market. Commodity ETFs are more focused, but they are new and so far somewhat illiquid. We address each investment option in turn.

INDIVIDUAL EQUITIES

Investors may also choose to buy stock in a company that produces a commodity. A major issue, however, is that extractive industries in particular are subject to the risk of radical contract renegotiation (e.g., Venezuela and the oil companies in 2006) or outright nationalization whether de facto (Russia bankrupting Yukos in 2005) or de jure (when the Chilean congress transferred ownership of all Chilean copper resources to Codelco in the 1970s).

As a result of government ownership sometimes only a small portion of worldwide production rights are available for purchase in the equities markets. For example, in the crude oil market Saudi-owned Saudi Aramco stated its proven oil reserves as of 2007 to be about 260 billion barrels of oil, 12 times as large as those of the largest publicly traded company. Even if a company's extraction rights are not changed, replacing capacity may prove to be challenging. On the other hand, public companies may be used by nationalized companies as contractors for their expertise and thus may still provide directional exposure to the price of the relevant commodity.

Major natural resources companies are listed in Table 21.5, along with the ticker symbol and the country of main listing. For oil companies we also list the 2006 year-end reserves in terms of millions of barrels of oil equivalents (BOE). For companies with at least five years' history, we list the correlation of the monthly percentage total returns of the equity with a relevant commodity—for example, crude oil for the energy companies. Mining companies whose returns are dominated by one metal are compared with that metal; we compare returns of diversified mining companies with an equally weighted index of the three major industrial metals—copper, aluminum, and zinc. The companies are typically correlated with both the returns of the commodities and the returns of the stock market, as measured

TABLE 21.5 Natural Resource Companies

	Company	Ticker	Country of Listing	Correlation to... Change in Commodity	Correlation to... S&P 500 Total Return	2006 Energy Reserve
Oil Companies	Exxon Mobil	XOM	US	0.15	0.46	22,110
	BP Plc	BP	UK	0.32	0.38	16,769
	Lukoil	LKOH	Russia	0.07	0.39	15,931
	Rosneft Oil	ROSN	Russia			12,597
	PetroChina Co. Ltd.	857	China (H.K.)	0.35	0.28	11,627
	Chevron Corp	CVX	US	0.25	0.45	11,620
	Royal Dutch/Shell	RDSA	UK/Netherlands			11,554
	ConocoPhillips	COP	US	0.30	0.41	11,169
	Total SA	FP	France	0.21	0.36	10,728
	ENI SpA	ENI	Italy	0.30	0.42	6,436
Copper	Antofagasta Plc	ANTO	London	0.35	0.24	
	Freeport-McMoRan	FCX	US	0.47	0.36	
	Grupo Mexico–B	GMEXICOB	Mexico	0.47	0.30	
	Kazakhmys Plc	KAZ	London			
	Sociedad Minera	SMCV	Peru	0.38	0.14	
	Southern Copper	PCU	US/Peru	0.44	0.29	

Aluminum	Alcoa, Inc.	AA	US	0.39	0.57
	Aluminum Corp of China (Chalco)	2600	China (H.K.)	0.46	0.48
	Alcan Inc	AL	Canada	0.42	0.59
Zinc	Zinifex Ltd	ZFX	Australia	0.80	0.12
	Korea Zinc Co	010130	Korea	0.33	0.27
	Hindustan Zinc	HZ	India	0.36	0.05
	Boliden AB	BOL	Sweden	0.51	0.42
Diversified Metals	BHP Billiton Ltd	BHP	Australia	0.41	0.36
	Anglo Amer Plc	AAL	UK/South Africa	0.49	0.47
	Xstrata Plc	XTA	UK/Australia	0.50	0.46
	Teck Cominco	TCK/A	Canada	0.43	0.32
	Rio Tinto	RIO	UK/Australia	0.44	0.45

Notes: Correlations are of monthly percentage returns, 1990–2006. Energy reserve in millions of barrels of oil equivalent.

by the total returns of the S&P 500 index. This analysis is similar to that undertaken in Chapter 2, "Commodity Futures as Investments," where we compared returns of equity indexes with returns of related commodities.

MUTUAL FUNDS

Another option for individual investors who are not prepared to speculate on individual futures contracts may be mutual funds that specialize in natural resources equities. Morningstar tracks the returns of mutual funds specializing in this sector in its Specialty Natural Resources Index. This index consists of roughly 50 mutual funds (collapsing share classes differing only in fees) that are focused on the equities of companies producing, refining, transporting, or retailing natural resources. These funds can be as narrowly focused as natural gas or may span the gamut of natural resources companies.

There is no investment vehicle currently offered that offers the performance of the Morningstar Specialty Natural Resources Index, so it is not the ideal representation of its class; nevertheless, it should prove informative. The mutual fund index, however, does include fees, which the other assets do not. This will reduce the Morningstar returns. The returns of this index are shown in Table 21.6. In broad terms, the average mutual fund has somewhat outperformed both our equally weighted commodity futures index and the broader stock index, though with somewhat more risk. The natural resources funds have substantially outperformed the S&P GSCI total return index. The correlations in Table 21.6 suggest that the natural resources mutual funds combine aspects of both commodities and stocks.

EXCHANGE TRADED FUNDS

As commodities diffused into the zeitgeist, several commodity Exchange Traded Funds (ETFs) were launched beginning in 2005. As far as commodities go, these funds either replicate an index or buy and fully collateralize a single commodity future. While there are now several dozen of these, most are thinly traded. Large professional investors have their pick of customized over-the-counter investments to choose from. ETFs open the world of commodity investing to anyone who can trade stocks, so they could be a good option for those who do not wish to open a futures account. The largest U.S. listed commodity ETFs are presented in Table 21.7. In September 2006, ETF Securities Ltd. launched a series of index and single commodity ETFs on the London Stock Exchange.

TABLE 21.6 The Returns of Natural Resources Mutual Funds

	Morningstar Specialty Natural Resources	S&P GSCI Total Return	Collateralized Equally Weighted Portfolio	S&P 500 Total Return
Analysis of Returns				
Annualized Geometric Return	12.3%	5.9%	9.3%	10.9%
Annualized Std. Dev. of Return	19.1%	19.3%	10.1%	13.6%
Avg.*	0.64	0.31	0.93	0.80
Max. Month	16.5%	16.9%	8.1%	9.8%
Min. Month.	−19.2%	−14.4%	−6.1%	−14.5%
Correlation of Monthly Returns				
Morningstar	1	0.58	0.59	0.51
S&P GSCI Total Return	0.58	1	0.73	0.00
Equally Weighted Portfolio	0.59	0.73	1	0.20
S&P 500 Total Return	0.51	0.00	0.20	1

Notes: All data begins with the inception of the Morningstar Natural Resources Index, May 1992 to December 2006. Morningstar Specialty Natural Resources Index © Morningstar, Inc.
*This row is the average monthly return divided by the standard deviaiton of monthly return, hence avg./std. dev./Std. Dev.

TABLE 21.7 ETF Market Capitalization

ETF Name	ETF Tracks	2007 Market Cap ($ billion)	Ticker
Streettracks Gold Trust	Gold	$14.60	GLD
iPath DJ-AIG Commodity Index	DJ-AIG index	$2.30	DJP
Deutsche Bank Commodity Index	DB index	$1.30	DBC
Powershares DB Agricultural	Deutsche Bank Agricultural Index	$0.70	DBA
US Natural Gas Fund LP	Natural Gas	$0.50	UNG
US Oil Fund LP	WTI Oil	$0.40	USO
iShares GSCI Commodity	S&P GSCI	$0.40	GSG
iPath S&P GSCI	S&P GSCI	$0.20	GSP

CONCLUSION

Allowing someone else to invest for you inevitably has good and bad points. Many investors will be unable or simply unwilling to buy commodity futures on their own and will want to pick some sort of passive vehicle, targeted on one commodity or on a collection of commodities. The vehicles explored in this chapter aim to do just that with little effort on the investor's part. A natural resources mutual fund will expose investors to the vagaries of the equity market along with the volatility of the commodities markets, to say nothing about relying on the skills of the fund manager. At the other extreme, a commodity future index involves an investment scheme that may go through periods of low expected returns, such as the S&P GSCI, when the crude oil curve is in contango, as was the case during most of the 2005–2007 period. As we have said repeatedly in this book, the first step to successful investing is understanding the market and the instruments you are investing in.

CHAPTER 22

Conclusion

Without doubt, commodities are one of the major investment themes at the beginning of the twenty-first century. Billions of dollars have flown into passive, long-only strategies, and over the past several decades such strategies have done well. But will they do well in the future?

A desirable property of any investment strategy is that it satisfies two criteria: (1) it makes sense, and (2) it has worked historically. Many make the case that (1) is easily satisfied for commodities. The world is producing more and more people and more and more purchasing power, but the Earth contains finite natural resources and thus prices must rise, the argument goes. We put more stock in the counter-argument that commodities are not investment assets, they exist to be consumed and do not naturally produce cash flows by virtue of their possession as stocks and bonds do.

Furthermore, although in some absolute sense the world's resources are finite, it is very difficult to say where the terminus is or how close we are to it. For example, the combination of technology and a well-incentivized population could presumably bring large amounts of additional land into cultivation. Of course, no one knows for sure what lies ahead for commodity prices. They will probably go up over time—inflation tends to be positive so most things do—but whether they will go up in real terms or by enough to compare favorably with other investment alternatives, such as equities, is another matter.

The question of historical performance can be answered more definitively. During the past several decades, investments in portfolios of commodity futures, including interest, have done well. They have earned equity-like returns with equity-like volatility and little correlation with equities. The overall roll yield or *creep* has been negative in general, but in certain salient cases, such as crude oil, it has been significantly positive.

As shown in Chapter 3, "Commodities for the Long Run," however, reaching deeper back into history clouds the picture. The Economist Commodity Price Index (an index of cash commodities, not futures) has yielded negative real returns since its inception in the mid 1800s, and its nominal returns have been far outpaced by stocks. Furthermore, during the stock market crash of the late 1920s commodity prices went down along with equities.

More recently, in the early part of the twenty-first century there have been long stretches during which the crude oil futures curve has been steeply contangoed. Should another such period occur, this would present a significant hurdle for index investors to overcome, given that many of the common indexes have a significant weighting in petroleum. As was shown in Chapter 21, "The Rise of the Indexes," if the recent contango had obtained throughout history, investors in the Goldman Sachs Commodity Index (now the S & P GSCI Index) would not have made any money during the past two decades.

Investors considering a commodity index should study the situation carefully. To proceed forward, some combination of the following should hold: (1) a firm conviction that commodity prices will rise, (2) backwardated futures markets, and (3) high short-term interest rates.

If it turns out that commodity indexes do not offer attractive opportunities does that mean that the whole subject of commodities should be turned aside? No. One of the themes of this book is that there is much of use that investors can acquire by studying commodities from an investment perspective. Understanding the commodities and their markets will help one assess the potential for various other commodity-based strategies, which have also grown tremendously in recent years. For example, there are the simple commodity equities (e.g., oil companies), commodity-based ventures, commodity hedge funds, tactical commodity strategies, and even the prospect of locking in the price of heating oil for the winter.

For some commodities the long-term outlook for prices will be stronger than for others. Over the long term, commodities that are naturally scarce or do not have substitutes are likely to have stronger price performance than commodities that are plentiful or easily substituted. For example, copper is relatively rare compared with aluminum. The world economy is effectively structured so that oil has no ready substitute. On the other hand, if wheat becomes expensive people can choose to eat something else or bring more land into wheat cultivation. Presumably companies that own that which is scarce will earn higher margins than those that own that which is plentiful.

As the chapters on the individual commodities have made clear, supply shocks are a common theme. Weather, strikes, political unrest, natural disasters, political interference—all of these can send the price of commodities sharply upward. This is unique to commodities; financial assets do not have supply shocks.

It is possible to attempt to collect and quantify important information to use in a model. We have given some direction for this in Chapter 20, "Some

Building Blocks of a Commodity Trading System." Constructing models that work in practice is always difficult, and success is not guaranteed and probably not even likely. However, the process of constructing a model forces one to precisely structure one's thinking and allows one to explore how various factors have interacted with prices in the past. This deepens one's understanding. It also provides a context to help evaluate strategies that may be presented to you ("I tried that, it didn't work").

Finally, for most readers, neither commodities nor investing can be avoided, and it is only a matter of time before the two cross paths. We hope that this book has provided some of the data, analysis, and modes of thinking to help you determine the path on which you may wish to take them.

The London Metal Exchange

The London Metal Exchange, LME, hosts actively traded markets for six primary industrial metals: aluminum, copper, lead, nickel, tin, and zinc.[a] In this book, the discussion focuses on the three most liquid metals: aluminum, copper, and zinc.

LME OVERVIEW

The LME differs substantially from the other exchanges that have been discussed in this book, representing a hybrid between a futures market and a forward market. The unique characteristics of the LME derive from its historically strong orientation toward the physical side of the industry: Every contract is presumed capable of physical delivery. These commercial needs have resulted in more delivery dates and rather elaborate contract specifications as compared with the other exchanges.

A typical commodity futures market offers one expiry date (contract) per month, and it is up to the participants to hedge away basis risk between the desired delivery date and the limited set of expiry dates. Not so for the LME, where every market date is in principle a prompt date. Contract dates begin with *cash,* two market days from the current day, and extend outward daily for three months. The LME then offers contracts that settle every Wednesday for months 3 to 6 and then every third Wednesday for months 6 to 63.[b]

The most important and most liquid contract is the three-month. Typically prices of other contracts are quoted in dollars of backwardation

---

[a] The LME also offers contacts for aluminum alloy, silver, an industrial metal index, and two plastics—polypropylene and linear low-density polyethylene.
[b] Copper and aluminum trade out to 63 months. The other metals extend out to 27 months.

or contango relative to the three-month. For instance, 6c means six dollars of contango relative to the three-month whereas 6b means six dollars of backwardation relative to the three-month. Coordination on the three-month arises for historical reasons. Copper was the first LME contract, and three months corresponded to the amount of time required to ship copper to Europe from Chile. Among the more distant contracts, the 15-month, 27-month and 63-month also play important roles as foci for liquidity.

A trader who wishes to exchange metal on a date other than the 3-, 15-, 27- or 63-month dates simply requests an adjustment. For example, a buyer can purchase three-month copper for delivery on June 15 and then have it adjusted to the desired delivery date, say June 8. If the copper market is in contango between these dates, the buyer receives a discount to the three-month price; if the copper market is in backwardation, the buyer pays a premium to the three-month rate. If you do this, however, be aware that the adjustment market is particularly opaque and you may be paying, at least implicitly, commissions twice—once to exchange the metal and once to adjust it to the target date. If you do adjust your metal, try to keep it on a (third) Wednesday, as these dates are the most liquid.

Worldwide, LME prices provide the reference point for trading much of the metal that is directly exchanged (notably including material that does not pass through LME warehouses). Trade publications quote metals at a premium to the LME. These premiums reflect differences in grade and location. For example, U.S. Midwest P1020 refers to 99.7% high-grade aluminum deliverable in the Midwest of the United States and might be quoted at a premium of 3.5 cents per pound. Many market participants actively track these premiums as indicators of market availability, with larger premiums indicating scarcity.

Like a typical futures exchange, every LME contract is standardized. However, the standardization takes a somewhat laborious form. Physical metal traded on the LME must belong to a list of more than 450 LME-registered brands approved as good for delivery. Furthermore, deliveries and withdrawals of metal in response to closure of a contract must occur in one of more than 400 LME-registered warehouse. After delivering acceptable metal into a warehouse, the owner receives a warrant that serves as title to the metal. The warrant records the weight, brand, origin, and location of material. Metal in an LME warehouse for which a warrant has been issued is known as *on warrant*. Cancellations occur when someone redeems a warrant for the underlying metal. The material is now *off warrant* but may stay in the LME warehouse for as long as desired. The liquidity of a warrant relative to the metal itself can be very valuable to the seller. The warrant may be sold, traded for another warrant, held speculatively, employed as collateral, or even transferred to a customer.

For a trader who has no intention of delivering or of taking delivery, brand and warehouse differences are mostly immaterial. For someone playing the physical market, however, they can be extremely important. On the LME, delivery is at the discretion of the seller. Thus, a seller can hand over any warrant that she desires. Which warrant will she deliver? Rest assured, it will be the warrant with the lowest value. Of course, she would be free to exchange that warrant for a more desirable brand at a more desirable location for a modest premium (fee). But that is the way the game is played.

This leads to another curiosity: The LME price generally sets the floor for standard-grade metals prices. If the foregoing were not sufficient to show you why, there is another reason. An exchange warehouse is not a place that a seller wants to place her metal. She would prefer to sell it directly to a consumer without having to pay extra warehouse charges. Furthermore, the buyer would rather receive the metal at a more convenient location, which is typically more expensive.[c] The LME is the dumping house for unwanted metal. Of course, it is a very useful dumping house that serves a very important purpose, but it is a dumping house nonetheless.

TRADING DETAILS

There are a variety of membership classes for the LME but the key players are the 11 ring-dealing members. Each of the ring-dealing members sits at a fixed point on the ring, a circle with, not surprisingly, eleven seats. Open outcry trading occurs across this ring. Given the small number of ring-dealing members, this is admittedly a far more stately affair than the chaotic pit-style open outcry of the CME.

The LME trading day has a carefully designed structure. The core trading day is broken up into ring sessions and kerbs. Each metal has four 5-minute ring sessions, two in the morning and two in the afternoon, during which dealer attention focuses squarely on that particular metal. The ring sessions are where the real liquidity lies. In principal, other metals may be traded, but it may be hard to get a market. The day's *official* prices are set during the precious second ring.[d]

In addition to the rings, there are two kerbs during which any metal may be traded. Think of a kerb as walking over to the curb to conduct a deal. The morning kerb lasts 90 minutes while the afternoon kerb lasts

---

[c] Common delivery arrangements are cif (cash, insurance, freight), fob (freight on board), c&f (cash and freight), and fas (free alongside).

[d] One ring to rule them all, one ring to find them, one ring to price them all and to the market bind them.

45 minutes. Kerbs serve as general-purpose, lower-intensity rings. If trading volume is low enough, ring members may even walk away from their seats. Liquidity thus tends to be lower than during the rings but may well pick up as the kerb comes to a close. At the end of the last kerb, the end of day *evaluation* prices are established. Trading can occur outside rings and kerbs through the interoffice phone market, but trading during these times typically involves substantially lower liquidity.

In addition to the open outcry ring and interoffice phone markets the LME has an electronic trading platform called LME Select. LME Select is open between 1:00 AM and 7:00 PM London standard time and trades side-by-side with the open outcry ring. LME member firms are connected to LME Select and are able to execute trades for clients. This electronic platform has increased liquidity for the market, especially outside the designated ring times for a specific metal.

In December 2006 the LME launched LMEmini contracts, which are small-sized, cash-settled monthly futures contracts available for trading on LME Select or through the interoffice telephone market. LMEmini contracts are available for aluminum, copper, and zinc and in the future may be a useful tool for smaller speculative investors. The LMEmini contracts have not generated much interest through the summer of 2007, so investors should verify that sufficient liquidity exists before entering one of these contracts.

For further information, see the perpetual favorite, *Wolff's Guide to the London Metal Exchange* or the LME's website (www.lme.co.uk).

Be aware also that many LME contracts formerly were traded in pounds sterling rather than U.S. dollars. This becomes important when constructing long price histories.

Notes

CHAPTER 2

1. Two papers that deal with many of the issues discussed in this section are Gorton and Rouwenhorst (2006) and Erb and Campbell (2006).
2. According to the *Oil and Gas Journal* (Dec. 18 2006), world proven oil reserves increased 2% in 2006.

CHAPTER 3

1. © The Economist Newspaper Limited, London.

CHAPTER 4

1. William L. Leffler. *Petroleum Refining in Non-technical Language,* PennWell: Tulsa, OK, 2000, pp. 9–12.
2. Oil Sands Discovery Center, Alberta, Canada.
3. Organization of Petroleum Exporting Countries.
4. BP. *BP Annual Statistical Review of Energy 2006,* 2006.
5. M.K. Hubbert. "Nuclear Energy and the Fossil Fuels," Lecture presented at the Spring Meeting of the Southern District, American Petroleum Institute, San Antonio, Texas, March 7–9, 1956, pp. 22–25.
6. BP. *BP Annual Statistical Review of Energy 2006,* 2006.
7. Marilyn Radler. "Oil production, reserves, increase slightly in 2006," *Oil and Gas Journal,* December 18, 2006. pp. 20–23.
8. BP. *BP Annual Statistical Review of Energy 2006,* 2006.
9. Henry R. Linden. "Global oil, gas outlook bright; US gas production nears plateau," *Oil and Gas Journal,* November 27, 2006.
10. Ibid.
11. Canadian Association of Petroleum Producers.
12. International Energy Agency.
13. Bob William. "Heavy hydrocarbons playing key role in peak oil debate, future energy supply," *Oil and Gas Journal,* July 28, 2003, p. 20.

14. Energy Information Administration. *Annual Energy Outlook 2006,* p. 53.
15. Energy Information Administration. *Annual Energy Outlook 2006,* p. 54.
16. BP. *BP Annual Statistical Review of Energy 2006,* 2006.
17. Energy Intelligence Group. *The International Crude Oil Market Handbook,* 2004, pp. E1, E287 and E313.
18. BP. *BP Annual Statistical Review of Energy 2006,* 2006.

CHAPTER 5

1. Energy Information Administration. *Residential Heating Oil Prices: What Consumers Should Know,* January 2003.
2. Energy Information Administration.
3. Energy Information Administration. Form EIA-810, "Monthly Refinery Report" and Form EIA-815, "Monthly Terminal Blenders Report."
4. Energy Information Administration. Form EIA-821, "Annual Fuel Oil and Kerosene Sales Report," 2005.
5. Energy Information Administration. Petroleum Supply Monthly, February 2006.
6. Ibid.
7. Energy Information Administration. Weekly Petroleum Status Report Data.
8. New York Mercantile Exchange.
9. Energy Information Administration. Form EIA-821, "Annual Fuel Oil and Kerosene Sales Report," 2005.

CHAPTER 6

1. Chevron Products Company. "Technical Bulletin on Fuel Economy of Gasoline Vehicles."
2. Environmental Protection Agency. *Clean Air Act Amendments of 1990.*
3. Ibid.
4. Environmental Protection Agency. "Achieving Clean Air and Clean Water: The Report of the Blue Ribbon Panel on Oxygenates in Gasoline."
5. Environmental Protection Agency. "Regulation of Fuel and Fuel Additives: Removal of Reformulated Gasoline Oxygen Content Requirement."
6. Environmental Protection Agency. "Renewable Fuel Standard Program."

7. American Coalition for Ethanol.
8. Bureau of Transportation Statistics. National Transportation Statistics, September 2006 update, Table 1–11.
9. US Department of Energy. *Energy Efficiency and Renewable Energy, Gasoline Gallon Equivalent Conversion Factors.*
10. Energy Information Administration. Forms EIA 810–EIA 817.
11. American Coalition for Ethanol.
12. US Department of Agriculture. World Agricultural Supply and Demand Estimates, December 2006.
13. Energy Information Administration.
14. Energy Information Administration. Form EIA-810, "Monthly Refinery Report" and Form EIA-815, "Monthly Terminal Blenders Report."
15. Energy Information Administration. Forms EIA 810–EIA 817.
16. Ibid.
17. Ibid.
18. Ibid.
19. Ibid.
20. Ibid.
21. New York Mercantile Exchange.
22. Ibid.
23. Ibid.
24. Ibid.
25. Ibid.
26. International Energy Agency, IEA Statistics.

CHAPTER 7

1. BP. *BP Annual Statistical Review of Energy 2006*, 2006.
2. Ibid.
3. Energy Information Administration. Form EIA-23, "Annual Survey of Domestic Oil and Gas Reserves," 2005.
4. Ibid.
5. United States Geological Survey. "National Oil and Gas Assessment 2006—Updated Results."
6. United States Geological Survey. "Methane Hydrates Fact Sheet."
7. BP. *BP Annual Statistical Review of Energy 2006*, 2006. (Average 1996–2005, tons equivalent).
8. BP. *BP Annual Statistical Review of Energy 2006*, 2006.
9. Ibid.
10. Energy Information Administration. "US LNG Imports: The New Wave," January 2007.

11. BP. *BP Annual Statistical Review of Energy 2006,* 2006.
12. Energy Information Administration. "US LNG Imports: The New Wave," January 2007.
13. BP. *BP Annual Statistical Review of Energy 2006,* 2006.
14. Energy Information Administration. "Natural Gas Processing: The link between natural gas production and its transportation to market." January 2006.
15. Marilyn Radler. "Oil production, reserves, increase slightly in 2006," *Oil and Gas Journal,* December 18, 2006. pp. 20–23.
16. Energy Information Administration, *International Energy Outlook 2006.*
17. "Potential Gas Supply of Natural Gas in the United States," Report of the Potential Gas Committee, December 31, 2004, Potential Gas Agency, Colorado School of Mines.
18. Energy Information Administration, Annual Energy Review 2005.
19. Energy Information Administration, Form EIA-895, "Monthly and Annual Quantity and Value of Natural Gas Production Report," and the U.S. Mineral Management Service.
20. Ibid.
21. Energy Information Administration, "US Natural Gas Storage Developments: 1998–2005" October 2006.
22. Ibid.
23. Ibid.
24. Ibid.
25. New York Mercantile Exchange.

CHAPTER 8

1. U.S. Grains Council.
2. USDA. "World Agricultural Supply and Demand Estimates," January 12, 2007.
3. USDA. National Agricultural Statistics Service, Agricultural Statistics Database.
4. Ibid.
5. USDA. "World Agricultural Supply and Demand Estimates," January 12, 2007.
6. USDA. Economic Research Service, Sugar Briefing Room, Table 52.
7. USDA. "World Agricultural Supply and Demand Estimates," January 12, 2007.
8. Ibid.
9. Environmental Working Group, Farm Subsidy Database.

CHAPTER 9

1. The Commodity Center Corporation, *The Practical Grain Encyclopedia*, 2007.
2. USDA. Foreign Agricultural Service.
3. Ibid.
4. Ibid.
5. USDA. "World Agricultural Supply and Demand Estimates," January 12, 2007.
6. Ibid.
7. USDA. Economic Research Services.
8. Ibid.
9. Ibid.
10. Ibid.
11. Ibid.
12. USDA. "World Agricultural Supply and Demand Estimates," January 12, 2007.
13. Ibid.

CHAPTER 10

1. USDA, Foreign Agricultural Service, PS&D Online.
2. "The Practical Grain Encyclopedia," The Commodity Center Corporation.
3. USDA, Economic Research Services.
4. P.D. Goldsmith, B. Li, J. Fruin, and R. Hirsch. "Global Shifts in Agro-Industrial Capital and the Case of Soybean Crushing: Implications for Managers and Policy Makers," *International Food and Agribusiness Management Review*, 7 (2) 2004: 87–115.
5. USDA, Foreign Agricultural Service. PS&D Online.
6. Ibid.
7. USDA, Foreign Agricultural Service. Oilseeds: World Markets and Trade, March 2007.
8. Ibid.
9. Ron Kotrba. "Pressing the Possibilities," *Biodiesel Magazine*, September 2006.
10. The Commodity Center Corporation. *The Practical Grain Encyclopedia*, 2007.
11. National Biodiesel Board.
12. Ibid.
13. Ibid.

14. European Biodiesel Board.
15. Ibid.
16. USDA, Foreign Agricultural Service. "Commodity Intelligence Report: Biodiesel Demand Continues Pushing Rapeseed Area Up in the EU," June 2006.
17. USDA. "World Agricultural Supply and Demand Estimates."

CHAPTER 11

1. Grain Inspection Packers and Stockyards Association (GIPSA), USDA. "Spot and Alternative Marketing Arrangements in the Livestock and Meat Industries," Interim Report, July 2005.
2. National Agricultural Statistics Service (NASS), USDA. *US Hog Breeding Structure*, September 2006.
3. Informa Economics, Inc. *The Changing US Pork Industry and Implications for Future Growth*, prepared for the Indiana State Department of Agriculture, October 2005.
4. USDA Economic Research Service.
5. Ibid.
6. Informa Economics, Inc. *The Changing US Pork Industry and Implications for Future Growth*, prepared for the Indiana State Department of Agriculture, October 2005.
7. Ibid.
8. Marvin Hayenga, Ted Schroeder, John Lawrence, Dermot Hayes, Tomislav Vulkina, Clement Ward, and Wayne Purcell. *Meat Packer Vertical Integration and Contract Linkages in the Beef and Pork Industries: An Economic Perspective*, the American Meat Institute, May 2000.
9. John D. Lawrence and Glenn Grimes, "Production and Marketing Characteristics of US Pork Producers, 2000 (Staff Paper No. 343)," Department of Economics, Iowa State University, August 2001.
10. Ronald L. Plain. "Structural Change in the Pork Industry: What It Means for Hog Prices, Meat Consumption and the Future of Family Farms," Lecture presented at the Sixteenth Annual Farm Outlook Seminar, Marshall, MN, March 9, 2000.

CHAPTER 12

1. RTI International. "GIPSA Livestock and Meat Marketing Study," Final Report, January 2007.

2. Rodney Jones. *Farm Management Guide: Finishing Beef*, Manhattan, KS; Kansas State University Agricultural Experiment Station and Cooperative Extension Service, MF-592, October 2006.
3. Ted C. Schroeder, Clement Ward, John Lawrence, and Dillon M. Feuz. "Fed Cattle Marketing Trends and Concerns: Cattle Feeder Survey Results," Kansas State University, June 2002.
4. RTI International. "GIPSA Livestock and Meat Marketing Study," Final Report, January 2007.
5. Steven Kay, *Cattle Buyers Weekly*, October 16, 2006.
6. Kenneth H. Matthews, Jr.; William F. Hahn; Kenneth E. Nelson; Lawrence A. Duewer; and Ronald A. Gustafson. "US Beef Industry: Cattle Cycles, Price Spread and Packer Concentration," *Market and Trade Economics Division, Economic Research Service, USDA, Technical Bulletin No. 1874*, April 1999.
7. Ibid.
8. William Hahn. "Beef and Pork Values and Price Spreads Explained," *USDA ERS*, May 2004.
9. Robert C. Taylor. "Where's the Beef? Monopoly and Monopsony Power in the Beef in the Beef Industry," mimeo, Auburn University, March 2002.
10. USDA. National Agricultural Statistics Service.
11. William F. Hahn; Mildred Haley; Dale Lueck; James Miller; Janet Perry; Fawzi Taha; and Steven Zahniser. "Market Integration of the North American Animal Products Complex," *USDA ERS*, May 2005.
12. Kenneth H. Matthews Jr.; Monte Vandeveer; and Ronald A. Gustafson. *An Economic Chronology of BSE in North America*, USDA, June 2006.

CHAPTER 13

1. David R. Lide (ed.). *CRC Handbook of Chemistry and Physics, 85th Edition*. CRC Press: Boca Raton, Florida (2005).
2. Copper Development Association. *The US Copper-base Scrap Industry and Its By-Products—2006*, 2006, pp. 50, 58.
3. Copper Development Association. *Annual Data 2006: Copper Supply & Consumption 1985–2005*, 2006.
4. Robert Ayres, Leslie Aures, and Ingrid Rade, "The Life Cycle of Copper, Its Co-Products and By-Products," International Institute for Environment and Development, World Business Council for Sustainable Development, p. 34, January 2002.
5. Sucden. *Metals Insider*, December 22, 2006.

CHAPTER 14

1. International Aluminium Institute. "Aluminium in History," 2007. Available online at www.world-aluminium.org.
2. Alcoa, Inc. "Aluminum Smelting," 2002. Available online at www. alcoa.com/global/en/about_alcoa/pdf/Smeltingpaper.pdf
3. World Bureau of Metal Statistics.
4. International Aluminium Institute "The Aluminium Industry's Sustainable Development Report," 2001.
5. World Bureau of Metal Statistics.
6. Ibid.
7. Natural Resources Canada. "Aluminum," *Canadian Minerals Yearbook*, 1998.
8. Trevor Tarring, "Corner!," *Metal Bulletin*, 1997.
9. James H. Jolly. U.S. Bureau of Mines. *Mineral Yearbook*, 1990–1994.
10. U.S. Bureau of Mines. *Mineral Yearbook*, 1990–1994.

CHAPTER 15

1. David R. Lide (ed.). CRC Handbook of Chemistry and Physics, 85th Edition, CRC Press: Boca Raton, Florida (2005).
2. International Lead and Zinc Study Group Web site.
3. Ibid.
4. ILZSG, CRU as quoted by Xstrata in July 2003 presentation to analysts in Asturias, Spain.
5. James H. Jolly, *Minerals Yearbook,* U.S. Bureau of Mines.

CHAPTER 16

1. International Coffee Organization.
2. Mark Pendergrast. *Uncommon Grounds*, Basic Books: New York, NY, 1999.
3. "Coffee Futures and Options," New York Board of Trade.
4. Data from ICO, calculation by authors.
5. "Tropical Products: World Markets and Trade," December 2006, USDA.
6. "Coffee Futures and Options," New York Board of Trade.

CHAPTER 17

1. American Sugar Alliance.
2. USDA, Foreign Agricultural Service, PS&D Online.

3. Ibid.
4. American Sugar Alliance.
5. New York Board of Trade.

CHAPTER 18

1. See, for example, www.cocoapro.com, a Mars company website that contains links to research in the area and a discussion of their efforts to maintain flavanols through processing.
2. Data from International Cocoa Organization, calculation by authors.

CHAPTER 19

1. USDA, Foreign Agricultural Service. PSD Online.
2. National Cotton Council of America.
3. Economic Research Service of the USDA. "The Forces Shaping World Cotton Consumption After the Multifiber Arrangement," April 2005.
4. USDA, Foreign Agricultural Service. PSD Online.
5. USDA. *World Supply and Demand Estimates*, December Issues 1997–2006

CHAPTER 20

1. Liz Moyer. "In the Wild West of Energy Trading," *Forbes* magazine online, September 22, 2005.
2. "MotherRock Energy Hedge Fund Closing After Losses," *Bloomberg* news online, August 3, 2006.
3. "Amaranth's $6.6 Billion Slide Began with Trader's Bid to Quit," *Bloomberg* news online, December 6, 2006.
4. Doug Alexander and Sean B. Pasternak. "Bank of Montreal Has Trading Loss of C$450 Million," *Bloomberg* news online, April 27, 2007.
5. See, for example, Philippe Jorion, *Value at Risk*, 1997.

References

Andersen, T.G., T. Bollerslev, F.X. Diebold, and P. Labys, "Modeling and Forecasting Realized Volatility," *Econometrica*, 71, 579–625, 2003.

Bernstein, Peter L. *The Power of Gold*, Wiley, New York, 2000.

Bodie, Zvi and Victor I. Rosansky. "Risk and Return in Commodity Futures," May–June, 1980, *Financial Analysts Journal*.

Business Cycle Indicators Handbook. U.S. Department of Commerce, Bureau of Economic Analysis. The Conference Board Inc., 2001.

Clark, Gregory. "The Price History of English Agriculture, 1500–1914," University of California—Davis, Working Paper, 2003.

Commodity Center Corporation. *The Practical Grain Encyclopedia*.

Energy Information Administration. "Annual Energy Outlook 2006." pp. 53–54.

Energy Information Administration, "Form EIA-895: Monthly and Annual Quantity and Value of Natural Gas Production Report," and the U.S. Mineral Management Service.

Energy Information Administration, "Natural Gas Processing: The Link between Natural Gas Production and Its Transportation to Market." January 2006.

Energy Information Administration, "Residential Heating Oil Prices: What Consumers Should Know," January 2003.

Energy Intelligence Group, "The International Crude Oil Market Handbook 2004." pp. E1, E287 and E313.

Environmental Protection Agency, "Achieving Clean Air and Clean Water: The Report of the Blue Ribbon Panel on Oxygenates in Gasoline.

Environmental Protection Agency, Clean Air Act Amendments of 1990.

Environmental Protection Agency, "Regulation of Fuel and Fuel Additives: Removal of Reformulated Gasoline Oxygen Content Requirement."

Environmental Protection Agency, "Renewable Fuel Standard Program."

Erb, Claude B. and Campbell R. Harvey, "The Strategic and Tactical Value of Commodity Futures," March–April, 2006, *Financial Analysts Journal*.

Feng, Lu and Peng Kaixiang, "A Research on China's Long-term Rice Prices (1644–2000)," *Frontiers of Economics in China*, Vol. 1, No. 4, December 2006.

Germain, Shanna. "Ready for Robustas?" *Roast Magazine*. March/April 2006. Grain Inspection, Packers and Stockyards Administration (GIPSA), USDA. "Spot and Alternative Marketing Arrangements in the Livestock and Meat Industries," Interim Report, July 2005.

Goldsmith, P.D., B. Li, J. Fruin, and R. Hirsch. "Global Shifts in Agro-Industrial Capital and the Case of Soybean Crushing: Implications for Managers and Policy

Makers." International Food and Agribusiness Management Review. 7(2) 2004: 87–115.

Gorton, Gary B. and K. Geert Rouwenhorst, "Facts and Fantasies about Commodity Futures," March–April, 2006, *Financial Analysts Journal.*

Hahn, William. "Beef and Pork Values and Price Spreads Explained," *USDA ERS,* May 2004.

Hahn, William F., Mildred Haley, Dale Leuck, James J. Miller, Janet Perry, Fawzi Taha, and Steven Zahniser, "Market Integration of the North American Animal Products Complex," *USDA ERS,* May 2005.

Hayenga, Marvin, Ted Schroeder, John Lawrence, Dermot Hayes, Tomislav Vulkina, Clement Ward, and Wayne Purcell, "Meat Packer Vertical Integration and Contract Linkages in the Beef and Pork Industries: An Economic Perspective," for the American Meat Institute, May 2000.

Hubbert, M.K. "Nuclear Energy and the Fossil Fuels Presented before the Spring Meeting of the Southern District, American Petroleum Institute, Plaza Hotel, San Antonio, Texas, March 7–9, 1956, pp. 22–25.

Informa, "The Changing US Pork Industry and Implications for Future Growth," prepared for the Indiana State Department of Agriculture, October 2005.

Kaldor, Nicholas. "Speculation and Economic Stability," The Review of Economic Studies, Vol. 7, No. 1, October 1939, pp. 1–27.

Kotrba, Ron. "Pressing the Possibilities." Biodiesel Magazine. September 2006.

Lawrence, John D. and Glenn Grimes, "Production and Marketing Characteristics of US Pork Producers, 2000," Staff Paper No. 343, Department of Economics, Iowa State University, August 2001.

Leffler, William, L. *Petroleum Refining in Nontechnical Language.* Penn Well. 3rd Edition, 2000.

Linden, Henry R. "Global oil, gas outlook bright; US gas production nears plateau", Oil and Gas Journal, November 27, 2006.

Matthews, Jr., Kenneth H., William F. Hahn, Kenneth E. Nelson, Lawrence A. Duewer, and Ronald A. Gustafson, "US Beef Industry: Cattle Cycles, Price Spread and Packer Concentration," Market and Trade Economics Division, Economic Research Service, USDA, Technical Bulletin No. 1874, April 1999.

Matthews Jr., Kenneth H., Monte Vandeveer, and Ronald A. Gustafson, "An Economic Chronology of BSE in North America," USDA, June 2006.

National Agricultural Statistics Service (NASS), USDA. "US Hog Breeding Structure," September 2006.

Officer, Lawrence H., "Exchange rate between the United States dollar and the British pound, 1791–2005." Economic History Services, EH.Net, 2006. URL: http://eh.net/hmit/exchangerates/pound.php.

Officer, Lawrence H. and Samuel H. Williamson, "Annual Inflation Rates in the United States, 1774–2006, and United Kingdom, 1265–2006," Measuring-Worth.Com, 2007.

Pendergrast, Mark. *Uncommon Grounds: The History of Coffee and How It Transformed Our World.* Basic Books. 1999.

Plain, Ronald. "Structural Change in the Pork Industry: What It Means for Hog Prices, Meat Consumption and the Future of Family Farms," University of Missouri, presentation text, Marshall, MN; Austin, TX; and Nebraska City, NE, March 2000.

Radler, Marilyn. "Oil Production, Reserves, Increase Slightly in 2006," Oil and Gas Journal, December 18, 2006, pp. 20–23.

RTI International. "GIPSA Livestock and Meat Marketing Study," Final Report, January 2007.

Fed Cattle Marketing Trends and Concerns, KSU; RTI International, "GIPSA Livestock and Meat Marketing Study." 2007.

Taylor, Robert C., "Where's the Beef? Monopoly and Monopsony Power in the Beef Industry." Auburn University, March, 2002.

Ulrich, Hugh, "The Amber Waves of History: 200 Years of Grain Prices," Commodity Research Bureau, 1996.

USDA Agricultural Projections to 2016, Office of the Chief Economist, February 2007, p. 52.

USDA, Foreign Agricultural Service, "Commodity Intelligence Report: Biodiesel Demand Continues Pushing Rapeseed Area Up in the EU," June 2006.

US Department of Energy. "Energy Efficiency and Renewable Energy, Gasoline Gallon Equivalent Conversion Factors."

William, Bob. "Heavy Hydrocarbons Playing Key Role in Peak Oil Debate, Future Energy Supply," Oil and Gas Journal, July 28, 2003, p. 20.

About the Authors

ADAM DUNSBY is a principal at Cornerstone Quantitative Investment Group. He received both his undergraduate degree and PhD in finance from the Wharton School of the University of Pennsylvania.

JOHN ECKSTEIN is a principal at Cornerstone Quantitative Investment Group. He earned a BS from Brown University where he studied computer science and cognitive science. Mr. Eckstein developed investment application software for money management firms prior to his current position.

JESS GASPAR is the director of research at Cornerstone Quantitative Investment Group. He earned his undergraduate degree from MIT and his Ph.D. in economics from Stanford. After receiving his PhD, Mr. Gaspar was an assistant professor at the University of Chicago where he did research and taught international economics and computational methods in economics and finance. Mr. Gaspar worked as a consultant at McKinsey & Co. before joining Cornerstone.

SARAH MULHOLLAND is the head trader at Cornerstone Quantitative Investment Group. She earned a BS in Economics from the Wharton School of the University of Pennsylvania. Prior to joining Cornerstone, she traded energy derivatives for Enron North America and PSE&G.

Index

Alternative Energy, 54–55. *See also* Bio-Fuels
Aluminum
   Aluminum, consumption, 16–170
   Aluminum, forward contracts, 174–175
   Aluminum, grades, 175
   Aluminum, production, 165–166
   Aluminum, recycling, 168
Anchor Variables, 6–7, 224
Arabica. *See* Coffee.
Arbitrage Theory, 100–101, 224–238
ARCH. *See* Volatility Forecasting

Backwardation, 253. *See also* Creep
Barclay's CTA Index, 259
Bayer Process. *See* Aluminum
Bio-Diesel, 124–125, 138–139.
Bio-Fuels, 54, 64, 200–201. *See also*
   Bio-Diesel
Bovine Spongiform Encephalopathy (BSE),
   147

Calendar Spreads, 224
Cattle
   Cattle, feeder, 142
   Cattle, futures, 149–150
   Cattle, grade designations, 142–143
Clear Air Act of 1990, 68–69
Cocoa
   Cocoa, consumption, 208–210
   Cocoa, futures, 210–211
   Cocoa, history, 207–208
   Cocoa, processing, 208
   Cocoa, production, 208–210
Coffee
   Coffee, consumption, 193–194
   Coffee, futures, 194–195
   Coffee, history, 189
   Coffee, processing, 190–191
   Coffee, production, 191–193
   Coffee, types, 189

Contango, 8, 17, 24, 27, 102, 112, 229–231,
   253. *See also Creep*
Convenience Yield, 227
Copper
   Copper, forward contracts, 163
   Copper, processing, 154
Corn
   Corn, consumption, 98–100
   Corn, drought-resistant corn seeds, 95
   Corn, futures, 102–103
   Corn, harvest, 98
   Corn, production, 96–98
Cost of Carry, 18, 100–102, 112, 226–227,
   253
Cotton
   Cotton, consumption, 214–217
   Cotton, futures, 217–218
   Cotton, production, 214
   Cotton, gin, 213–215
Cottonseed. *See* Cotton
Crack Spread, 60–61, 75. *See also* Crude
   Oil
Creep, 17, 27, 224, 233, 238, 240, 253, 255,
   265
Creutzfeld-Jacob disease (CJD), 147
Crude Oil
   Crude Oil, distillation curve, 39
   Crude Oil, futures, 50–51
   Crude Oil, grades, 49
   Crude Oil, refining, 48–50
   Crude Oil, West Texas Intermediate
      (WTI), 11
Commodity Trading Advisor (CTA),
   257–258
Curve Fitting. *See* Data Mining

Data Mining, 241
Dried Distillers Grains (DDG), 99–100, 123,
   139
Dual-Fuel Power Plants, 89

E85 Fuel. *See* Ethanol
Ethanol, 27, 54–55, 69–71, 98–100, 123, 141, 199
Exchange Traded Funds (ETFs), 262

Flavanols, 207

GARCH. *See* Volatility Forecasting
Gasoline
  Gasoline, consumption, 72–74
  Gasoline, futures, 74–75
  Gasoline, MTBE, 27, 69
  Gasoline, octane rating, 67
  Gasoline, production, 71–72
  Gasoline, reformulated blendedstock for oxygen blending (RBOB), 27, 68–70
  Gasoline, reformulated unleaded (RFG), 68–69
GSCI. *See* S&P GSCI

Hall-Heroult Process. *See* Aluminum
Heating Oil
  Heating Oil, Consumption, 58–60
  Heating Oil, Futures, 51, 60
  Heating Oil, Production, 58
High Fructose Corn Syrup (HFCS), 95, 98, 199, 200
Hogs
  Hogs, futures, 140
  Hogs, production, 134
Horizontal Drilling, 40
Hotelling's Theory of the Economics of Exhaustible Resources, 7, 229
Hubbert's Peak, 7, 43–44

Java. *See* Coffee.

Keynes' Theory of Normal Backwardation, 4, 224, 228–229, 232

Lean Hogs. *See* Hogs
Live Hogs. *See* Hogs

Mutual Funds, 262

Natural Gas
  Natural Gas, futures, 89–90
  Natural Gas, liquids (NGL), 83
  Natural Gas, liquified (LNG), 80–82
  Natural Gas, storage, 85

Oil Sands, 40–41, 45–46
Organization of Petroleum Exporting Countries (OPEC), 41–42

Petroleum Administration for Defense Districts (PADD), 62–63, 77

Renewable Fuel Standard Program. *See* Ethanol
Robusta. *See* Coffee
Roll Yield, 224. *See also* Creep

S&P GSCI, 7, 9, 29, 235, 246–264
Shale Oil, 40–41, 45–46
Simon-Ehrlich Wager, 3, 10
Solvent Extraction-Electrowinning (SX-EW). *See* Copper
Soy Complex. *See* Soybeans
Soybean Meal, 98, 118, 122, 133. *See also* Soybeans
Soybean Oil, 54, 64, 118, 123–124. *See also* Soybeans
Soybeans
  Soybeans, futures, 125–126
  Soybeans, gross processing margin (GPM), 120
  Soybeans, production, 119–121
  Soybeans, products, 118
Sugar
  Sugar, consumption, 199–201
  Sugar, futures, 202–203
  Sugar, government subsidies, 201–202
  Sugar, production, 197–199
Sugar Beets, 197. *See also* Sugar
Sugarcane, 197. *See also* Sugar

Trend Following, 5, 7, 235–237

Ultra Low Sulfur Diesel, 60

Value-at-Risk, 243–244
Volatility Forecasting, 244

Wet Distillers Grains (WDG), 99
Wheat
  Wheat, categories, 107, 109
  Wheat, consumption, 110–111
  Wheat, futures, 112–114
  Wheat, production, 107–109

Zinc
  Zinc, consumption, 179–182
  Zinc, forward contracts, 182–184
  Zinc, production, 177–179

Printed in the United States
By Bookmasters